CREATIVE  TOUCHES™

Stone Finishes

ETC.

THE HOME DECORATING INSTITUTE®

Copyright© 1996 Cy DeCosse Incorporated 5900 Green Oak Drive Minnetonka, Minnesota 55343
1-800-328-3895 All rights reserved Printed in U.S.A.

Library of Congress Cataloging-in-Publication Data Stone finishes etc. p. cm. — (Creative touches)
Includes index. ISBN 0-86573-997-8 (softcover) 1. House painting. 2. Stone in art. 3. Marble in art. 4. Interior decoration. I. Cy DeCosse Incorporated. II. Series.
TT323.S82 1996 698'.14 — dc20 96-15846

CONTENTS

Getting Started

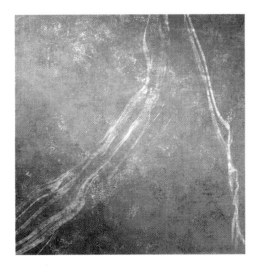

Faux Stone Finishes

Faux Marble Finishes

Stone Finishes ETC.

The art of faux finishing can be the practical solution to some decorating problems, while at the same time offering hours of creative enjoyment. When you want the look of real marble, but the expense forbids it, a painted marble finish may be the answer. Not only will you save lots of decorating dollars, you will thoroughly enjoy yourself in the process.

Use stone and marble faux finishes to enhance your decorating scheme in many ways. Apply a faux granite finish to decorative boxes or picture frames. Create the look of semiprecious stones, such as tigereye or malachite, on decorative accessories or furniture. Or, on a larger scale, paint a travertine finish on a fireplace surround.

Stone and marble finishes that look like the genuine article are also easy to create, using a few specially designed tools along with some common household items. For the safety of the environment as well as ease in cleanup, all the faux finishes in this book are created using water-based paints and glazes. Even the amateur faux finisher can get great results with just a little practice, following these clear instructions with color photography.

All information in this book has been tested; however, because skill levels and conditions vary, the publisher disclaims any liability for unsatisfactory results. Follow the manufacturers' instructions for tools and materials used to complete these projects. The publisher is not responsible for any injury or damage caused by the improper use of tools, materials, or information in this publication.

GETTING STARTED

Primers & Finishes

PRIMERS

Some surfaces must be coated with a primer before the paint is applied. Primers ensure good adhesion of paint and are used to seal porous surfaces so paint will spread smoothly without soaking in. It is usually not necessary to prime a nonporous surface in good condition, such as smooth, unchipped, previously painted wood or wallboard. Many types of water-based primers are available; select one that is suitable for the type of surface you are painting.

A. FLAT LATEX PRIMER is used for sealing unfinished wallboard. It makes the surface nonporous so fewer coats of paint are needed. This primer may also be used to seal previously painted wallboard before you apply new paint of a dramatically different color. The primer prevents the original color from showing through.

B. LATEX ENAMEL UNDERCOAT is used for priming most raw woods or woods that have been previously painted or stained. A wood primer closes the pores of the wood, for a smooth surface. It is not used for cedar, redwood, or plywoods that contain water-soluble dyes, because the dyes would bleed through the primer.

C. RUST-INHIBITING LATEX METAL PRIMER helps paint adhere to metal. Once a rust-inhibiting primer is applied, water-based paint may be used on metal without causing the surface to rust.

D. POLYVINYL ACRYLIC PRIMER, or PVA, is used to seal the porous surface of plaster and unglazed pottery, if a smooth paint finish is desired. To preserve the texture of plaster or unglazed pottery, apply the paint directly to the surface without using a primer.

E. STAIN-KILLING PRIMER seals stains like crayon, ink, and grease so they will not bleed through the top coat of paint. It is used to seal knotholes and is the recommended primer for cedar, redwood, and plywood with water-soluble dyes. This versatile primer is also used for glossy surfaces like glazed pottery and ceramic, making it unnecessary to sand or degloss the surface.

FINISHES

Finishes are sometimes used over paint as the final coat. They protect the painted surface with a transparent coating. The degree of protection and durability varies, from a light application of matte aerosol sealer to a glossy layer of clear finish.

F. CLEAR FINISH, such as water-based urethanes and acrylics, may be used over painted finishes for added durability. Available in matte, satin, and gloss, these clear finishes are applied with a brush or sponge applicator. Environmentally safe clear finishes are available in pints, quarts, and gallons (0.5, 0.9, and 3.8 L) at paint supply stores and in 4-oz. and 8-oz. (119 and 237 mL) bottles or jars at craft stores.

G. AEROSOL CLEAR ACRYLIC SEALER, available in matte or gloss, may be used as the final coat over paint as a protective finish. A gloss sealer also adds sheen and depth to the painted finish for a more polished look. Apply aerosol sealer in several light coats rather than one heavy coat, to avoid dripping or puddling. To protect the environment, select an aerosol sealer that does not contain harmful propellants. Use all sealers in a well-ventilated area.

Tools for Faux Finishing

Many tools and paintbrushes have been developed for creating specialized faux finishing effects. Depending on how they are used, some tools may create more than one effect. Working with the various tools and learning their capabilities is an important step in becoming a successful faux finisher. Most tools and paintbrushes are available in a range of sizes. As a general rule, use the largest size tool or brush suitable for the surface size.

D

F

C

G

B

A

H

Some tools and brushes are designed for manipulating the wet glaze on the surface, such as A. FLOGGERS, B. BLENDING BRUSHES or SOFTENERS, C. MOTTLERS, and D. STIPPLERS.

Certain faux effects are achieved using removal tools, such as E. COMBS, F. GRAINERS, G. OVERGRAINERS, and H. WIPE-OUT TOOLS. I. ARTIST'S ERASERS can be notched (page 28) and used as combs.

Specialty brushes designed for applying paints and glazes include artist's brushes, such as J. ROUNDS, K. LINERS, or L. DAGGERS. These may be used for veining in marble finishes or graining in wood finishes. M. STENCILING BRUSHES are available in ¼" to 1¼" (6 mm to 3.2 cm) diameters. Other tools, such as N. FEATHERS or O. SEA SPONGES are also used for applying paints and glazes. P. CHECK ROLLERS are specialty tools used for applying pore structure in a faux oak finish.

Preparing the Surface

To achieve a high-quality and long-lasting paint finish that adheres well to the surface, it is important to prepare the surface properly so it is clean and smooth. The preparation steps vary, depending on the type of surface you are painting. Often it is necessary to apply a primer to the surface before painting it. For more information about primers, refer to pages 8 and 9.

PREPARING SURFACES FOR PAINTING

SURFACE TO BE PAINTED	PREPARATION STEPS	PRIMER
UNFINISHED WOOD	1. Sand surface to smooth it. 2. Wipe with damp cloth to remove grit. 3. Apply primer.	Latex enamel undercoat.
PREVIOUSLY PAINTED WOOD	1. Clean surface to remove any grease and dirt. 2. Rinse with clear water; allow to dry. 3. Sand surface lightly to degloss and smooth it and to remove any loose paint chips. 4. Wipe with damp cloth to remove grit. 5. Apply primer to any areas of bare wood.	Not necessary, except to touch up areas of bare wood; then use latex enamel undercoat.
PREVIOUSLY VARNISHED WOOD	1. Clean surface to remove any grease and dirt. 2. Rinse with clear water; allow to dry. 3. Sand surface to degloss it. 4. Wipe with damp cloth to remove grit. 5. Apply primer.	Latex enamel undercoat.
UNFINSHED WALLBOARD	1. Dust with hand broom, or vacuum with soft brush attachment. 2. Apply primer.	Flat latex primer.
PREVIOUSLY PAINTED WALLBOARD	1. Clean surface to remove any grease and dirt. 2. Rinse with clear water; allow to dry. 3. Apply primer, only if making a dramatic color change.	Not necessary, except when painting over dark or strong color; then use flat latex primer.
UNPAINTED PLASTER	1. Sand any flat surfaces as necessary. 2. Dust with hand broom, or vacuum with soft brush attachment.	Polyvinyl acrylic primer.
PREVIOUSLY PAINTED PLASTER	1. Clean surface to remove any grease and dirt. 2. Rinse with clear water; allow to dry thoroughly. 3. Fill any cracks with spackling compound. 4. Sand surface to degloss it.	Not necessary, except when painting over dark or strong color; then use polyvinyl acrylic primer.
UNGLAZED POTTERY	1. Dust with brush, or vacuum with soft brush attachment. 2. Apply primer.	Polyvinyl acrylic primer or gesso.
GLAZED POTTERY, CERAMIC & GLASS	1. Clean surface to remove any grease and dirt. 2. Rinse with clear water; allow to dry thoroughly. 3. Apply primer.	Stain-killing primer.
METAL	1. Clean surface with vinegar or lacquer thinner to remove any grease and dirt. 2. Sand surface to degloss it and to remove any rust. 3. Wipe with damp cloth to remove grit. 4. Apply primer.	Rust-inhibiting latex metal primer.
FABRIC	1. Prewash fabric without fabric softener to remove any sizing, if fabric is washable. 2. Press fabric as necessary.	None.

Water-based Paints & Glazes

Latex and acrylic paints can be used successfully for a wide range of faux finishes and techniques. Because they are water-based, they are easy to clean up with just soap and water, and they are also safer for the environment than oil-based paints.

Water-based paints also dry quickly, which is not necessarily an advantage in faux finishing, especially for techniques that require some manipulation of the paint on the surface. To increase open time, or the length of time the paint can be manipulated, several paint additives have been developed. These include latex paint conditioner, such as Floetrol®, and acrylic extender.

For some faux finishing techniques, it is preferable to use a paint glaze, which is usually thinner and more translucent than paint. There are some premixed acrylic paint glazes available in limited colors. These may be mixed to acquire additional glaze colors. Untinted acrylic mediums in gloss, satin, or matte finishes are also available for mixing with acrylic or latex paint to make glazes. The glaze medium does not change the color of the paint; generally a small amount of paint is added to glaze medium, just enough to give it the color you want. Latex or acrylic paint can also be mixed with water-based urethane or varnish for a very translucent glaze.

GLOSS GLAZE. Faux marbles and semiprecious stones have high-gloss finishes that give them a more realistic appearance. Premixed glazes generally will dry with a gloss finish. To mix a glaze that will dry with a gloss finish, use acrylic medium that specifies gloss finish, or mix a urethane glaze. Follow instructions on glaze mediums or mix one part urethane, one part paint, and one part water.

SATIN OR MATTE GLAZE. For a translucent glaze that dries with a satin or matte finish, mix latex or acrylic paint with matte or satin acrylic medium, or mix matte finish acrylic medium into premixed glaze to cut the gloss.

FLAT PAINT GLAZE. For a faux finish with a naturally flat appearance, such as unpolished stone (page 23) or travertine (page 57), a flat paint glaze can be used. For small surface areas, this may simply mean mixing two parts paint and one part water. For extended open time, desired on a larger surface, use a recipe of one part paint, one part paint conditioner, and one part water. Vary the recipe to suit your own needs.

WASH. A wash is often applied as a final step in a faux finish to add a hint of color tone, or to give the illusion of depth. A wash is created by diluting latex or acrylic paint with water to the consistency of ink. Washes generally have a flat finish.

1. LOW-LUSTER LATEX ENAMEL PAINT is used for the base coat under faux finishes. The slightly sheened surface gives the finish a base to cling to, while allowing manipulation tools to move easily on the surface.

2. PREMIXED ACRYLIC PAINT GLAZES are available in a variety of colors for faux finishing. They are slightly translucent and contain additives for extended open time.

3. CRAFT ACRYLIC PAINTS are available in a wide range of colors. They can be used alone for stenciling, or mixed with acrylic mediums to create glazes for faux finishing.

4. ACRYLIC MEDIUMS can be mixed with acrylic or latex paint to create paint glazes with gloss, satin, or matte finishes.

FAUX STONE
FINISHES

Faux Granite Finish

Duplicating the look of natural granite is very easy. By combining the techniques of sponge painting and specking, you can create a simulated granite that is so realistic, people may actually have to touch it before they realize it is a painted finish.

Natural granite is formed from molten stone and has a crystalline appearance. Granite colors from different regions of the world vary greatly, depending on how fast the molten lava cooled. The most common types of granite in America are composed of earth tones in burnt umber, raw umber, warm gray, black, and white. Some exotic granites consist of a rich combination of burgundy, purple, black, and gray; a fiery mix of copper, umber, black, and gray; the cool opalescence of metallic blue, black, pearl, and gray; or a warm combination or orange, red, and salmon.

OPPOSITE: METAL LAMP AND WOODEN FRAME are finished in two coordinating colors of granite.

COLOR EFFECTS

Granite colors vary from one part of the world to another. Use the color combinations below to simulate some of the natural granites that exist.

Apply a black base coat. Use sea sponge to apply paints in medium gray, light gray, and metallic silver. Speck with more light gray paint (A).

Apply a dark ivory base coat. Use a sea sponge to apply paints in brown, medium gray, dark gray, and black. Speck with more black paint (B).

Apply a medium gray base coat. Use sea sponge to apply dark gray, black, and metallic copper. Speck with more black paint (C).

MATERIALS

- Flat latex or craft acrylic paint, for base coat.
- Flat latex or craft acrylic paint in desired colors, for sponging and specking; metallic paint may be used for one of the colors.
- Natural sea sponge.
- Fine-bristle scrub brush or toothbrush.
- Matte aerosol clear acrylic sealer or matte clear finish.

How to apply a faux granite finish

1. Prepare surface (page 13). Apply a base coat of flat latex or craft acrylic paint in white, gray, or black.

2. Dilute one paint color for sponging, one part paint to one part water, or to the consistency of ink; it may not be necessary to dilute metallic paint. Apply paint to surface in an up-and-down motion, using sea sponge.

3. Blot paint evenly with a clean, dampened sea sponge, immediately after applying it. This mottles the paint, blends it slightly with background color, and increases transparency. If the effect is not pleasing, wipe it off with a damp cloth before it dries.

4. Repeat steps 2 and 3 for remaining colors of paint for sponging, allowing each color to dry before the next color is applied. Allow some of the base coat to show through the other layers to create depth.

5. Apply diluted white, gray, or black paint to surface, using the specking technique, below. Speck the surface evenly in a light or moderate application.

6. Apply a matte aerosol clear acrylic sealer or clear finish to add sheen and depth and increase durability.

How to add specking

1. Dilute the paint for specking with water as in step 2, opposite. Test the paint consistency and technique by specking on cardboard before specking the actual project. Dip the bristles of a fine-bristle scrub brush or a toothbrush into the paint mixture. Dab once on a dry paper towel, to remove excess moisture and prevent drips.

2. Hold the brush next to surface; run craft stick or finger along bristles, causing specks of paint to spatter onto surface. Experiment with how fast you move the craft stick and how far away you hold the brush. Too much paint on the brush may cause paint to drip or run.

Faux Unpolished Stone Finish

Unpolished stone, in many colors and textures, is used extensively by the building industry, both in its natural state and cut into stone blocks. Just as genuine unpolished stones vary in surface textures, different faux painting techniques can be used to create faux unpolished stone finishes that are very different from each other. The painting technique of stippling results in a relatively smooth textured finish with blended colors. A stippler is repeatedly pounced over the surface, blending glazes and creating a fine-grained texture. Another method, using newspaper, results in an unpolished stone finish with depth, color variation, and rough visual texture.

Flat earth-tone glazes are used in all methods to create faux finishes that mimic real unpolished stones. Use the glazes suggested here, or select other earth-tone colors, as desired. For a faux finish resembling stone block, mask off grout lines and apply the finish to each stone individually. This allows you to vary the depth of color in adjacent stones. If applying the finish to a large, undivided surface, work in smaller areas at a time, leaving a wet edge. When dry, the painted stone may be left unsealed, or sealed with a matte finish.

MATERIALS

- White low-luster latex enamel paint, for base coat; sponge applicator or paintbrush, for smaller surface; sponge or low-napped roller, for larger surface.
- Flat paint glazes (page 14) in a variety of earth-tone colors, black, and white.
- Stippler (page 10), for stippling method.
- Newspaper, for newspaper method.
- White wash; earth-tone wash (page 14); cheesecloth.
- Matte aerosol clear acrylic sealer or matte clear finish, optional.

How to apply a faux unpolished stone finish using the stippling method

1. Prepare the surface (page 13). Apply base coat of white low-luster latex enamel to the surface, using applicator suitable to surface size. Allow to dry. Mask off grout lines, if desired.

2. Apply flat earth-tone glaze in random strokes, using sponge applicator or paintbrush; cover about half the surface. Repeat with another color glaze in remaining areas; leave some small areas of base coat unglazed.

3. Stipple over surface, using stippler; blend colors as desired, leaving some areas quite dark and others very light where base coat shows through. Add white and black glazes, if desired; add earth-tone glazes as necessary. Stipple to blend. Allow to dry.

4. Apply white wash to the entire surface. Dab with wadded cheesecloth to soften. Allow to dry. Apply matte clear finish or matte aerosol clear acrylic sealer, if desired.

How to apply a faux unpolished stone finish using the newspaper method

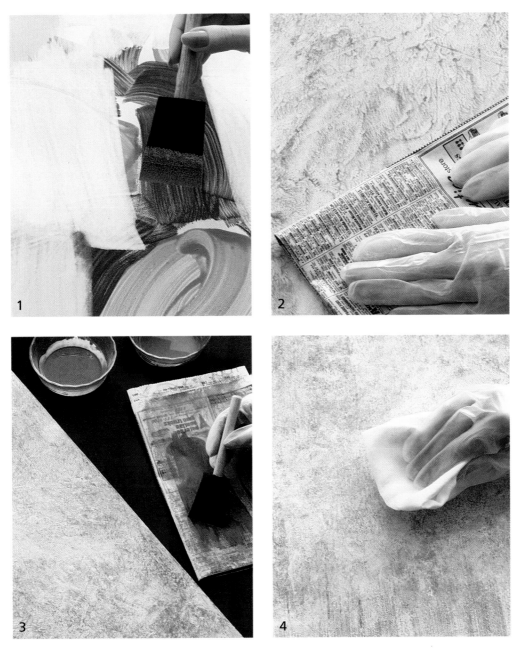

1. Follow steps 1 and 2, opposite. Apply white wash in areas desired; apply earth-tone wash in areas desired.

2. Fold a sheet of newspaper to several layers. Lay it flat over one area of surface and press into the glaze. Lift, removing some glaze. Repeat in other areas, turning same newspaper in different directions to blend colors roughly.

3. Add more color to an area by spreading glaze on newspaper and laying it flat on surface. Repeat as necessary until desired effect is achieved. Leave some dark accent areas in finish; also leave an occasional light spot. Use same newpaper throughout. Allow to dry.

4. Apply white wash to entire surface. Dab with a wadded cheesecloth to soften. Allow to dry. Apply matte clear finish or matte aerosol clear acrylic sealer, if desired.

Faux Tigereye Finish

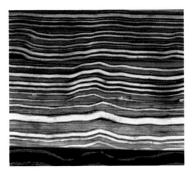

Tigereye is a semiprecious stone often used in jewelry or small ornamental pieces. This dark, glassy stone is characterized by undulating narrow bands of gold that have a changeable luster, like the eye of a cat.

The gold bands of a faux tigereye finish are created by first covering the surface with gold metallic paint, or, for a rich, luminous look, gold leaf. A raw umber gloss glaze is applied over the gold surface and combed, using the notched edge of an eraser, to reveal irregular bands of gold. After drying, a final wash (page 14) is drawn across the bands in the opposite direction, forming shadowy streaks that give the tigereye its undulating quality. A high-gloss finish is an essential last step, giving the tigereye finish a glassy brilliance.

Tigereye finish is appropriate for small, flat surfaces, such as a wooden box lid or picture frame. For an inlaid effect, a border of tigereye finish can be applied around the outer edge of a small table or tray.

MATERIALS

- Acrylic or latex paint in metallic gold color, for base coat; sponge applicator.
- Soft artist's eraser; mat knife.
- Raw umber gloss glaze; sponge applicator or paintbrush; newspaper.
- Cheesecloth.
- Raw umber wash.
- High-gloss clear finish or high-gloss aerosol clear acrylic sealer.

How to apply a faux tigereye finish

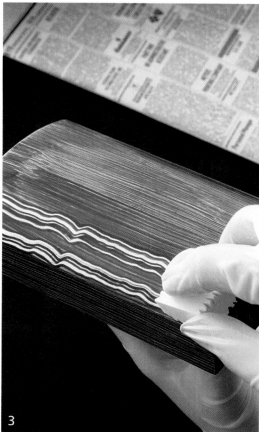

1. Prepare the surface (page 13). Apply base coat of gold metallic paint, or apply gold leaf and sealer. Notch edges of eraser in irregular pattern, using mat knife. Test notch patterns by pulling eraser edges through thin glaze spread on tagboard scrap. Each notched edge should leave clean, irregularly spaced stripes of varying widths from fine lines to 1/4" (6 mm) wide. Adjust the notches, if necessary.

2. Apply raw umber gloss glaze to surface, using sponge applicator or paintbrush; draw brush across surface in parallel lines.

3. Comb through glaze in direction of brush strokes, using notched edge of eraser. Start at outer edge of surface; move eraser slowly from top to bottom in continuous motion, creating gold bands with irregular small waves, dips, and peaks. Wipe excess glaze from eraser onto newspaper.

4. Comb through glaze next to previous bands, using another notched edge of eraser; vaguely follow pattern of previous bands. Wipe excess glaze from eraser. Repeat until entire surface has been combed, varying width of bands and spaces between them.

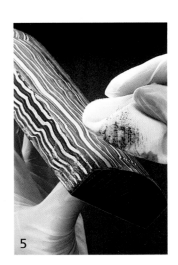

5. Dab surface with wadded cheesecloth, slightly softening gold bands. Allow to dry thoroughly.

6. Apply wash to the surface with sponge applicator, stroking in the opposite direction of gold bands and making wash more visible in some areas than others; allow hand to tremble, creating shadowy streaks. Allow to dry thoroughly.

7. Apply several thin coats of high-gloss clear finish or high-gloss aerosol clear acrylic sealer, allowing the surface to dry between coats.

Faux Malachite Finish

The distinctive banding pattern and vibrant green color of malachite make this semiprecious stone instantly recognizable. A cross-section of malachite reveals egg-shaped nodules surrounded by multiple bands, varying in width and intensity, that seem to echo from the nodules like ripples of water. The bands of malachite will vary from nearly straight to sharply curved. Genuine malachite in solid form is used in jewelry and carved objects, while thin slices of the stone are often inlaid in mosaic fashion on tabletops or other flat surfaces.

The painting technique used to simulate malachite is combing, using an irregularly notched edge of an artist's eraser. Malachite is usually depicted as pieced geometric sections on a small, flat surface, with the banding direction changing at each adjoining line. Some sections may show a partial nodule, created by combing in a tight, oval shape, with surrounding bands that echo from the nodule. Other sections may contain only bands with varying degrees of curve. The bands often have a characteristic V-formation, created by combing in an arc, hesitating, and then changing direction into a new arc. A final high-gloss finish gives faux malachite its characteristic depth and luster. It is helpful to sketch the layout of the sections and the pattern of banding in each section before beginning to paint. Also, practice the combing method to achieve the look of genuine malachite.

MATERIALS

- Paper and pencil, for sketching design.
- White low-luster latex enamel paint, for base coat; sponge applicator or paint brush.
- Bright green or blue-green latex or craft acrylic paint, acrylic urethane, for urethane glaze.
- Painter's masking tape.
- Very dark hunter or forest green gloss glaze (page 14).
- Sponge applicator or paintbrush, for applying glazes.
- Soft artist's eraser; mat knife or razor blade.
- Newspaper.
- Cheesecloth.
- Denatured alcohol; round artist's brush.
- High-gloss aerosol clear acrylic sealer or high-gloss clear finish.

URETHANE GLAZE

Mix together the following ingredients:

One part bright green or blue-green latex paint or craft acrylic paint.

One part acrylic urethane.

One part water.

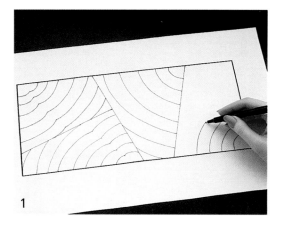

Making a sketch of the design

1. Outline design area to scale on piece of paper. Divide design area into sections, avoiding acute and square angles whenever possible. Sketch banding pattern in each section, including partial nodules in some sections; vary banding direction and degree of curve in adjoining sections.

How to apply a faux malachite finish

1. Prepare surface (page 13). Apply base coat of white low-luster latex enamel to surface, using sponge applicator. Allow to dry. Mix urethane glaze (page 31); apply to entire design area, using sponge applicator or paintbrush. Brush entire area first in one direction and then in opposite direction, leveling glaze. Allow to dry thoroughly. Divide design area into sections with light pencil lines, following sketch. Mask off first section to be glazed. Notch eraser edges as in step 1 on page 28.

2. Apply very dark green gloss glaze to first design section, using sponge applicator or paintbrush. Comb notched eraser edge through glaze, following sketched banding pattern, beginning and ending combing motion just beyond design area. If pattern contains nodule, comb it first. Allow hand to waver occasionally. Wipe excess glaze from eraser onto newspaper.

3. Comb through glaze next to previous bands, using another notched edge of eraser; follow pattern of previous bands, gradually widening arc on curved banding patterns. Repeat until section is completely combed. Remove tape.

4. Mask off next section that does not adjoin previously glazed section. Apply glaze; comb, following sketch. Remove tape. Repeat for remaining sections that do not adjoin. Allow to dry.

5. Mask off a section that adjoins a previously glazed section; position tape edge so hairline of glazed section is exposed. Apply glaze; comb, following sketch. Remove tape. Repeat for remaining unglazed sections until design is complete. Allow to dry.

6. Dilute dark green glaze with water to consistency of wash (page 14). Apply over entire design; dab with wadded cheesecloth to soften.

7. Spatter immediately with denatured alcohol, using round paintbrush in random, sparse application. Allow to dry thoroughly.

8. Apply several thin coats of high-gloss aerosol clear acrylic sealer or high-gloss clear finish, allowing the surface to dry between coats.

Faux Lapis Finish

Lapis is a deep blue semiprecious stone flecked with lustrous, golden mineral deposits. The blue color builds and recedes in drifts, in spots revealing pale gray tones. Because of its scarcity, it is generally used in fine jewelry or small, ornate accessories.

Faux lapis is applied, using a stippling technique. Two different deep blue paint glazes are stippled onto the surface in diagonal drifts, sometimes blending with each other and at other times remaining separate, thus creating the characteristic depth of color. Droplets of denatured alcohol, sprinkled over the wet glaze, cause amorphous rings in the glaze. Gold powder is sprinkled over the wet glaze and gently pressed into the surface to resemble mineral deposits. After drying, a high-gloss aerosol acrylic sealer is applied for a glassy appearance.

For a realistic appearance, faux lapis can be applied to any small paintable surface, such as a ceramic vase. It can also be applied as inlaid sections on a flat surface.

When using metallic powders, avoid any drafts that may blow the powder around and wear a protective mask to prevent inhaling the fine particles.

MATERIALS

- Light gray low-luster latex enamel paint, for base coat; sponge applicator or paintbrush.
- Prussian blue gloss glaze (page 14).
- Cobalt blue gloss glaze (page 14).
- Stippler (page 10), in size suitable to project.
- Denatured alcohol; round artist's paintbrush.
- Cheesecloth.
- Gold powder; protective mask.
- High-gloss aerosol clear acrylic sealer.

How to apply a faux lapis finish

1. Prepare surface (page 13). Apply base coat of light gray low-luster latex enamel to surface, using sponge applicator or paintbrush. Allow to dry. Apply Prussian blue gloss glaze in random strokes, using sponge applicator or paintbrush; cover about half the surface. Repeat with cobalt blue gloss glaze in remaining areas; leave some small areas of base coat unglazed.

2. Stipple over entire area, blending colors slightly and leaving lighter small areas where base coat shows through.

3. Spatter droplets of denatured alcohol over wet glaze, using round artist's brush; apply droplets in diagonal drifts. Allow alcohol to react in glaze.

4. Dab some alcohol droplets with wadded cheesecloth to soften; leave other droplets undisturbed. Apply more Prussian blue glaze onto surface in diagonal drifts; repeat, using cobalt blue glaze. Stipple, blending colors slightly.

5. Repeat steps 3 and 4. Load small amount of gold metallic powder on dry round artist's brush. Hold brush about 12" (30.5 cm) above surface; tap the brush gently, allowing the powder to fall onto darker areas of the surface in small concentrations.

6. Press gold powder gently into the surface with wadded cheesecloth.

7. Repeat steps 5 and 6 as desired. Apply more Prussian blue glaze in some areas, deepening color; soften with cheesecloth. Repeat step 3 over fresh glaze. Allow entire surface to dry thoroughly. Apply several thin coats of high-gloss aerosol clear acrylic sealer, allowing surface to dry between coats.

FAUX MARBLE FINISHES

Faux Onyx Finish

Onyx is a black semiprecious mineral with wispy bands of white that resemble the veins found in many marbles. It has long been used for small carvings or accessories, accentuating the high contrast between the black background and white bands.

To create the white bands in a faux onyx finish, acrylic extender and acrylic thickener are applied alongside white paint, using a turkey feather. This results in wispy bands that fluctuate from opaque to translucent. A high-gloss finish gives the faux onyx a glassy, polished look.

MATERIALS

- Black craft acrylic or flat latex paint, for base coat.
- White craft acrylic paint.
- Acrylic paint thickener.
- Acrylic paint extender.
- Natural sea sponge.
- Two turkey or pheasant feathers.
- Disposable plate.
- High-gloss aerosol clear acrylic sealer.

How to apply a faux onyx finish

1. Prepare surface (page 13). Apply a base coat of black craft acrylic or flat latex paint. Allow to dry.

2. Apply a long pool of white paint onto a disposable plate. Apply pool of thickener on one side of white paint and extender on the other.

3. Run edge of feather through pools, picking up some thickener, paint, and extender on feather; cover the entire length of feather. Blot excess onto paper towel.

4. Zigzag the feather across base coat in 3" to 4" (7.5 to 10 cm) irregular diagonal bands, with some of the bands meeting or intersecting. Work on only two or three bands at a time, because paint dries quickly.

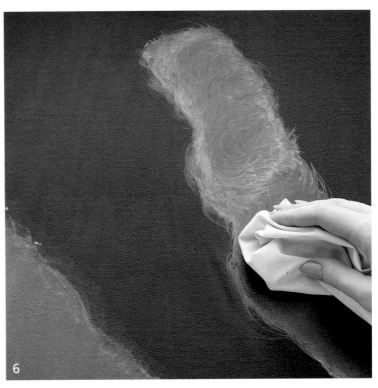

5. Smear the bands of white in a circular motion, using moist sea sponge, for the look of softened light clouds.

6. Rub the bands lightly while still wet, using a dry rag, to give them the appearance of dust on a chalkboard; do not rub over the black base coat. Reapply white paint if too much is rubbed away. If surface dries too quickly, apply water, then rub with rag to soften. Allow to dry.

7. Run edge of the feather through pools of thickener, paint, and extender; blot on paper towel. Place tip of feather onto surface; drag the feather along, fidgeting it and turning it slightly in your hand to create veins. Outline chalky bands with veins; apply more veins in a diagonal direction, crisscrossing them as desired. The thickener and extender vary the veins so some areas are opaque and some are translucent. Allow the paint to dry. Apply several coats of high-gloss aerosol clear acrylic sealer.

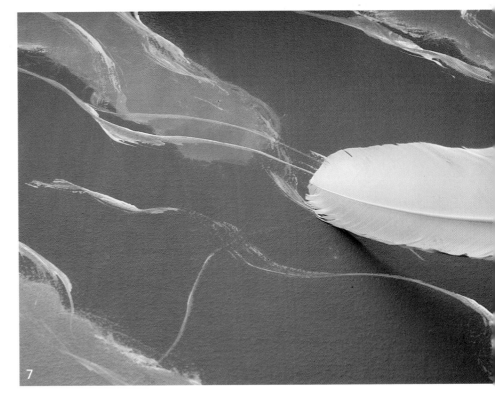

Faux Serpentine Finish

Serpentine is the general name given to a variety of green marbles that contain deposits of the mineral, serpentine. The different varieties vary in visual texture and color tone, often with traces of black and white. Some serpentines may be characterized by a network of fine veining, while others contain little or no veining. As with other marbles, the serpentines have various architectural uses, including floors, walls, and pillars.

Just as genuine marble is cut into workable pieces for installation, a faux serpentine finish applied to a large surface is more realistic if applied in sections with narrow grout lines. By masking off alternate sections, the finish can be applied to half the project, following steps 1 to 9. When the first half has been allowed to dry completely, the completed sections can be masked off, and the finish can be applied to the remaining sections. A high-gloss finish is then applied to the entire surface, giving the faux finish the lustrous appearance of genuine marble.

MATERIALS

- Medium green low-luster latex enamel paint, for base coat; sponge applicator or paintbrush, for small surface, or low-napped roller, for larger surface.

- Black gloss glaze (page 14).

- Green gloss glaze (page 14), in darker shade than base coat

- White gloss glaze (page 14).

- Newspaper, cheesecloth, stippler, for applying and working glaze.

- Spray bottle; water.

- Turkey feather, for veining.

- High-gloss clear finish or high-gloss aerosol clear acrylic sealer.

How to apply a faux serpentine finish

1. Prepare surface (page 13). Apply base coat of medium green low-luster latex enamel to surface, using applicator suitable to surface size. Apply black, green and white gloss glazes separately in random, broad, diagonal strokes, using sponge applicator or paintbrush; cover most of surface, allowing small patches of base coat to show through.

2. Stipple the glazes in adjoining areas to blend slightly, pouncing stippler rapidly over the surface.

3. Fold a sheet of newspaper to several layers; lay flat over an area of surface, in the same diagonal direction as original strokes. Press newspaper into glaze; lift, removing some of glaze.

4. Repeat step 3 over entire surface, using same newspaper; turn paper in opposite direction occasionally. Add glazes as desired to develop color. Dab areas of high contrast with wadded cheesecloth, to soften. Mist surface with water, if necessary, to keep glazes workable.

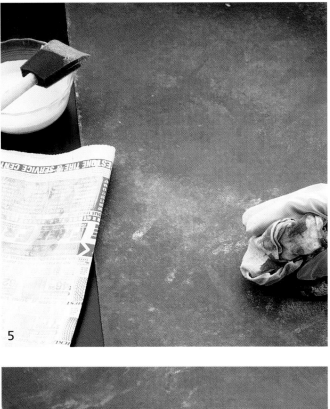

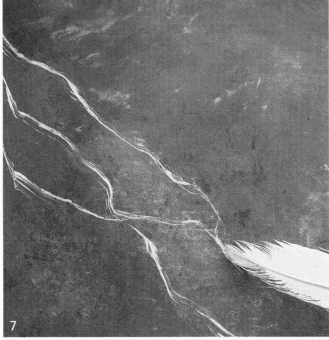

5. Brush black glaze onto newspaper and touch to surface diagonally in scattered areas, adding drama and depth. Soften with cheesecloth, if necessary. Repeat, using white glaze in small, lighter areas.

6. Dilute mixture of white and green glazes with water to consistency of light cream. Run edge and tip of feather through diluted glaze. Place tip of feather onto surface in desired placement for vein; lightly drag feather diagonally over surface, fidgeting and turning slightly and varying pressure, to create irregular, jagged vein. Begin and end vein lines off edge of surface.

7. Repeat step 6 as desired to build veining pattern; connect adjacent vein lines occasionally, creating narrow, oblong, irregular shapes. Dab veins lightly with wadded cheesecloth to soften, if necessary. Allow surface to dry.

8. Dilute glazes to consistency of wash (page 14); apply randomly to surface. Dab with wadded cheesecloth to soften. Allow to dry. Apply several thin coats of high-gloss clear finish or high-gloss aerosol clear acrylic sealer, allowing surface to dry between coats.

GOLD VEINING GLAZE

Mix together the following ingredients:

One part gold metallic craft acrylic paint.

One part acrylic urethane.

One part water.

Faux Portoro Finish

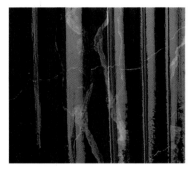

Portoro, also known as black and gold marble, has been used for centuries in architecture and for smaller-scale decorative work. It is characterized by networks of fibrous veining, usually 1″ to 3″ (2.5 to 7.5 cm) wide and running in very linear patterns through wide expanses of black marble. The veining networks are often gold in color, though the color can be more off-white or beige. Distinctive white secondary veins intersect the networks at opposing angles, threading over or under the veining in staggered lines.

Select faux Portoro for a dramatic finish on a bathroom wall or fireplace surround. On a smaller scale, paint a faux Portoro finish on a table base or pedestal. Apply the finish with the veining networks running horizontally or vertically. If possible, turn the work so that you are working vertically from top to bottom, since the veining brush will be held at right angles to the veining network. Start and end veining networks off the surface, implying visually that they continued beyond the cut marble.

OPPOSITE: THE FAUX PORTORO FINISH makes it look as though this pedestal has been carved from solid marble. A high-gloss finish makes the illusion even more believable.

MATERIALS

- Black low-luster latex enamel paint, for base coat; sponge applicator or paintbrush, for small surface area, or roller, for larger area.
- Gold metallic acrylic paint, acrylic urethane, for gold veining glaze.
- Round artist's brush.
- White gloss glaze (page 14).
- Black wash (page 14).
- Cheesecloth.
- High-gloss clear finish or high-gloss aerosol clear acrylic sealer.

How to apply a faux Portoro finish

1. Prepare surface (page 13). Apply base coat of black low-luster latex enamel to surface, using applicator suitable to surface size. Allow to dry.

2. Mix gold veining glaze (page 48). Dip round artist's brush into water, then into glaze. Hold the brush sideways at upper edge of surface, at right angle to line of veining network; hold brush between thumb and fingers near end of handle, with thumb on top. Pull brush toward lower edge, rolling brush handle back and forth and fidgeting to create irregular, jagged veining line.

3. Repeat step 2 in second vein alongside first vein; add third vein as desired.

4. Dip brush into water, then into glaze. Paint thin, fidgety lines connecting adjacent veins, using the tip of the brush; also, form small nodules here and there along one side of each main vein by connecting jagged points.

5. Allow gold veining networks to dry. Dip brush into water, then into white glaze. Paint a few thin, fidgety lines at opposing angles to veining networks; avoid right angles. Cross directly over the top of some veining networks; on others break the white line as it passes behind gold veins. Allow to dry.

6. Apply black wash to entire surface. Dab with wadded cheesecloth to soften. Allow to dry.

7. Apply several thin coats of high-gloss clear finish or high-gloss aerosol clear acrylic sealer, allowing surface to dry between coats.

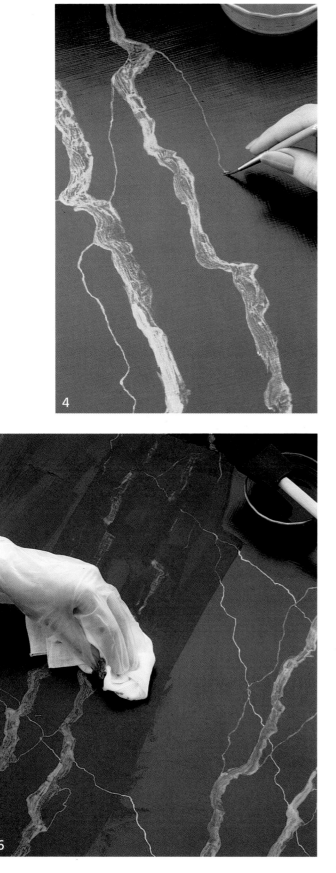

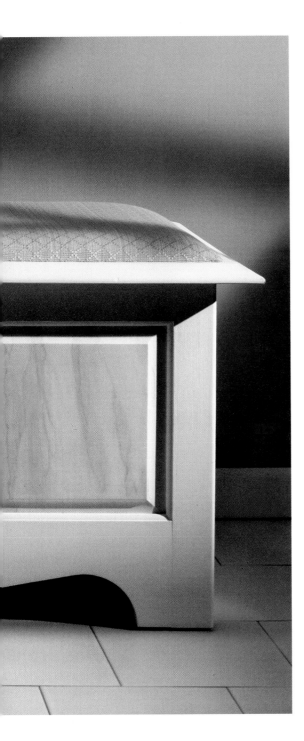

Faux Norwegian Rose Finish

Norwegian rose is a white marble with patches of pink and green mineral deposits that give the marble its striking contrast of colors. Patchy drifts of dusty pink color fade into hues of taupe and tan, surrounded by a gray-green veining structure.

The decorative uses for a faux Norwegian rose marble finish include floor or wall tiles, pillars, accessories, and tabletops. The marble pattern, determined by the direction of the veining structure, can be set up vertically, horizontally, or at an angle, depending on the desired effect.

MATERIALS

- White low-luster latex enamel paint, for base coat; sponge applicator or paintbrush, for small surface, or low-napped roller, for larger surface.
- White gloss glaze (page 14).
- Pink gloss glaze (page 14).
- Tan gloss glaze (page 14).

- Raw umber gloss glaze (page 14).
- Sponge applicator, cheesecloth, feather, blending brush, for applying and working glazes.
- White wash (page 14).
- High-gloss clear finish or high-gloss aerosol clear acrylic sealer.

How to apply a faux Norwegian rose finish

1. Prepare surface (page 13). Apply base coat of white low-luster latex enamel to surface, using applicator suitable to surface size. Apply pink gloss glaze to surface in a few random oval patches, angling ovals in desired direction of marble pattern.

2. Apply narrow patches of tan gloss glaze along the sides of some pink patches, running tan areas together. Avoid any regular pattern or balanced placement. Apply white gloss glaze in remaining areas. Dab with wadded cheesecloth to soften and blend adjoining colors.

3. Whisk over the surface in desired direction of the marble pattern, using blending brush (page 10) to soften and elongate patches of color. Whisk occasionally in the direction perpendicular to pattern to widen patches slightly.

4. Apply more glaze, dab with cheesecloth, and whisk as needed to achieve the desired look. Repeat for all areas of surface.

5

5. Run edge and tip of feather through the raw umber glaze; drag the feather over the surface, roughly outlining patches of color. Connect adjacent vein lines, creating narrow, oblong, irregular shapes.

6. Dab veins lightly with wadded cheese-cloth to soften. Whisk with blending brush to elongate and blur vein lines. Allow to dry.

7. Apply white wash to the surface; dab with wadded cheesecloth to soften. Whisk with blending brush. Allow to dry. Apply several thin coats of high-gloss clear finish or high-gloss aerosol clear acrylic sealer, allowing the surface to dry between coats.

6

7

*F*aux Travertine Finish

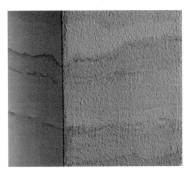

Travertine is a type of limestone used extensively in architecture, especially for large surfaces, such as floors and walls. It is formed when water from underground springs deposits layer upon layer of minerals in faulted horizontal bands. Throughout the layers of mineral deposits, small pits are created as the water evaporates. These open pits are very evident in unpolished travertine, the form used most often. For some uses of travertine, the surface pits are filled and the stone is polished. Because of its very linear structure, travertine can be used vertically, horizontally, or diagonally for different effects.

For a faux travertine finish, flat earth-tone glazes are applied in narrow, blended bands over a white base coat. Denatured alcohol is applied to the wet glaze, mottling the bands with swirls and voids that resemble the mineral deposits and pits in the stone. These mottled bands are separated by wide, pale bands that are very lightly streaked. When applying the finish to a large, unbroken surface, such as a wall or tabletop, apply all mottled bands first. Repeat steps 2 through 5 for each mottled band, working in rough 24" (61 cm) lengths and keeping a wet edge until the entire band is complete. When all mottled bands are dry, apply thinned glaze, as in steps 7 and 8. Then apply all separating layers (steps 9 and 10). When all layers have been completed, the final wash and optional matte finish can be applied to the entire surface. The finish may also be applied in sections, resembling stone blocks, allowing you to work on one block at a time.

How to apply a faux travertine finish

MATERIALS

- White low-luster latex enamel paint, for base coat; sponge applicator, paintbrush, or roller.
- Flat raw sienna glaze (page 14).
- Flat raw umber glaze (page 14).
- Flat white glaze (page 14).
- Stippler.
- Spray bottle with water.
- Denatured alcohol; round artist's paintbrush.
- Cheesecloth.
- Blending brush or softener.
- Ivory wash (page 14).
- Matte clear finish or matte aerosol clear acrylic sealer, optional.

1. Prepare surface (page 13). Apply base coat of white low-luster latex enamel to surface, using applicator suitable to surface size. Allow to dry.

2. Apply narrow bands of flat raw sienna glaze, flat raw umber glaze, and flat white glaze next to each other on surface, breaking and staggering bands randomly.

3

4

3 Stipple bands of glaze in adjoining areas, blending colors slightly. Mist with water to keep surface moist.

4. Dip round artist's paintbrush into denatured alcohol; touch tip of brush into wet glaze, applying small amounts of alcohol throughout stippled band. Reload brush as needed.

5. Roll brush through band, redistributing alcohol. Allow alcohol to react with glaze, creating swirls and voids throughout the band. Dab with cheesecloth as needed, to soften effect.

Continued

5

How to apply a faux travertine finish

(CONTINUED)

6. Repeat steps 2 through 5 for each mottled band, allowing spaces for separating bands two to four times the width of mottled band. Allow mottled bands to dry.

7. Thin white glaze with water to consistency of light cream. Apply to mottled band, using sponge applicator or paintbrush; dab with wadded cheesecloth to soften.

8. Spatter denatured alcohol throughout band; stipple. Add more thinned glaze as desired; repeat alcohol application.

9. Repeat steps 7 and 8 for each mottled band. Sideload the brush with small amount of raw umber glaze; dip in thinned white glaze. Draw the brush through separating band several times, forming watery, pale streaks. Allow to dry slightly.

10. Brush over the slightly dry separating band with light strokes in opposite direction, using dry blending brush.

11. Repeat steps 9 and 10 for all separating bands. Allow the entire surface to dry thoroughly. Apply ivory wash, using sponge applicator or paintbrush; dab with wadded cheesecloth to soften. Allow to dry. Apply matte clear finish or matte aerosol clear acrylic sealer, if desired.

Index

CY DECOSSE INCORPORATED

President/COO: Nino Tarantino
Executive V.P./Editor-in-Chief: William B. Jones
Chairman Emeritus: Cy DeCosse

Creative Touches™
Group Executive Editor: Zoe A. Graul
Managing Editor: Elaine Johnson
Editor: Linda Neubauer
Associate Creative Director: Lisa Rosenthal
Senior Art Director: Delores Swanson
Art Director: Mark Jacobson
Contributing Art Director: Judith Meyers
Copy Editor: Janice Cauley
Desktop Publishing Specialist: Laurie Kristensen
Sample Production Manager: Carol Olson
Studio Manager: Marcia Chambers
Print Production Manager: Patt Sizer

COWLES
Enthusiast Media

President/COO: Philip L. Penny

STONE FINISHES ETC.
Created by: The Editors of Cy DeCosse Incorporated

Also available in the Creative Touches™ series:

Stenciling Etc., Sponging Etc., Valances Etc.,
Painted Designs Etc., Metallic Finishes Etc., Swags Etc.,
Papering Projects Etc.

The Creative Touches™ series draws from the individual titles of
The Home Decorating Institute®. Individual titles are also available
from the publisher and in bookstores and fabric stores.

Printed on American paper by:
  R. R. Donnelley & Sons Co.
99 98 97 96 / 5 4 3 2 1

Cy DeCosse Incorporated offers a variety of how-to books.

For information write:
  Cy DeCosse Subscriber Books
  5900 Green Oak Drive
  Minnetonka, MN 55343

SMALL
WORLD

SMALL WORLD

A MICROCOSMIC JOURNEY

BRAD HERZOG

POCKET BOOKS

New York   London   Toronto   Sydney

POCKET BOOKS, a division of Simon & Schuster, Inc.
1230 Avenue of the Americas, New York, NY 10020

ISBN: 0-7434-6470-2

First Pocket Books trade paperback edition May 2004

10   9   8   7   6   5   4   3   2   1

Manufactured in the United States of America

For information regarding special discounts for bulk purchases,
please contact Simon & Schuster Special Sales at 1-800-456-6798
or business@simonandschuster.com

To Luke and Jesse,
my small world

The gentle reader will never know what a consummate ass he can become until he goes abroad. I speak now, of course, in the supposition that the gentle reader has not been abroad, and therefore is not already a consummate ass. If the case be otherwise, I beg his pardon and extend to him the cordial hand of fellowship and call him brother. I shall always delight to meet an ass after my own heart when I have finished my travels.

— MARK TWAIN, *THE INNOCENTS ABROAD*

CONTENTS

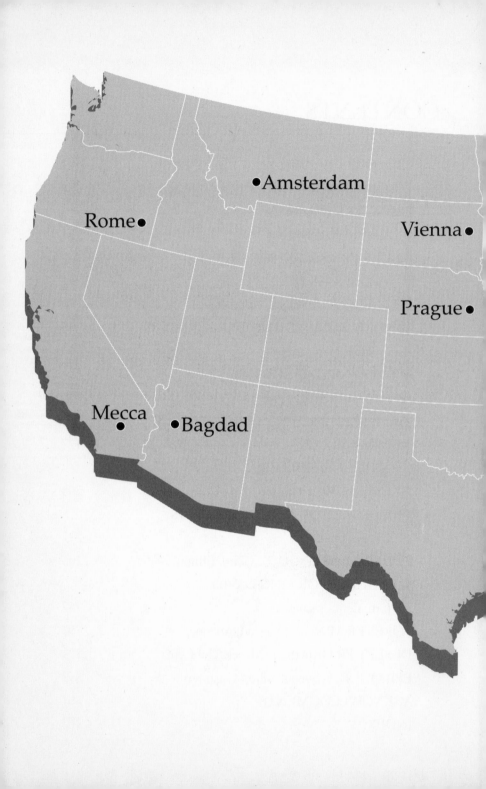

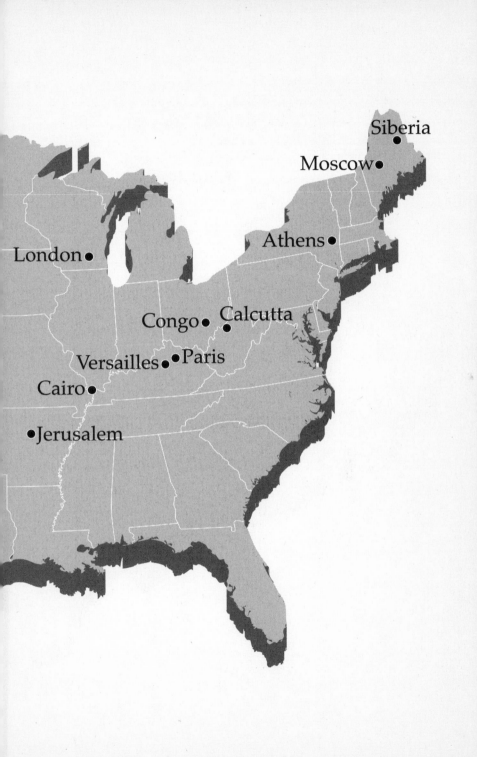

PROLOGUE

FREEBIRD

It was a place immersed in unreality.

And there I was, staring down at a dwindling pile of play money atop a faux felt blackjack table, sipping a watered-down drink served by a woman with silicone breasts and collagen-puffed lips, suffering disingenuous banter with false companions and insincere sympathy from a dealer wearing fake fingernails to match her smile, surrounded by bent and bleary-eyed folks reflexively dropping quarters into slot machines with illusory names like Life of Luxury and Carnival of Wonders, all in the pursuit of unattainable jackpot dreams.

Ah, Reno, Nevada. God bless America!

I had arrived there, appropriately, along a trail blazed by greed—I-80 through the Sierra Nevada, once the site of hundreds of mining camps with names like Poker Flat and Gouge Eye. Just over a century-and-a-half earlier, a man named Johann Augustus Sutter had trodden much the same trail. Like me, he had been in his mid-thirties and had set off from California's Monterey Peninsula toward lands unknown, dreaming of great discovery. But the similarities end there. He found gold by his sawmill, launched the great Gold Rush, and eventually died penniless. Nowadays, the gold seekers go to Reno. This is where I began my hunt for the sociological equivalent of buried treasure—at a point of embarkation as artificial as neon in the desert.

There was a campground alongside the casino, but it was a

1

KOA carved out of a parking lot. There was a lake alongside the lot, but it was a man-made lake, designed as a target for golfers at a driving range. And there was live music blaring from an outdoor amphitheater nearby, where I glimpsed a stage backed by a massive Confederate flag and heard the familiar opening guitar pick of "Sweet Home Alabama." But it was still only an approximation of the real thing. The soul of Lynyrd Skynyrd had died in an airplane crash a quarter-century earlier. This was simulated Skynyrd, the remnants of the band, a sound soon replaced by a cacophony of electronic bells and whistles and crap-game shouts.

Later, my pockets lighter, I left the casino and returned to the fresh air of a July evening grown cooler. The band was still on stage, and I stood there for a moment, listening. It was the quiet between songs, and I could hear voices shouting requests into the night: "Freebird! Freebird!" Then came the tinkling of a piano, answered by the wail of an electric guitar and the roar of an arena.

"If I leave here tomorrow . . . will you still remember me? . . . I must be traveling on now . . . 'Cuz there's too many places I've got to see. . . ."

This was hardly a setting for poignancy, yet there it was.

Mine was a journey undertaken with some misgivings. A few days earlier, I had bid farewell to my wife and two little boys, as they boarded an airplane that would take them from California toward a summer with the grandparents in Chicago. I had become a father twice-over in the past twenty months, an experience that tends to shrink your world by focusing your priorities. But for me, it had also become an occasion for large-scale assessment. Into what kind of world did I bring my children? What were the neighbors like (the neighborhood being a continent wide)? Hence, this journey.

I had planned an itinerary that would take me through Chicago a couple of times, allowing me to see my family every few weeks. Still, I wondered if this trip was the right thing to do. I could only hope that someday my sons would understand that their father had to leave them for a while one summer because he was on a mission to take stock of their world. Perhaps they would someday see the attempt as a lesson in exploration. Maybe they would follow in my footsteps—take the road less traveled, try to understand the overlooked, shift the boulder to discover the teeming life beneath it.

Or not. But as long as they remember to call . . .

It struck me as an interesting time to take on the responsibility of parenting. As my expedition began, many of the nation's other iconic institutions were reeling. The once-venerated U.S. intelligence community had become fodder for late-night TV monologues. A stunning series of Wall Street scandals had revealed that some of the highest floors of corporate America were inhabited by some of the lowest forms of life. The stock market was in a freefall. Leaders of the Catholic Church had forsaken their flock, choosing the status quo over the safety of children. And baseball—geez, baseball—was dominated by talk of steroids and work stoppages and Ted Williams' children arguing over what to do with his lifeless body. At any moment I expected to hear that apple pie causes cancer.

There was a collective crisis of confidence in those entrusted with our safety, our money, our faith, our future. And hovering above it all was a big bold headline that trumped the rest—AMERICA UNDER ATTACK—along with the daily apprehension that the words still applied.

Following the shock of 9/11 the great majority of Americans reveled in allegiance to country, more so than at any time in the past half-century. It may be a mess of a place at the moment, we said, but it's our mess, and we'll defend it. Ask what we were defending, however, and the usual reply offered only sound bites and vague abstractions. Listening to the typical American describe the provenance of his patriotism is a bit like listening to a book report by an eighth-grader who read only the back cover. A great many patriots have largely lost touch with America.

There is an irony of scale. The modern world is small, indeed. We send faxes to Tokyo and emails to Madrid. We retrieve television signals from Belfast and Beijing. In no time in history have we been more familiar with more places than we are now. But as the world's size diminishes, so too has our familiarity with places closer to home.

Like a New Yorker who hasn't gotten around to visiting the Statue of Liberty, Americans tend to take the neighborhood for granted. We translate distance to wonder—the longer the journey, the greater the destination. In the process, we seem to be missing the trees for the forest. How many U.S. citizens have been to India, but not Indiana? How many have vacationed in the south of France, but couldn't find South Dakota on a map if you spotted them North Dakota? Indeed, I would bet that there are a great many Americans who have never actually seen the amber waves of grain.

Disregard for the nation's so-called flyover spaces has become such a coastal and urban reflex that America has become merely a patchwork quilt of stereotypes and rumors. Whole regions have become punch lines. I recall a joke from *Saturday Night Live* in which a Weekend Update anchor related a sordid and absurd news story about someone from a rural region, and then she said simply, "And that's the news from Tennessee." The audience howled. Sure, most in the New York crowd had never had an actual conversation with a blues singer in Memphis or a banker in Chattanooga or an antiques dealer in Gatlinburg. But, oh, that backward-ass Tennessee!

Some months later, Fox Television, which never met a bar it couldn't lower, came up with a show called *The Simple Life* in which notoriously spoiled hotel-chain heiress Paris Hilton and an equally pampered friend were "forced" to spend a few weeks in Altus, Arkansas (pop. 817). It could be argued that half the country's population lives in a place much like Altus. But to Hollywood, it is a culture so foreign that it is akin to being stranded on an island: *Survivor: The Ozarks.*

Likewise, I came across a cartoon in *The New Yorker* depicting a car racing along the highway, clearly in one of those places deemed the Middle of Nowhere. On the side of the road was a lonely sign announcing, YOUR OWN TEDIOUS THOUGHTS NEXT 200 MILES. The implication: There's nothing out there, and any place without Starbucks and sushi bars is unworthy of exploration.

The problem isn't that many Americans don't know what's out there. It's that they don't care. This attitude has become endemic. In schools, geography appears to be going the way of Latin. A 2002 *National Geographic* survey of college-aged Americans found that only half could locate New York on a map. One in ten couldn't even find Texas or, when given a blank world map, the United States itself.

On the bright side, apparently people are beginning to, as Paul Simon put it, "look for America" again. September 11th was quickly christened The Day That Changed The Nation, but look around. Detached irony didn't die. The political arena is as partisan as it ever has been. We seem to have learned few lessons about global cooperation or the futility of violence or the excesses of religious fundamentalism. It didn't even take long for folks to start complaining about overzealous airport security. But one thing has happened: People are increasingly taking to the road. Blame flying fears, perhaps, but the road trip seems to have emerged as a comforting option, an exodus from urban angst. Or maybe we're beginning to realize the benefit of exploring that which we're defending.

We understand our world by expanding our reach, and it begins with the small world close to home. So I decided to hit the highway in an effort to explore the real America. Not the America of tabloids and talk shows, not the America of post-9/11 should-be and could-be, but the America that is and long has been—wonder and warts and all.

Lynyrd Skynyrd's "Freebird" is one of those tunes that masquerades as a ballad in the early going, then shifts into hard rock mode. As I listened and the song segued into a frenzied guitar solo, I was transported to another reflection, to summer camp in the North Woods a quarter-century earlier. Once each July, an eager group of us campers would grab our racquets and race down to the tennis courts knowing there was no tennis on the agenda. Instead, a counselor would flip a tape into a cassette player, and southern rock's anthem would waft into the Wisconsin sky.

" 'Cuz I'm as free as a bird now . . . and this bird you'll never change. . . ."

By the time the song played out, a few dozen sweaty eleven-year-olds would have air-guitared our hearts out. None of us knew who the hell Lynyrd Skynyrd was. Half of us thought it was some guy named Leonard. But we tried hard—a little Chuck Berry here, a Pete Townsend there, maybe a Mick strut or an Elvis snarl. And we improvised. I distinctly remember wearing my racquet cover on my head. The best performer of the evening was usually awarded an ice cream bar, an unmatched prize in summer camp, where sugar is like gold. But I was never much interested in the ice cream. I reveled in the experience. On that night I could aspire to greater things. Like being a preteen Jewish lead guitarist in a band of good ol' boys.

Such was the subtext of my journey—humble American aspirations. New York City may be the cultural center of the world and the nerve center of a nation, but it isn't the heart of America. For that one needs to head for the wide-open spaces and quirky crossroads that many folks speed past or fly over in a hurry to get to somewhere else. The United States is less a melting pot than a masterpiece of pointillism, a dot painting defined not by the broad strokes of mainstream media and metropolitan muscle, but by the smallest dots on the map. The colors blend from a distance; they stand out boldly from up close. If you want to understand America, you have to connect the dots.

Reno calls itself "the biggest little city in the world." I would take it one step further. There is a world of stories along the American highway, so I decided to attempt a global expedition of sorts—Magellan in microcosm. My itinerary included visits to hamlets with names like Cairo and Calcutta, Athens and Amsterdam, Paris and Prague. It was merely a means to an end, an excuse to canvas the country. My hypothesis: One can find the fascinating, the exotic, the eccentric and eclectic in one's own backyard.

You just have to squint a little.

In Jules Verne's classic, *Around the World in 80 Days*, protagonist Phileas Fogg completed his arduous trek by rail, by steamship, even by elephant. I was shooting for fifty days in a state-of-the-art RV. I am of the opinion, once articulated by Howard Vincent O'Brien, that discomfort can be endured but should be avoided. My twenty-one-foot Winnebago Rialta offered well-designed self-sufficiency (bed, toilet, microwave, refrigerator, freezer) and a Volkswagen engine powerful enough to let me reach triple digits on the speedometer—if I were so inclined. All in all, it's what James Bond would drive if Her Majesty's Secret Service ever sent him to Yellowstone. Verne's description of Fogg well described my vehicle: "an enigmatical personage" who "talked very little and seemed all the more mysterious for his taciturn manner." So I named him Phileas, and we got along famously.

Still, I identified less with Verne than with a contemporary of his—Mark Twain. More than once, Twain lugged his uniquely American perspective around the world, passing through, as he put it, "the strangest, funniest, undreamt-of old towns." His were some of the earliest travel narratives, accounts sprinkled with insight and amazement and scorn and disillusion and bemusement. I expected to experience the same range of emotions closer to home. Along the way, I hoped to gather some historical perspective, something that also seems to be increasingly foreign to many Americans.

A friend of mine tells a story about parking himself at an overlook at the North Rim of the Grand Canyon. He watched as a young boy and his father peered over the edge and marveled at how the Colorado River carved out such massiveness.

"Wow! How long did it take, Dad?" asked the boy, staring at the canyon formed over the epochs.

"Son," said the father, placing a hand on the boy's shoulder and standing tall while imparting his knowledge, "it took *hundreds* of years."

Somewhere along the line, we seem to have lost a grasp of time and place, a sense of the scope of things. I aimed to tighten my grip. It has been said that tourists leave home to escape the world, while travelers aim to experience it. Let me be a traveler then, an innocent abroad. Let me take to the open road and allow myself those rare moments devoted only to reflection. Let me watch a motion picture of America unfold before me, stop the film intermittently and enter the celluloid. Let me trek to the so-called Middle of Nowhere and ask myself how I got here, while maybe learning how we all did.

Geography is the residue of time, and every small town tells a tale. The towns come and go, their stories often fleeting and easily lost, like candles flickering in the wind. If I could save a few flames still smoldering off the beaten path, so much the better. Of course, every tale is at the mercy of the teller's state of mind. Or as Twain put it following his final global excursion, "The very ink with which all history is written is merely fluid prejudice."

Let this be mine.

OH GIVE ME A HOME

ROME, OREGON

As a rule, men worry more about what
they can't see than about what they can.
—JULIUS CAESAR

One road leads to Rome. It is U.S. 95 through south-eastern Oregon, a forlorn stretch of highway that yawns thirty miles at a time without so much as an exit, a house or any sign of life save sagebrush. I reached it by way of Interstate 80, which covers 2,909 miles from San Francisco to Teaneck, New Jersey, although I used only the 164 miles through northwestern Nevada.

Shortly after I exited Reno, the splash of neon became a distant memory. The desert announced itself immediately, shouting its odd mix of colors—mustard yellow tall grass, mint sagebrush, brown maroon mountains on the horizon. Dust devils swirled and danced under the midday sun, some of them growing into wispy dirt tornados reaching dozens of feet into the sky.

I quickly came upon the town of Fernley, marking the western end of the 40-Mile Desert—a barren, waterless wasteland reaching all the way to the next desert outpost, Lovelock. This was once the most dreaded section of the California Emigrant Trail, which was traveled by some 165,000 people between 1841 and 1867. If possible, travelers passed through at night to avoid the worst of the heat. But starvation was the real killer. A survey made in 1850 counted 3,750 dead cattle, nearly 5,000 dead horses, more than 1,000 dead mules and 953 human graves. As I rushed through it a century-and-a-half later, I passed sculpted messages in the form of rocks placed carefully on roadside mounds. These weren't quite the last words of dying pioneers. One was in the shape of a smiley face. Another announced, "I Love Tony."

At Lovelock, the trickle of a river made an appearance, a waterway of many names. It had been called the Unknown River, Paul's River, Swampy River, Mary's River, Ogden's River, Barren River and finally the Humboldt River, so named by John C. Fremont, who praised its "prospective value in future communications with the Pacific Ocean." Most emigrants were less impressed, which is why the Humboldt was often called Humbug.

Those who bestow designations in the desert tend to call it as they see it. The names of things are evocative, if not inviting—Disaster Peak, Furnace Creek, Black Rock Desert, Devils Playground. On the other hand, the town of Unionville, about five miles west of me as I wheezed along I-80, was essentially named by the prevailing winds. It was called Dixie by the southern sympathizers who settled it, but became Unionville when neutral and Northern preferences gained a voting majority. That was in 1861, when Mark Twain lived there, just before he moved to Virginia City. For some reason, as I raced a Union Pacific freight train across the desert, I thought of the first day of Twain's unprecedented around-the-world voyage, chronicled in *The Innocents Abroad,* as his ship found itself anchored to the ocean bottom during a driving rain. "This," he commented with typical drollness, "was pleasuring with a vengeance."

I turned onto U.S. 95 at a city named after a Northern Paiute chief—Winnemucca, a would-be desert metropolis that tries to draw wayward tourists with curiosities like the largest piece of driftwood ever collected and temptations like loose slots. BUTCH CASSIDY LEFT HERE RICH. SO CAN YOU, said the billboard plea. The Oregon state line arrived seventy-four lonely miles later, just past the Fort McDermitt Indian Reservation, which has the unique incongruity of being named after a lieutenant colonel killed by Indians.

The eastern third of Oregon, an enormous tract of land roughly as large as South Carolina, is home to fewer than two hundred thousand people. U.S. 95 is the only highway through what the locals call I.O.N. Country. I have discovered, in my travels, that America isn't really fifty states, but rather dozens of regional designations, trumpeted by local news promos in an effort to reckon their viewing market. Shreveport, for example, is situated where Arkansas, Louisiana and Texas meet, so they refer to the region as Ark-La-Tex. The twenty-two-county area around Abilene, Texas, is Big Country. El Paso dominates the Borderlands. Florida's central coast is the Treasure Coast. The Albany-Schenectady area is the Capital Region. Western South Dakota is Kota Territory; eastern South Dakota is the Sioux Empire. We are a patchwork quilt constructed of places like the Bay Area, the Hill Country and Kentuckiana.

I.O.N. Country is where the remote corners of Idaho, Oregon and Nevada come together, a rugged, undeveloped expanse where wild horses and bighorn sheep roam, where deer and antelope play, and where many globally rare species—spotted bats, loggerhead shrikes, ferruginous hawks—maintain critical habitats. Fossil records, too, reveal more than three thousand mammal species that once inhabited the region, exotic creatures like the sabre-toothed salmon, the scimitar-toothed cat and the giant beaver. Human inhabitants, however, are rarest of all.

The highway led me into Malheur (a French word for "misfortune") County, 95 percent of which is rangeland. It may be as close as America comes these days to a frontier. At nearly ten thousand square miles, it is the second largest county in the state. New Jersey is approximately the same size. There are 8.4 million people in New Jersey; there are fewer than 32,000 in Malheur County. Or put another way, there are more than one hundred people per square acre in New York County; there are about three people per square mile in Malheur County.

It is a peculiar sensation to be utterly alone on a country highway. I passed no farmhouses, no ranch gates, no service stations, no turnoffs, no pullouts, just a row of telephone poles hinting at unseen civilization and highway signs—PASS WITH CARE—that amused through irrelevance. I continued northward, over Blue Mountain Pass, across Crooked Creek, into Burns Junction, which was a fork in the road featuring fuel pumps and a huge pile of broken and twisted black rock, remnants of an ancient lava flow, which looked almost as if it had been placed there for decorative effect.

I took the northeast fork, and soon the land grew dramatic and uneven, a panorama of white chalky cliffs overlooking deep green slopes, intermingled with the occasional black lava outcrop—a beautiful landscape sculpted by geological cataclysm. I glided over a rise, and then down, steeply, into a valley of sporadic residence. The suggestion of a settlement only seemed to emphasize the open spaces. This part of Oregon began in the 1890s as an encampment of Basque sheepherders. Today, it is dominated by sprawling cattle ranches, meaning folks are neighbors only in the relative sense of the word. But just after the sign for ROME along the empty road was another sign, and this one was either a further lesson in rural relativity or an exercise in sarcasm. The sign said simply, CONGESTION.

One river leads to Rome, too. The Owyhee, pronounced O-waa-hee and named in memory of three Hawaiian trappers killed by the natives in its deep reaches in 1819, has been called the loneliest river in America due to its isolated, back-of-beyond location. Although it is a whitewater destination in springtime, it is a relatively undiscovered jewel, a wonderland of hot springs, petrified trees, towering spires and sheer-walled canyons. In four hundred miles from the Owyhee's headwaters in northern Nevada to its confluence with the Snake River on the Oregon-Idaho border, Rome is the only community it passes.

Where the lonely river and the remote road intersect, there sits Rome Station, the only commercial establishment in this hiccup of a hamlet. It is a tiny café—seven low stools at a counter and a handful of booths—that doubles as a service station and moonlights as an RV campground. I would be the only overnight guest.

As afternoon segued into evening and distant Oregon forest fires painted a pink and lavender sunset, I backed Phileas into a spot alongside the café and took a stroll around the environs. Alongside the parking area, a large satellite dish was being periodically sprayed by a moving sprinkler, the mesmerizing *ch-ch-ch-ch* sound being interrupted every once in a while by a tinny gong. Farther back in the lot, the remains of every type of vehicle imaginable—a bulldozer, a propane truck, an old camper, a van—lay half-hidden in the weeds like highway triage. There were mobile homes, too, in various states of disrepair, and I couldn't tell if they were inhabited or abandoned. There is a fine line between the two in the high desert, where things that have outlived their usefulness linger as rusted monuments and lawn ornaments. Indeed, an empty, unpaved airstrip next to Rome Station was surrounded by lawnmowers, refrigerators, boilers, wash basins and other assorted appliances whose death throes left them contorted into nearly unrecognizable shapes. The liveliest sight in Rome was the lit-up Pepsi sign above the Rome Station entrance, a red-white-and-blue beacon to weary travelers and black flies.

I stepped into the café and sank (a little too much) into a booth. A few hours earlier, near the Nevada-Oregon border, I had passed a billboard: JUST 71 MILES TO ROME STATION. QUITE POSSIBLY THE BEST FOOD IN THE WORLD. Sacrificing cholesterol caution for custom (after all, when in Rome . . .), I ordered a chicken-fried steak, chewed on it a bit and mused that I was quite possibly hungry enough to enjoy it.

The television behind the counter was turned to a feature film—*Gone in 60 Seconds,* which rather well describes my early impressions of life along the lonely highway. The road flattens at Rome after steep downgrades from both directions, meaning the motorcycles, cars, pickup trucks, RVs and eighteen-wheelers that zoom past every few minutes are doing so at speeds of at least seventy-five miles per hour. During the day, each passing vehicle causes the tables at Rome Station to shake slightly, accompanied by a fleeting shadow passing across the café. It is a rural version of living next door to the elevated train tracks in Chicago. At night, the headlights appear first, long before the roar of the engines. They pass in a blur and quickly fade into a distant hum and taillights. The world literally seems to be passing by.

ROME STATION

Thomas Wolfe once wrote, "The city had not existence save that which he conferred on it: he wondered how it had lived before he came, how it would live after he left." Most of us traveling down a dark country highway tend to confer nothing on a place like Rome. It can't be found on many maps. It is a blurred Pepsi sign in the night, a hint of life amid the blackness and nothing more. But most of us don't see it from Rome's perspective. I found it remarkable how, in only a few hours of Rome residence, I already caught myself wistfully watching the taillights disappear into the gloaming.

But that is an outsider's perspective from the wayside. They don't see it that way in Rome. Indeed, there is life here, in the so-called Middle of Nowhere. The next day, I lunched and lingered at Rome Station, enjoying a front row seat as a series of visitors entered Rome's world, briefly but eternally. Over the course of a few hours, transients and regulars with various purposes and pedigrees pulled off the highway. Stanford coeds on the way to school. A family of four en route to Yellowstone. A sheriff and deputy making rural rounds and debating the merits of certain car stereos.

A denim-and-leather couple in their forties, both wearing black Harley-Davidson T-shirts, sidled up to the counter and traded banter with a grinning trucker. The TV featured an old black-and-white western with the sound off, and as they all kept an eye on it, I kept an ear on them and enjoyed a paddle down a small-talk stream of consciousness.

"These guys sure use a lot of bullets and never hit no one," said the male biker, which led to comments about the fake-looking riding and the lame fight choreography . . . which somehow led the conversation to Steve Irwin, the alligator guy, how his wife is from Oregon, how his dog is smarter than its master . . . which got them talking about Mutual of Omaha's *Wild Kingdom* and Marlin Perkins and how it was always his assistant Jim who got the crap beat out of him . . . which led to a discussion of animal encounters around these parts ("I bet I've hit more deer with my truck than most people will ever see," said the trucker) . . . which turned to talk of California drivers ("Californians," said the female biker, spitting the word out and shaking her head. "We call them Californicators.") . . . which made me grateful that Phileas came adorned with Iowa license plates.

Ironically, the proprietor of Rome Station was a repented Californicator, himself. Joel McElhannon was a stocky fellow in his early fifties, and he held a fly swatter in his hand, which he occasionally wielded with surprising agility. Before purchasing Rome Station in 1991, he had lived southeast of Sacramento. Having just retired after twenty-two years in the army, he had been going through a divorce and had been looking for a change. "I was getting tired of California. Too many people. Too much politics and bureaucracy," he said. It seems they were planning a 250-house subdivision across the highway from his house in Pine Grove, California. It was time for him to leave. "I like people," he explained "but not all at one time."

"Interesting that you chose to enter the service industry. . . ."

"I don't mind people stopping and spending money," he explained and then allowed half a smile, "as long as they keep on going."

As he told me of his tour of duty with the 25th Infantry in Vietnam, where the entertainment consisted of sitting in lounge chairs behind the barracks and counting the tracer rounds bouncing off the rooftops in Chu Chi, I wondered if perhaps he had chosen to settle in a spot where the options were equally limited. Here, the nearest movie theater is two hours distant. The nearest law enforcement is thirty-three miles away in Jordan Valley. Then again, said Joel, "Most crooks who are halfway intelligent, they've gotta realize that if they come in here and steal something, there's only two ways they can go, and it's a long way in either direction."

I asked Joel to estimate the population of Rome, and he ran his hands through his thick black hair. "Oh, let's see, there's my son and I here. Then there's Royle Hogan over at the ranch. That's three. There's Pam and Jesse and their son, Timmy. . . ."

When his head count was complete, he figured twenty-nine sounded right. Twenty-nine. That's the size of an aerobics class, a Super Bowl party. But then Joel told me about the huge wedding scheduled for six days hence, just up the road in the hamlet of Arock. Not surprisingly, the wedding planners soon walked in.

The Fretwells, Terry and Robert, and the Lequericas, Mary and Tony, invited me to share some beers with them outside on the Rome Station patio. The Fretwells were hosting the wedding of the Lequericas' daughter, who was marrying a local legend of sorts, one of the nation's top professional team ropers. Rodeo cowboys and their lariats are to this Rome what gladiators and their swords were to the other. The groom was also a full-blooded Basque with a large family, and the combination of heritage and hype apparently translated to an incongruously massive wedding. Six hundred people were expected to attend. Joel McElhannon had ordered 560 pounds of beef. "When you know everybody in all the little communities around here, it's hard to draw the line and leave anybody out," said Terry, "because you've known them all your life."

Mary and Terry were sisters. Their husbands were longtime best friends who shared a mischievous sense of humor. Robert poked fun at Tony's Basque heritage; Tony lamented how the gringos diluted the breeding.

Various theories hypothesize about the Basques' origin— that they are a lost tribe of Israel, even refugees from Atlantis—but there is no evidence that they lived anywhere other than where they have always been centered, in the Pyrenees Mountains of northern Spain. They are an enduring people, having outlasted the Celts, the Romans, the Goths, Charlemagne, Napoleon and Franco. Some fifty thousand Basques live in the United States, a large portion of them in the vicinity of I.O.N. Country, although the image of the solitary Basque sheepherder has diminished with time and economic reality.

The Basque language is unique—ancient and unrelated to any of the other six thousand languages in the world. There is an old story that the devil lived among the Basques for seven years trying to learn their language, but he only managed to learn three words, which he promptly forgot on the way home.

"When we were kids, they talked it all the time," said Tony, whose great-grandparents migrated from the Iberian Peninsula. But he claimed to remember only about a dozen words. "Half of them are yes, no and cuss words."

A dark-haired woman who had been behind the counter at the café joined us at the picnic table. She also taught kindergarten in Arock, and she, too, was Basque. Her name was Cecilia Yturriondobeitia. Wonder why the Basque language is dwindling? Imagine being five years old on the first day of school, and the teacher writes on the chalkboard: Mrs. Y-T-U-R-R-I-O-N-D-O-B-E-I-T-I-A. . . .

I asked the assembled Romans (well, Arocknoids) if they had ever considered living somewhere else. "Nope," they replied in unison. The bride-to-be, Marcia Lequerica, had flouted convention and set out for college in central New York state. "We drove her there and went through a lot of different places," said Mary. "And you know what? Home looked pretty good."

"You oughta show him the video from your trip out there." Robert elbowed Tony.

Tony, a grizzled fellow with a sideways grin, shrugged. "Yeah, we have a videotape of the trip."

"Three and a half minutes, from coast to coast," Robert laughed. "You see a pop machine in Montana, corn fields going past the window, then crossing the Mississippi, then the college. Then the river going back, a few corn fields and that was it."

Added Terry, with thick sarcasm, "I just felt like I'd been there."

Following the September 11th terrorist attacks, Marcia Lequerica got home even quicker. She was at school in Binghamton, perhaps two hundred miles from Manhattan, no closer to Ground Zero than folks in Boston or Baltimore. But to her friends and family in the Oregon outback, she was in *New York*. Marcia jumped in her car and drove straight through to Malheur County.

I told them that I, too, had attended college in upstate New York, adding, "I would probably live there if the weather was more agreeable."

"I would," Tony muttered into his beer, "if my car broke down and I couldn't get home."

Yes, around here, they pull no punches. There is a local tale, retold in *Owyhee Graffiti*, a book for sale at Rome Station, that well describes the sort of people who scrape out a living in southeastern Oregon. It is about a man who etched his name into a canyon wall along the river and carved under it: TRAPPER . . . MINER . . . HERO . . . AND ALL AROUND GOOD HAND. Below that, a subsequent visitor less carefully chiseled: AND A SON-OF-A-BITCH.

Robert had his own canyon-carving story. He pointed to some outcroppings overhanging the river a half-mile away. "See that rock outcrop right straight across over there? The square white one at the bottom of the cliff. My grandfather rode in here in nineteen one. He come from up the river, from Watson, and he carved his name and the date up there while sittin' up in a saddle horse about ten feet high. Carlton Fretwell, nineteen one. And he said, 'This is the spot.' He went back to Watson and married my grandmother. They moved here and took all this ground across the river and built waterwheels to pump the water out of the river to irrigate that. And when he come back he wrote his and her name in the rock a year later."

And that's why Tony had wanted to rush home. This was civilization built from scratch, the legacy of pioneer ancestry. It was uncomplicated and entrenched. There were buffalo roaming not three miles north of Rome and deer eating clover alongside the highway and rangers conducting aerial antelope surveys. This was the song come to life, as near as it gets to the proverbial home on the range. The people here were *of the land*. The two were inseparable. This I discovered with great clarity later that evening at a ranch house along the river.

*   *   *

Pam and Jesse White, a couple in their forties, had stopped in Rome Station the previous evening, after another in an endless series of sweat-and-blood days on the ranch. He was filthy, tired, tilting back his straw hat as he slumped onto a stool, such a genuine cowboy that he made me feel somehow inauthentic. I introduced myself, and we made an appointment to chat the next day at sunset. But by the time I arrived at their house, just a few hundred feet down the road from the café and right alongside the Owyhee, my reputation had apparently preceded me.

I had fallen into a friendly but earnest political conversation with Joel McElhannon at the café, and we had found ourselves on opposite sides of the spectrum. The sore subject was Bill Clinton, which I discovered to be a still tender one in these parts. Indeed, a few days later in South Dakota, I noticed a Republican senatorial candidate declare, in a television campaign ad, that his opponent supported Clinton's "War on the West," as if James Carville had led tanks into the Black Hills. Apparently, gossip moves like a brush fire in a town of twenty-nine. So, just a few hours later, Pam White was waiting for me with a fistful of opinions.

"Joel warned me about you," she said, her eyes frowning, as she joined me in her living room, "that you were liberal, that you supported Clinton, that you were—"

"Pro-choice," I said, just so I wouldn't have to hear the word "pro-abortion." I tried to smile as she frowned some more.

"You know, when we stop being able to live our lifestyle, you will certainly have to stop living your lifestyle."

"I don't understand what my politics have do with not supporting your lifestyle," I countered, gently, for I was a guest in her house. "And anyway, that liberal label . . . I mean, I have conservative views, too, on certain issues. . . ."

"If you were hungry, your views would be more conservative," she said, rather imperiously. "If you had to pray for your food, rather than dish it up. If you had to not know where your next meal was coming from . . ."

And here I thought I had been supporting the party of the poor and oppressed. "But that has nothing to do with being, say, pro-choice—"

"Oh, yes it does! Yes it does!" She nearly leapt out of her chair. "Your fundamental fiber comes from somewhere, and it comes from your beliefs. I can't understand how people can be pro-choice. I mean, we've seen people protect fish. . . . Or seatbelts—oh my gosh, seatbelts! We don't have laws against abortion. We do have laws that we have to wear a seatbelt. I have a cousin. She lived down there in Winnemucca. She got pregnant, and it was late term, and she was scared to death. She gave herself an abortion with a coat hanger. She did an abortion on herself. The baby was born alive. They took it out in the desert, and they ran over it. They tried her as if the baby was alive, but in my mind there was never a difference, whether she gave herself an abortion in the first week or in the eighth month. She killed a baby. When she should have given herself a choice is before. She should have taken birth control pills. I'm not against birth control. But once you conceive, it's alive."

"What if the mother's health is at risk?" I asked, searching for a sliver of agreement.

Pam shook her head. "The Lord Jesus Christ gives life, and he takes it away. . . ."

I could see I was in for a long night. There is an old Basque proverb, one of many old Basque proverbs, that says: "*Amen: Zu hor eta ni hemen.*" It translates roughly to: "Let's agree to disagree." No such luck. It was as if I had a scarlet letter—*L* for liberal—on my chest. I might as well have chained myself to a redwood.

"The environmental movement is a worship of nature, rather than a worship of the Lord Jesus Christ," Pam continued. "We're being attacked. Three major environmental groups in Oregon brought a lawsuit to close the river corridor to cattle grazing. But for a great many allotments the river is the only source of water, so once you close it to cattle grazing, you close entire areas. And they won their lawsuit." She leaned forward and pointed a finger at me accusingly. "And you can't tell me, sir . . . you can't look at this vastness, at nothing going on out here, and tell me that what's wrong with the environ-

THE WHITES' RANCH

ment is out here when we have the municipal waste and the crap going on in cities." She sat back in her chair and folded her arms. "We got on a plane and flew to Portland. We were sixteen floors above the Willamette River, and we could see probably thirty thousand people. Every one of them had a Styrofoam cup in their hands, and the river was paved to the water's edge. And no environmental group is trying to stop that."

It was another Roman, Marcus Cicero, who said, "A good deed in the wrong place is like an evil deed." Such, I think, was Pam White's point, that folks whose hearts might be in the right place were sticking their noses in the wrong place. It was an affirmation of the maxim, too, that all politics is local. Pam had lived in Rome all her life. Her mother had lived there all her life. Her grandparents had first homesteaded there in 1913. She and Jesse, who was descended from Basques, owned several hundred Angus cows, running them on public lands for seven months out of the year and then struggling to feed them during the wintertime. Theirs was a constant battle against the elements. If they weren't trying to raise hay amid a drought—and this in a region that receives perhaps ten inches of annual precipitation—then they were worrying about the river flooding or the desert catching fire or the dust invading or the winters biting.

And on top of it all, there were a series of court battles. The Whites had spent tens of thousands of dollars in legal fees—not to mention countless sleepless nights—over the years, trying to save their livelihood from what they considered the irrational whims of misguided tree huggers. The way they see it, their way of life is being attacked. They and their fellow ranchers are circling the wagons, trying to keep pace with their deep-pocketed adversaries. Every September, for instance, the locals hold a "Rope and Ride" fundraising event, associated with the nearby Jordan Valley Big Loop Rodeo. Proceeds are used to protect property rights of landowners throughout the county and to aid the Oregon Owyhee River Defense Fund.

"Environmental groups are kicking me off the river for environmental issues. I let my kids swim in the river!" Pam grumbled. "Here, in America, the logic is missing. Here, the farmer can't do this, he can't do that, he can't do another thing. And God forbid that he spray his field so that it doesn't have bugs in it, so he can reap a larger harvest and feed the fat people of America. I mean, I can go on and on and on."

This was becoming apparent. Another Basque proverb: *"Bihotzean dagoena, mihira irten"*—What is in the heart comes out of the mouth. "I hope I haven't offended you," she said, "but I believe what I believe." I have always preferred opinions to apathy, and I had to admire her for trumpeting her convictions. I also appreciated the lesson, however strident, about real struggles in the face of abstract policy. On the other hand, when Jesse, just as filthy and tired as the previous evening, walked in from the hayfields and slumped silently in a chair, it became apparent that he was a man of few words. Maybe he was just too exhausted to berate.

Pam took a deep breath and then resumed her diatribe. "Have you ever seen a coyote eat a cow? Have you ever seen five, six, seven blackbirds come around and pick your baby calf's eyes out? And the calf may still be alive. And even if you can stop the shock and stop the bleeding, one hundred percent of the time it will die. You get a gun and you shoot it yourself. You have a bad dog, you shoot it yourself. Your horse gets down and can't get up, you shoot it yourself. If you saw the gun closet in our bedroom, you would think we were ready to do battle with Afghanistan at any moment. There's a gun under our bed. We abhor school shootings. But we can understand why they happen because people are not raising children, they're raising depraved minds. They're watching too much crap on television. There's so much emphasis in cities on things like appearance. We're teaching our young girls— way too young—to be attractive. They all have the same personality. They all dress out of the same stores. They all cultivate the same sexuality. And it's ignorant! And it's luxurious! They're way more aware of that sort of thing than they need to be. They need to ride bikes and ride horses, and they need to have to worry about something else besides entertainment and titillation. It's not a good thing to be allowed this sort of luxury."

By luxury, I believe she meant any high-minded (or lowbrow) considerations and complications spawned by too much leisure time and not enough focus on the nuts and bolts of life.

"So you value your life of simplicity, of daily necessities?"

"Yes," she nodded, "and we resent the fact that environmental groups are trying to take it away from us."

Somewhere along the river, there is treasure, or so the story goes. In August 1860, fifty-four immigrants in eight wagons left what is now eastern Idaho along the Oregon Trail. They brought whatever possessions they could carry, along with enough gold to buy land when they arrived in the Willamette Valley—an estimated $10,000 in coins, which was kept in a strongbox. But it was an ill-fated trek. A Snake Indian attack took nineteen lives, then starvation took another twenty. The rest, only fifteen people, resorted to cannibalism to survive. Mark Vanorman, the leader of the wagon train, was killed, but

not before he buried the strongbox—"Vanorman's Cache"—
on the north side of the Owyhee River and etched his initials
into a nearby rock. He wrote a letter revealing this information, a letter that wasn't discovered until years later. The treasure has never been found, but I sort of hoped it washed up
into the Whites' hayfield someday, if only to even the odds in
court.

"Do you know why Rome fell?" Pam asked.

"You mean Rome, Italy?" Rome, Oregon, as far as I knew,
had never reached heights lofty enough for a plummet.

"Yeah, well, it probably had a lot to do with crucifying
Jesus," she said, "but we won't go there. What happened was,
people sat around in bathhouses and debated politics. And
they didn't do their work."

It was a unique take on the fall of an empire, and I'm not
sure where this left me in her estimation, even had I not been
a Bubba-enabling, spotted owl-loving, baby-killing Jew. Here I
was on a meandering tour of American subcultures, a sweat-
free trip down a high-concept highway, which offered me
nothing but time to mull over mega-thoughts.

"But in all fairness," I tried, "you don't have to look at the
big picture here because you're so consumed with your daily
survival. There have to be some people somewhere looking at
these situations. Whether they're making the right decisions,
regarding the river for instance, is another matter. But there
have to be people examining these issues, don't you think?"

Pam wasn't buying it. "I think our team of examiners far ex-
ceeds what needs to be examined. I think we should all live in
our own areas."

The thing is, not everyone chooses to stay there. This, as I attempted to explain, was one of the reasons I had set a course for America's forgotten hamlets. They were losing their younger generations to greater opportunity elsewhere and thus dwindling with each passing decade. I was hoping to chronicle what was still there.

"Our youngest boy is the first one in his generation who wants to stay home," Jesse agreed. "Most of the parents don't want their kids to stay because there's no future in it. And one of these days, this will be gone. It's just going to take the stroke of one pen. One national monument, one whatever, and it's going to be over for us."

The next morning, I steered Phileas onto a gravel road across from the café and rumbled into the desert for a couple of miles until I reached an imposing sandstone formation known as the Pillars of Rome, which is how the settlement got its name. It was sufficiently impressive, but these rampartlike cliffs were hardly representative of the Rome I found. No, were I to choose a logo for the community, I would turn instead to the banks of the Owyhee River and the hackberry tree.

At the river launch ramp, just a few hundred yards up the highway from the café, where dust-colored lizards skittered silently and dragonflies hovered above the slow-moving current, there was a bulletin board notice about the wild, gnarly looking trees that line the riverbank. The notice might as well have been describing Rome and the will of its twenty-nine inhabitants:

"They may look dead, but they are very much alive. During the spring float season, hackberry trees appear to be ready for the firewood pile. Don't believe it. They are only dormant, just getting ready to come to life. Please let the trees live and grow without human pruning."

To the highway travelers, just passing through, the little café and the ranch houses are but a barely noticed interruption in the long yawn of U.S. 95, a burp of civilization, appearing half-dead. To them, the high desert hamlet is merely a bathroom break, a burger for the road or, most often, an entity unworthy of pause. This was reaffirmed every few minutes, at about seventy-five miles per hour.

"I like the highway because, like everyone else, we have to go places," Jesse told me. "But every dog we've ever owned has been run over on that highway. Fifteen or twenty of them. We've never had a dog die of old age." You can't brake for what you don't see.

Sure, the ranchers would like to see their hard work appreciated, their generational ties to the land recognized, their intimacy with the environs at least taken into account. But mostly, they want nothing more than to be left alone.

"We pretty much consider ourselves the environmentalists anyway," said Jesse, "because we're the ones living here. Her family has lived here for close to a hundred years. But then folks come out here and tell us this is a pristine canyon and they have to save it. Well, we been using it a hundred years and it's still pristine. So what are we saving it from?"

There is yet another old Basque saying, in that language unrelated to any other on earth: *"Izena duen guztiak izatea ere badauje."* Everything with a name exists.

This was Rome.

PRIVY TO THE DREAM

AMSTERDAM, MONTANA

The strength of a tree lies in its roots, not in its branches.
— DUTCH PROVERB

On the outskirts of Amsterdam, on the edge of Bozeman, in Montana's Gallatin River Valley, there lives
a fifty-eight-year-old woman who is part Czech, part
Cherokee and all vim and verve. Her small trailer house,
which she shares with her husband and grandson, sits across
from two iconic examples of landscape architecture and
artistry—a golf course and a grain elevator. This woman is an
artist herself, a creator of quirky works constructed from whatever materials are at hand—a six-foot papier-mâché Santa
Claus, for instance, and a cowboy cobbled together from discarded pieces of wood. "I don't throw anything away," she ex-

plained. "And I use anything for a canvas, except a canvas."

Apparently, that includes her yard, too. Across from the fairways, she has discovered another method of making a canvas out of countryside, turning her grassy lot into an antique gallery of sorts, a celebration of history and country, and a statement about functionality being as beautiful as form.

You see, Brenda Clements collects outhouses.

There were a half-dozen of them, arranged carefully around the yard and decorated with flags and ribbons and patriotic prose. I LOVE THE U.S.A., said one wooden crapper. GOD BLESS GEORGE W. BUSH, shouted another. Her collection included an outhouse done up in Christmas lights, a forest service commode painted red-white-and-blue and a fancy two-seater beside the driveway. It was a rough-plank version of

BRENDA CLEMENTS AND HER OUTHOUSES

a Rodin sculpture garden. I could just imagine THE THINKER musing over some bit of profundity while doing his business behind one of the closed doors.

Brenda tried to explain her paean to the privy. "There's something about how people had to live back then. . . . It was simpler. I just find them beautiful, and I like what they represent—that I'm free to do what I want to do."

The outhouses draw visitors—busloads of camera-toting senior citizens, curious college students, even a crew filming a commercial. "I had this one guy, a dentist, he stopped and his wife wanted to use one," Brenda recalled. "I said, 'No, they're not functional.' I mean, everything's in them, but there's no hole underneath."

So at least it isn't performance art. But in the surface world of creativity, there is always a hole underneath. That is to say, there is an explanation for art in the experience of the artist.

"My family was Catholic, then they converted to Jehovah's Witness. So I was persecuted a lot as a child in school because I wouldn't salute the flag," Brenda explained. "I was obeying my parents, but it was pretty harsh."

Her husband, Gus, also had been raised a Jehovah's Witness, but he had been tossed from the church for going off to fight in Vietnam. So they were the perfect complement—one ostracized for being, if you will, too patriotic; the other maltreated for not being patriotic enough. It can make for a muddled sense of national pride, and, indeed, for several years they were just outhouses in the Clementses' yard. No nationalistic decorations, just stark wooden examples of a great societal humbler, where everyone sat as equals. But September 11th stirred something in Brenda, something she thought she had ignored into irrelevancy.

"It just frightened me so bad to think that this country could be like some in the Middle East, like Israel. Although I love my country, and I'm glad I live here, I'm not extremely patriotic or anything. But I felt compelled . . ." She motioned toward her outhouse art and shrugged. "It didn't make any difference. It didn't change anything. But I just wanted to let my feelings out somehow."

Art is to be interpreted, of course, at the mercy of the moment and the mood. Given the state of the union at the time of my expedition—corporate giants toppling like dominoes, middle-class retirement savings dwindling toward nothing, the rumblings of war, the still fresh paranoia of terrorism—one might surmise that Brenda's collection of starred-and-striped toilets was symbolic of just where the Land of Opportunity appeared to be headed. "God Bless George W. Bush," indeed. Of course, one would have to be cynical to think such things.

I seem to be somewhere in the middle, and perhaps that is my problem. I have trouble seeing the red-white-and-blue in simple black-and-white terms. In the wake of September 11th, when a great many Americans decided it was time to stop taking our freedoms for granted, Old Glory became cool again, almost faddy, like porch banners or fuzzy dice. Houses began to resemble embassies; cars looked as if they had been separated from a motorcade. My wife and I are hardly flag-waving types, but even we taped a small paper Stars and Stripes to our living room window. It was a sign of appreciation of democracy, a grasp at collective mourning, a symbol of resilience.

Then the dust cleared, and the bodies were finally counted, and our national reaction turned from horror to anger to revenge, and we started bombing. And I took down my flag.

It wasn't necessarily because I disagreed with my country's response. Indeed, I was all for ferreting out Osama bin Laden's army of murderous thugs. But I didn't want revenge as much as refuge. Sadly, I also could attach a face to the tragedy, an old fraternity brother of mine whose wife was seven months pregnant at the time. Freddy Gabler was his name. He was one of the hundreds of Cantor Fitzgerald employees who lost their lives when the towers collapsed. Many people were much closer to the pain, losing spouses and daughters and brothers and close friends, but like millions of others, I was profoundly pissed off. More than that, I was deeply depressed.

It went beyond despair about the shattered families and the depth of malevolence that had emerged. I was depressed because I was so uncertain. In the short term, Americans reacted to September 11th by putting up a united front. We were all for freedom and against mass murder. It was simple. But in the long term, the ripples from the event further polarized a nation already divided.

In the aftermath of the attacks, as various related issues arose, I found few satisfying answers to many questions. Is there any way to fight terrorism without killing innocent civilians? Is the blood of innocents on their soil worth preventing such bloodshed on ours? And who is innocent anyway? And who is not? Is a terrorist someone who merely supports a terrorist agenda? Are we only targeting Islamic terrorist organizations? Are we facing an impossible task, butting our head against two thousand years of deeply rooted conflict?

Are we judging Middle Eastern allies by their usefulness rather than their character? Is unilateral military action acceptable in today's global village? Does an unprovoked attack on Iraq tarnish the luster of American ideals? Or does it assure an

American future? Are we best served by flexing our muscles or by trying to win over foreign hearts and minds? Does one necessarily negate the other? Could it be that what is best for America is not best for the world? Which should be my aim?

To what extent should I trust the instincts and motives of my president? Is he doing his best under impossible conditions? Or is he too mired in politics, too removed from the consequences of his decisions? Should civil liberties be trumped by national security? Should we worry more about our government invading our own lives? Or is it foolish to place ourselves at greater risk by clinging to abstract notions of personal freedoms and unfounded concerns about slippery slopes? Are we a nation unprepared for the sacrifices of wartime? Are we a nation unwilling to change our ways, as well?

I found myself examining this whole new set of global and moral complications, and I could only come up with this conclusion: I just don't know. I get lost in the shades of gray. Voltaire once said, "Doubt is not a pleasant condition, but certainty is absurd." He seemed rather sure of it. I am certain only that terrorism is unacceptable and evil, and that the United States is largely benevolent but flawed. Beyond that, it gets murkier.

So the Stars and Stripes have taken on a different connotation to me. As I traveled the back roads, I saw flags hanging from street lights, rising from lawns, shouting from mud flaps, draped over balustrades, fastened to antennas, on hats and T-shirts and homemade banners. I know in my heart that most folks were flying it with righteous motives, but I fear that the flag has come to imply that its owner supports a hawkish plan of action. To me, at this moment, with the world in this particular mood, Old Glory represents a certainty—unconditional support of whatever course of action our leaders prescribe—that I cannot quite muster.

The bulk of my journey to Amsterdam had consisted of a wondrous drive through the heart of Idaho. From Boise, I followed the Ponderosa Pine Scenic Byway, a winding two-lane road through the trees that led me into Idaho City, which was once the most populous town in the Northwest, when there was gold in them thar hills. At its boomtown peak in the 1860s, it boasted more than 250 businesses and 20,000 residents. Today, about 300 folks call it home, not counting the couple hundred men and women buried at its famed cemetery, Boot Hill, only about 28 of whom are said to have died of natural causes.

From there, it was a 2,200-foot climb to Mores Creek Summit, then a zigzag plunge into the Canyon of the South Fork of the Payette River and the town of Lowman, where more than 45,000 acres of the Boise National Forest burned in July 1989. The mountainsides looked like a used matchbook, but the signs whispered other warnings: AVALANCHE AREA NEXT 23 MILES. Then it was up and over 7,056-foot Banner Summit to Stanley, the state's coldest and most breathtaking retreat, where my scenic thoroughfare became another—the Salmon River Scenic Byway.

I had planned on reaching the town of Salmon that evening (which was just north of a sign proclaiming: 45TH PARALLEL—HALFWAY BETWEEN THE EQUATOR AND THE NORTH POLE). But just past Stanley, as the sun began to grow late, a merger of light and locale beckoned me. I stopped at Torrey's RV Campground, where there were a handful of campsites alongside the Salmon River. Surrounded by three mountain ranges, with the famed River of No Return floating past, kept company by regal horses nibbling on wildflowers in an adjacent corral, at that perfect time of day, about an hour before sunset, when the world is vivid and the shadows come alive, I wondered if perhaps I was King of the Road.

I had experienced this before in my travels, the suspicion that it might not be possible to improve on the setting where I chose to set up camp. I recall a cliff's edge overlooking the ocean in Malibu, a crimson sunset in southwestern Montana, a pastoral panorama in California's Sonoma County, a red rock wonderland in Nevada's Valley of Fire State Park. Here was another to add to the list.

Of course, I wasn't actually King of the Road. That title belonged to Norm, the guy in the state-of-the-art thirty-eight-footer two sites over. But Phileas, who was now covered in a fine layer of Nevada dust, Oregon dirt, and Idaho grasshopper gook, appeared eminently satisfied. And I was most certainly the Duke of the Road.

The next morning I completed the staggeringly beautiful drive along the river, which sliced and weaved its way through the rust-colored mountains. As I approached Montana, I climbed through a pine forest, via a series of spectacular switchbacks, and chugged over Chief Joseph Pass to the Montana border. It was the kind of a drive that tempts you to belt out "America the Beautiful." But bracketing my Idaho experience, not far from the state line on each side, were a gravesite in Oregon and a battlefield in Montana, each with its own story to tell about a nation's muddled past.

The grave belonged to Jean Baptiste Charbonneau, the youngest member of the Lewis and Clark expedition. He was born to French Canadian trapper Toussaint Charbonneau and

Shoshone Indian Sacagawea during the voyage to the sea. The image of the child strapped to his mother's back was engraved onto the Sacagawea dollar, a symbol of the peaceful nature of the expedition. The boy, whom the explorers nicknamed Pompy, was a sort of embodiment of compassionate coexistence. He later lived with William Clark for a dozen years in St. Louis, where he attended school. Then he went to Europe as a guest of a German prince, becoming fluent in four languages. After returning to the United States in 1829, he dabbled in assorted pursuits—mountain man, magistrate, interpreter, prospector. Jean Baptiste Charbonneau was sixty-one in 1866, on his way to Montana to join its gold rush, when he was struck down by illness. He was buried just a few miles east of Rome, Oregon.

Back when Pompy was still an infant adventurer, in 1805, several starving and weak members of the Corps of Discovery came upon some of the Nez Perce tribe. The encounter was trouble free, the Indians choosing to follow the words of an elder, who counseled, "Do them no hurt." But the hurt would later come to the Nez Perce, who endured pioneers, prospectors and missionaries squabbling over their land and their souls for the next seventy-five years. They found themselves pushed onto smaller and smaller reservations until, in 1877, hundreds of them, led by Chief Joseph, decided to leave rather than forfeit their right to live how and where they chose. U.S. soldiers chased them through present-day Idaho, Oregon, Montana and Wyoming. The turning point of the conflict, sealing the natives' sad fate, occurred at Big Hole National Battlefield, about a dozen miles east of Chief Joseph Pass.

So there was an American dichotomy—the boy and the battlefield, underscoring a nation's capacity for inclusion and

arrogance, imagination and myopia, achievement and imperfection. As I made my way toward my destination, by way of
I-90 at eighty miles per hour, I crossed the indecisive Continental Divide three times. It was an apt metaphor for my state
of mind. What I needed was a red-white-and-blue reaffirma-
tion of sorts, a reminder of ideals worth protecting and a spirit
worth defending.

I found it in Amsterdam.

A number of hamlets dotting the prairies and valleys of Montana evoke international culture, but usually the relationship
to the namesake city is distant at best. The town of Belgrade,
for instance, was named in appreciation of Serbian investors in
the Northern Pacific Railroad. Lima merely pays homage to a
town—Lima, Ohio—that was itself an homage to the Peruvian
capital. Zurich and Dunkirk drew their names via a blind-
folded railroad employee and a spin of the globe. And Florence was the name of a landowner's wife. But Amsterdam . . .
this was the real deal.

This modest hamlet in the land of the Big Sky has its origins in the Big Apple, in the form of a fellow named Henry Altenbrand, the German-American president of the New York
and Brooklyn Malting Company. In the 1880s a railway line
opened the Gallatin Valley to settlement, and Altenbrand suspected it might offer a promising alternative to Canadian-
imported barley. He acquired land from the Northern Pacific
Railroad and, in 1889, formed the West Gallatin Irrigation
Company. The first crops are said to have caused a sensation
in Europe, although you don't hear much about the
nineteenth-century Barley Craze, do you?

The following year, Altenbrand and some partners formed

the Manhattan Malting Company, building a malting house on the railway line north of the irrigated fields. The little town that grew around it was called Manhattan. Almost immediately, there began a migration of Hollanders to the area— transplants from older Dutch settlements in the Midwest. Within a few years, there were a dozen families, a burgeoning community led by farmers with names like Harmannus Klugkist and Boudewijn Hijink.

The present-day Amsterdam area, south of Manhattan, wasn't settled until 1897, when another Dutchman, Jan Verwolf, arrived. He came from the Dakotas, by way of Iowa, by way of the Netherlands. After buying a farm in South Dakota, he returned to Holland and gathered his wife and three sons, whom he had not seen for ten years. The farm didn't prosper, and a few years later they moved on. Verwolf and two of his sons traveled to the Gallatin Valley in a covered wagon. Following them, in a train boxcar, were his wife, eldest son and younger children who had been born in the States. They set up stakes along Camp Creek. So arrived the "Father of Amsterdam."

By the time a railroad spur reached the area in 1911, Jan was calling himself John, and he had been joined by countryman John Kamp. And John Karp, too. And John Klaver. They built a grain elevator, and then coal and lumber yards. The railway stop became a tiny business center; the Dutchman's farm quickly became a Dutch settlement. When the railroad requested a name for the new community, old country regional distinctions came to the forefront. Half of the settlers wanted to name it Groningen. The other half wanted Friesland. They compromised and called it Amsterdam.

This certainly wasn't the only place in Montana where Dutch immigrants tried to tame the soil. For every successful farm or settlement, there were others that failed, ruined by the weather, misled by the rosy reports that had drifted back to the Netherlands. Would-be settlers relied on letters home (which tended to be overly optimistic) and the recruitment efforts of real estate agents (who were prone to exaggerate). They were, after all, paid to serve the interests of railroad or land development companies, not the countrymen who trusted them.

To some degree, for many Hollanders who chanced life in unforgiving Montana, it was an immigrant version of a *piskun*. Before exploring Amsterdam, I had exited the interstate five miles east, bouncing seven miles along an uneven gravel road to the site of the Madison Buffalo Jump, a high limestone cliff over which Native Americans stampeded herds of bison. Piskun, the Blackfoot word for such a place, literally means "deep blood kettle." Utilizing speedy runners in animal skins and cleverly placed rocks, the natives lured tens of thousands of buffalo to their deaths over the course of two millennium, the practice only fading with the arrival of horses. Some buffalo were killed by the fall, others by their falling neighbors, and still others by merciless arrows at the bottom. There, families went to work carving up the carcasses, using meat for food, hides for clothing and shelter, bone and sinew for tools. It must have been a spectacular and gruesome sight, hundreds of thundering half-ton animals plunging one after another, after another, after another.

Tons of bones were said to be buried at the cliff's base, but some two centuries after its final production, it looked rather ordinary. Were it not for the posted history at a viewing area a few hundred feet away, one would have no understanding of the earlier carnage that took place. Perhaps one could say the same for modern-day Amsterdam. During the Depression, farmers suffered through droughts and dust storms, plummeting grain and cattle prices, and hordes of crop-killing locusts and cutworms. But the community regained its strength during World War II, and from the war-ravaged Netherlands a new breed of Hollanders, like the buffalo, still kept coming. Or maybe, in this analogy, the Dutch settlers are the Native Americans, knowing the land, figuring out a way to survive.

The United States took in some fifty million immigrants during the twentieth century. The other four major powers in 1900 — England, France, Germany and Russia — saw a modest increase in population over those one hundred years, while America's almost quadrupled in size. The United States grew into the world's lone superpower, thanks in large part to its imported enthusiasm and ambitions.

Today, about one in every ten U.S. residents is from somewhere else, and recent trends suggest a permeation of ethnicity into America's hard-to-reach places. In the last decade of the century, the foreign-born population of Colorado is reported to have grown 190 percent. North Carolina's increased 189 percent. Kentucky's swelled 181 percent. But the Dutch found their way into western Montana long before, and Amsterdam provides less an example of permeation than assimilation. In fact, one Dutch professor — Rob Kroes, chairman of the American studies department at the University of Amsterdam — even spent several months in the Gallatin Valley and wrote a book about it. In *The Persistence of Ethnicity: Dutch Calvinist Pioneers in Amsterdam, Montana*, Kroes explains, "Immigrant groups have developed a variety of strategies for cultural survival in the midst of an overbearing, assimilative American culture."

For the immigrants, this landlocked, wide-open high country was in every way distant from the seaside, crowded Low
Countries of their homeland. Certainly, this Amsterdam bears
little resemblance to the modern-day version of its namesake.
There is no red-light district; indeed, there are no stoplights.
You won't find hash bars or triple-strength monk-made beer, as
there has never been a tavern or a restaurant in town. The
only canals are the ones used to irrigate the fields with water
from the West Gallatin River.

A WINDMILL IN AMSTERDAM

The region, once more than 90 percent Dutch, is closer to 50 percent now, and there are indications of a shift of power and perspective. In Manhattan, for instance, the local gardening club had donated a pretty little welcome sign featuring some cute Dutch figures. But somebody vandalized the sign, removing the Hollanders, and there were complaints that the icons didn't represent the greater population. The club replaced the sign with another, sans Dutch references.

This gradual Americanization of a place is not an uncommon development, of course, particularly in communities with old European origins. With the death of millions of older immigrants, increasing intermarriage and a slow but sure acceptance of the cultural mainstream, places like Amsterdam are immersed in what Kroes calls the "wide grey zone where an ethnic community tends to blur into its environment."

But while it may no longer be a slice of the Netherlands in the hinterlands, folks in the Amsterdam area remain very much aware of their origins. There are Dutch figurines here and there on front lawns, and large decorative windmills on either side of town, and names on mailboxes—Flikkema, Van Dijken, Alberda, Droge, Klompier—suggesting generations of endurance. And over the impressive Amsterdam-Churchill Bank at the center of town, three flags fly—that of Montana, the United States and Holland.

I turned down Amsterdam Road, kicking up bits of gravel, and set my sights on the most bustling business in town—Danhof Chevrolet, a rather incongruous establishment among the rolling hills and silos. There, I found Joe Danhof, eighty-six years old, whose parents came over from the Netherlands as young adults.

"My father didn't like the old country. He was upset with

the way he got treated. He said he would never go back," said Joe, as he sat in his wood-paneled office, surrounded by assorted Metros and Malibus and Camaros and Cavaliers. "My mother came here when she was nineteen years old, and she would have liked to have gone back to see her family—eight brothers and three sisters and her father and mother—but she never went back either."

Nick and Agnes Danhof first settled in Muskegon, Michigan, where Nick worked in a steel foundry. But when he developed health problems, a doctor suggested he would be better off out in the country. He had visited the Dutch settlement in Montana one summer, and he had liked it, so they moved there in 1919, settling about seven miles south of the Amsterdam area. Joe was three at the time.

The Danhofs raised wheat, and not too successfully. "We didn't have any money," Joe recalled. "We had plenty to eat— big gardens, lots of food—but no money." When Joe was a teenager, a fellow who owned a local garage asked if he wanted a job as a mechanic. Joe jumped at the chance to escape the farm, explaining, "I don't particularly like to stir around dirt."

Within four years, by the age of twenty-one, he had bought out his employer. Then he obtained a Chevrolet franchise. One of the first cars he sold went to his father-in-law, a four-door sedan, a black one, for $837 in 1940. More than six decades later, Danhof Chevrolet sells some seventy-five cars each month. And the man who founded it, who now resorts to a walker, still goes to work for a few hours each morning. He mostly sits in his office, under the plaque honoring him as 1990 Montana Car Dealer of the Year and within arm's reach of the signed photo of one G. W. Bush. "When he was running for president, I gave him twenty-five dollars one time," said Joe. "I guess he thought I was a pretty nice guy, so he sent me that picture." He said it as if Dubya himself had personally licked the envelope.

In the office next door to Joe's, I was introduced to Carly, his granddaughter, who was a twenty-three-year-old manifestation of assimilation. Professor Kroes compares the collective attempt at maintaining cultural heritage to a balloon that is losing altitude, requiring its occupants to cut ballast. "What was thrown out first," he writes, "has differed from one group to the next." In Amsterdam, the community consolidated around a Christian Reformed congregation, building a proud white church that still overlooks the rolling hills. These were the conservative Dutch, dedicated to protecting their way of life from America's prevailing secularism. But the preservation of their language was not a priority. In fact, by the 1920s, local students were no longer taught in Dutch, and succeeding generations were simply, as Kroes puts it, "linguistically disinherited."

Carly Danhof-Bellach couldn't speak a word of Dutch. But hers was very much a Dutch upbringing, or at least the Montana version. She received an elementary education at little Amsterdam School, not far from the dealership. Then she attended Manhattan Christian School, behind the proud white church on the hill, where there were twenty-one people in her graduating class. She started working, too, when she was about ten, weeding fields, then detailing cars. In fact, Carly was astounded, when she later moved beyond the confines of the Gallatin Valley, by how kids from other places *didn't* work. "Jeff, my husband, he never had a job until he got out of college. Never had a job!" She shook her head. "I was like, are you kidding me?"

That's what you did in Amsterdam. And if you were a good Christian, there were things you didn't do. You didn't dance. You didn't mow the lawn on Sundays. Carly played basketball, but only until the ball bounced up against an immovable object. "I competed in lots of tournaments, and I could play on Friday and Saturday," she shrugged, "but if we made it to the championship game . . ." Sunday was for church, sometimes twice. And then a big dinner with the extended Danhof clan. This was the ethnic ballast that Amsterdam held onto.

Most of Carly's classmates either married straight from high school or attended one of the several Christian Reformed colleges in the Midwest and found their partner there. "There are only a few people who marry someone from, say, Three Forks. That's considered the outskirts, the extreme," she chuckled. Three Forks is about twenty miles away. However, Carly went to Montana Tech on a basketball scholarship. She married a fellow from Seattle; he was of German-Irish descent. They even moved to Texas.

But you know what? Carly missed Amsterdam. Those were her people. That was her home. And now she is back, working at Danhof Chevrolet, in the office next to Joe Danhof himself. "I just look at all that he's done, and I think it's amazing," she marveled.

Someday, she hopes to take over the dealership herself. But for now, she watches her grandfather sit there contentedly, surrounded by the awards and the photographs and the president's signed approval, as he basks in the glow of the American Dream.

UNDER PRAIRIE SKYSCRAPERS

VIENNA, SOUTH DAKOTA

America is the most grandiose experiment the world has seen,
but I am afraid it is not going to be a success.
—*SIGMUND FREUD*

A century ago, maps still identified eastern Montana as the Great American Desert, an apt description of the sand dunes and summer-baked hills along I-90 from Bozeman to Big Timber to Billings. It would have been a breeze of a drive were it not for the construction crews. The interstate was getting a shiny, new charcoal veneer, but it didn't seem to match the surroundings—like wearing black pants with brown shoes.

At the town of Crow Agency, in the Crow Indian Reservation, I turned onto U.S. 212, which would be my only, lonely road for the next five hundred miles. In the first mile, I passed Little Bighorn Battlefield, a national monument to the "engagement"—on June 25, 1876, nine days before America's centennial—between the U.S. cavalry and several bands of Lakota Sioux, Cheyenne and Arapaho. Most of the local billboards seemed to refer to it as Custer Battlefield, as in a handful of fake tepees at Custer Battlefield Trading Post. And a business, twenty miles later, called Custer's Last Camp. And the Custer National Forest, which abuts Custer County.

Here was a guy, George Armstrong Custer, who had some success against the Confederacy during the Civil War, only to later earn that dubious postwar historical title—Indian fighter. During his first year as lieutenant colonel of the 7th U.S. Cavalry Regiment, he was court-martialed for misusing government materials, abandoning wounded men and ordering deserters shot without trial. After being suspended from rank and pay for a year, he returned to kill women and children during a raid in Indian Territory. Then, at Little Bighorn, he failed spectacularly in his final mission of genocide, getting himself killed in the process. He was a murderous egomaniac hunting down the last vestiges of a proud people, a government-funded thug on the wrong side of moral history. Yet his name is splattered throughout a region in which he never lived, but only died dishonorably. You don't see many monuments to white massacres of Native Americans, but here this jackass is martyred and preserved.

The drive through the Northern Cheyenne Reservation, adjacent to the Crow lands, was a reminder that, for the Indians, Little Bighorn was merely a fleeting battle won amid a long war lost. On land barely suitable for some agriculture and ranching, through frigid winters, with no appreciable resources on which to base an economy, more than two-thirds of the Northern Cheyenne residents are living below the poverty line. The unemployment rate is over 30 percent. Per capita income is less than $5,000. The future is as barren as the landscape. According to one report in *Indian Country Today*, more than one in ten girls there have attempted suicide.

But we call it Custer's Last Stand.

I sped through Montana's southeastern corner, a swarm of insects painting a yellow-and-gray Jackson Pollock masterpiece on my windshield. Then it was exactly twenty miles through the northeasternmost corner of Wyoming, where the road improved slightly and the speed limit got worse and the eleven or twelve folks who live there practiced minority rule over massive herds of Black Angus cows.

Just past the South Dakota line was the city of Belle Fourche. This was as close as I would get to the geographic center of the United States, which is about twenty miles north in the open prairie. There is said to be a monument there, but it is all rather contrived, considering it takes into account the addition of Alaska and Hawaii, which is about as relevant as locating the exact center of the former British Empire. More legitimate to me is the center of the continental United States (in Kansas) or the center of North America (in North Dakota) or the nation's ever-shifting population center, currently in Missouri. Then again, no region in the country is more a hodgepodge of historical curiosities, geological oddities and kitschy attractions than this section of South Dakota. It has Mount Rushmore and Wall Drug, the Black Hills and the Badlands, Deadwood casinos and ice caves, Crazy Horse Mountain and petrified forests. And for a week or two in early August every year, there is the Sturgis bike rally—hog heaven in the middle of cattle country.

I spent the night in Spearfish and awoke to the growl of

motorcycles. It was the eve of the rally, as well as the ninety-ninth anniversary of the arrival of the first-ever Harley-Davidson, and I had been passing an ever-expanding parade of road warriors since I entered the state. So curiosity got the best of me. After a short detour south, I reached the city named after J. G. Sturgis, a cavalry lieutenant who died with Custer. At the north end of town stood a bronze statue—Sturgis, himself, I assumed, astride a horse and tipping his hat. These days, the city would be better represented by a fellow straddling an iron horse and flipping the bird. Every year, during the dog days of summer, this sleepy hamlet of six thousand is transformed into the largest city in the state, its numbers swollen by well over two hundred thousand members of Harley Nation. What Woodstock is to classic rock, what Westminster is to standard poodles, Sturgis is to easy riders.

It would be a couple of days before the debauchery really started, the annual chaos that has been described as "a Gomorrah of steel and hobnail boots." But there were already thousands of Harleys on hand, parked at angles along the main strip in front of tattoo parlors and T-shirt shops and temporary establishments selling everything from chaps to turkey legs to pinstriping. Oddly, as I carefully piloted Phileas through the fray, I was struck not by a sense of two-wheeled rebellion but rather of antiquated belonging, a sort of throwback subculture in which the uniform never changes. Everyone was decked out in denim and leather, an R-rated version of those touristy couples who wear matching nylon sweat outfits.

Still, this was very much an incongruity amid the high plains, which became even more apparent as I returned to the highway, all golden brown and spread flat to the horizon. Waves of Harley convoys roared west while I continued east,

PHILEAS AT THE MISSOURI RIVER

fighting a tremendous wind that blew the roadside tall grass like a biker mama's trailing blonde hair. I noticed that the cows that I was passing kept their heads down, having grown accustomed to the steel stampede. I would guess that the humans did, too.

About one hundred miles later, I crossed the Missouri River and entered a new county, a new time zone and another state of mind. Ranchland morphed into tremendous fields of sunflowers, all facing the same direction like an audience of thousands straining to catch a glimpse of the pope or the president. Or maybe Pat Robertson. About a dozen miles later, just past Gettysburg, I came upon a large billboard: ABORTION: THE CHOICE THAT KILLS. Forty miles later, in Faulkton, another one: BABIES ARE PEOPLE, TOO. In Zell: UNBORN BABIES ARE PEO-

PLE, TOO. CHOOSE LIFE. And in Henry, as I turned south on Highway 25: CHOOSE LIFE . . . YOUR MOTHER DID.

If an oversized ad isn't going to convince me to buy a certain brand of cigarettes or stop at a certain hotel chain, is it going to spark some sort of epiphany about a profound social issue? The billboard exhortations seemed, instead, an attempt to announce the politics of a region and to morally admonish. Welcome to the Heartland, oh, heartless one.

It was when I was about five miles from Vienna that I first saw it, the real prairie welcome. From a distance, backlit by the sun filtering through the clouds, it looked like a gleaming white castle, a solitary upright image amid the endless plain. It was taller than the hay stacked in pyramids, taller than the church steeples, taller than the tallest trees, the silos, the water towers and the telephone poles rising from the flatlands like pegs on a cribbage board.

The great grain elevator.

Much of South Dakota was birthed in increments, towns spaced every six to ten miles along the railroad, close enough to gather the agricultural produce of the plains. Since the nineteenth century, the means of this gathering has been the grain elevator, the prairie sentinel, hundreds of them shouting the presence of town after town, forming the economic lifeline of rural America. I had passed by various versions since crossing the Missouri—a stately white elevator in Faulkton, a concrete behemoth in Redfield, rusted gray efforts in Zell and Doland and Clark. They were structural metaphors for the Heartland—no superfluous decoration, just perfect functional simplicity. Receive the grain, weigh it, store it, transfer it.

But in the great scheme of things, the grain elevator has

significance beyond function. It is all things always—an announcement of civilization, a pioneer legacy, a conduit to distant places, a historical touchstone, a welcome home, a truly American architectural invention. And increasingly, it is something else, too—a reminder that a town still exists, an exclamation point.

As I neared my destination and the elevator expanded to fill my view, I traversed nearly a dozen sloughs over as many miles, almost as if it were a drive across the Florida Keys. In several, the tops of trees poked out of the water, looking like a fleet of sunken ships. Eastward now, on a tree-lined rural road, past classic farmhouses with front porch rocking chairs, and suddenly I was flinching every twenty yards as hundreds of birds—sparrows, crows, blackbirds—darted and dive-bombed past Phileas, or stood motionless in the center of the highway, waiting until the last second to flap away, annoyed at my intrusion. Finally, the air cleared after one flock of flappers, and I encountered a sign: WELCOME TO VIENNA. Such as it was.

First note of import: they pronounce it "Vah-yenna" here, which, for some reason, painted an image for me of the von Trapp family in overalls. The source of the town's name seems to have been lost to history, although I did come across a brief reminiscence by a former resident whose father came from Vienna, Austria, which at least supports obvious assumptions. Josephine Wopat Stevens was born in 1887, the same year that Vienna was given life, when the Great Northern Railway began operation through the area. A town called Kent, about a mile south, was simply moved north and renamed Vienna, perhaps by Josephine's father, who built, indeed, a little house on the prairie. In fact, just twenty miles south, in the town of De Smet, sits the homestead where Laura Ingalls Wilder herself grew up.

Vienna was incorporated in 1900, and it grew quickly. The business district eventually included a hotel, restaurant, liquor store, meat market, drug store, furniture store, men's clothing store, harness shop, livery, lumber yard and barber shop. There was a newspaper and a Bank of Vienna, and a dance hall. Among those plying their trades were a hatmaker, an undertaker, a jeweler and a blind piano tuner named Keller. Apparently, the biggest excitement in those days revolved around the annual controversy between the "wets" (who wanted a saloon) and the "drys" (who didn't). A vote was taken every April, which, according to one recollection, "quite often got into a heated affair and generally left some sore spots."

The irony is this: A saloon is nearly all that remains of Vienna.

Perhaps the town's demise began with the fire in 1913, which destroyed six businesses on Main Street. Or maybe it was the closing of the bank a decade later. Or the arrival of the highways, reducing the need for self-sufficiency. Or the diminution of the railroads. Or the demise of the small family farm. In combination, these events produced the Vienna of today—the Bethlehem Lutheran Church surrounded by a few dozen modest houses. Vienna is bisected by railroad tracks and Main Street, which features only the Vienna Bar, a U.S. post office in a building that has seen better days and a brick edifice with its windows boarded up beneath the faint outline of a faded marquee. It seemed to say FENN'S ICE CREAM.

At the end of Main Street I found a tiny town hall, and next to it a pleasant park and basketball court. The population of the entire town—estimated at about seventy—could probably sit comfortably at the dozen picnic tables. As it was, on this early August Saturday, I sat alone.

But all was not quiet in Vienna. Just a few blocks away, I could hear the tremendous squeaking and cranking and moving of parts that announced a grain elevator open for business. Here, throwing shadows on a hushed hamlet that was in turn a shadow of its past glory, was the largest grain storage facility in South Dakota.

In the early twentieth century, the grain elevator was one of the first stateside building types to receive international attention, influencing a generation of Europeans who realized that America had created a whole new structural design. "In abandoning the problem of form," famed Italian building designer Aldo Rossi observed, "they rediscovered architecture." Le Corbusier, the renowned Swiss architect, described the elevators sprouting up across the American landscape as "the magnificent fruits of the new age," comparing them to automobiles, airplanes and ocean liners.

But nowadays, the smallish country grain elevator seems to belong in another category. Like the one-room schoolhouse, the covered bridge and the old barn painted with Mail Pouch Tobacco ads, it is a vanishing and increasingly obsolete icon. Many country elevators are being abandoned in the face of liability threats, failed equipment, unaffordable railroad leases, and especially the emergence of mega-farms, which has created a demand for more storage. One new, large, ultra-efficient concrete or steel facility can replace as many as a dozen old wood elevators. It may be far less photogenic, but it is far more functional.

Such is Vienna's elevator—a modernized rural symbol. Hardly the gleaming white castle I imagined from five miles out, it turned out to be a rather unsightly gray and black complex of chutes, conveyor belts and huge partitioned grain silos.

It is officially known as the Cargill AgHorizons Farm Service Center, Cargill being an international marketer, processor and distributor of food, agricultural, industrial and financial products with tens of thousands of employees in hundreds of locations scattered throughout dozens of countries. The company had taken over Vienna's facility less than a decade earlier, a development that repelled some farmers, the ones who would rather support a local franchise than some faceless global conglomerate. Still, even in the agricultural off-season, I watched a steady procession of heavily laden trucks cross the sloughs, scatter the birds, pass Main Street and inch up to the Cargill elevator's scales like an oxcart approaching a drawbridge. In a sense, Vienna, the dying town, was booming again, only as a transient destination.

I followed the path of a semi behind the grain elevator and found my way to the scale room, which was Mission Control, an array of computers and video monitors, in front of which stood thirty-eight-year-old facility manager Scott Borg, who had grown up just down the road in Willow Lake. "You run the whole elevator from here," he explained, and I watched him do it.

The elevator usually wasn't open on Saturdays, but it was the spring wheat harvest, so Scott was at his post. On a busy day, during the autumn harvest, two hundred trucks might come through. "With that many, you need two people," said Scott. "You can do a hundred trucks by yourself."

Well, *he* could.

An older gentleman in coveralls piloted a truckload of wheat onto the scales alongside the elevator. "That's Ralph," said Scott. "I've known him for as long as I can remember. A

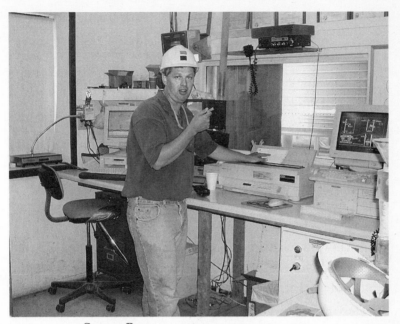

SCOTT BORG OPERATES THE ELEVATOR

couple of his kids were a few grades ahead of me in school."
Ralph's truck would be weighed again after the grain was
dumped, the difference being the weight of the haul. While it
was on the scales the first time, Scott worked a mechanical
arm with a joystick, dipping an eight-foot probe into the grain
heap and pulling out a six- to eight-pound sample. Within a
matter of seconds, it had made its way 250 feet to the scale
room. Scott dumped it into a machine to test its moisture and
protein value, weighed it, grinded it, graded it and gave me a
running commentary of his discoveries.

"Each bushel in this truck weighs fifty-six-point-nine
pounds. If it's really light, like below fifty-four pounds, there's a
discount 'cuz of quality. Now I'm grading it for splits—soybeans that have split in half—and FM. That's foreign material.

It's point-nine percent. He's allowed one percent. And it's about thirteen percent splits. You're allowed twenty percent before there's a discount. . . ."

By the time Scott had finished dissecting the sample, Ralph had maneuvered his truck alongside the scale room above a grate leading to a belowground conveyor belt. Scott opened the back of the truck and let the grain spill into a receiving pit. Ralph tipped the grain box higher and higher, letting gravity do the rest of the work, then he moseyed into the scale room and squinted at a dry eraser board revealing current price information throughout the area.

Meanwhile, Scott pointed and clicked on a computer terminal, working one of five elevator legs to continuously scoop the grain and carry it skyward to the distributor, which would direct it to a downspout leading to one of fifteen storage bins, each matched to a specific haul based on the type of grain or grade. The facility boasts a total storage capacity of two million bushels, a far cry from Vienna's first grain elevator, built about 112 years earlier, which had a capacity of about forty thousand bushels and was operated by horsepower, literally—horses walking in a circle. The animals would stop if they knew nobody was nearby to prod them, so blind horses were recruited if possible.

Scott tossed some more numbers my way. "The biggest bins—the three-hundred-thousand-bushel bins—are ninety feet high and ninety feet across. They're fun to clean up," he grimaced. "The main receiving leg is one hundred eighty feet tall."

"I guess that's why they call them prairie skyscrapers," I said, echoing an expression I had heard that well captured how the grain elevator's verticality and volume paradoxically emphasized the flatness and emptiness of its surroundings.

"Prairie skyscrapers. Never heard that," Scott replied. Then he winked. "Must be a city term."

I suppose it was a term coined by folks who had the time to consider poetic implications rather than protein content, but it fit. As did another I had come across—prairie cathedrals. The grain elevator is the Great Plains equivalent of a colonial church on a New England common. It is America's answer to the Gothic cathedrals of Europe or the Egyptian pyramids, a symbol of authority, vitality, continuity, even a certain majesty.

They are called prairie ironclads, too, likely for their fortresslike defenses. These facilities have to be built to withstand triple-digit temperatures and high humidity in the summer, month-long winter cold spells in which it doesn't warm up to zero all day, fierce prairie winds, mighty storms, high plains twisters. Not to mention the tremendous pressures of stored grain—and fire, the bane of the grain elevator.

"When grain dust is up in the air and it hits a certain condition, it's like dynamite," said Scott. "If you get a spark in the pit where the farmer dumped, it would follow up that leg, and there would be an explosion there. From that leg, it would follow the downspout into the bin, where you'd have another explosion. The main explosion is never the worst. It's the secondary one."

"And then what happens?"

He looked me straight in the eye. "Run like hell."

Fire isn't the only danger, of course. Before Cargill took over the elevator, one worker was killed in one of the bins. "They were pulling grain out of it, and if you get up to your thigh in grain that's moving, you're going to get sucked down in it and buried. You can't get out. They had to cut a hole in the bin to get his body out."

As he recalled this, Scott was grading another sample from another truck, this one brimming with soybeans. A fellow in a Stone Cold Steve Austin shirt and torn jeans was dumping his haul into the pit.

"That's Jerry," said Scott, beginning the process all over again.

When there came a lull in the truck parade, Scott handed me a hardhat and led me to a tiny room above the railroad tracks, the rail load out. This was the transfer part of the receive-weigh-store-transfer narrative. "This is a branch line," he said, pointing to the tracks. "They don't come here unless we order cars." During the fall harvest, that might mean three or four 54-car trains a week. In the summer, it translates to only a couple of trains per month.

We descended the stairwell and walked a few hundred feet to the company offices, where he pointed out a large United States map highlighting grain shipping points. The spring wheat might find its way to flour mills in Minnesota or Massachusetts. The corn might go to Ontario, California or to Hope, Arkansas. The beans might end up in Wichita, or they might be shipped to Seattle or Mobile or Galveston for export, or perhaps to Laredo, Texas, to be transported into Mexico.

There was something pleasingly efficient about the whole operation. Here was the transition from farmer to shipper, a key cog in the simple but profound journey from seed to sustenance. It was all satisfyingly circular. The trucks were weighed coming and weighed going. They arrived, dumped, departed, returned with more. The conveyor belts and elevator legs moved in a continuous loop. The trains arrived empty, left full, returned empty again. It all made the world go round.

*   *   *

Besides its functional capacity, there has also long been a social component to many old country grain elevators. They have been community gathering places, an opportunity to shoot the shit, as it were, to talk politics or farming, each generally inseparable from the other. But in Vienna, the grain elevator didn't serve that purpose. Instead, the community paid a visit to the post office.

I strolled back over to Main Street and stepped into the building, where a white-haired woman named Myra Cluts welcomed me warmly. It was less a post office, actually, than a clubhouse decorated like a 1970s den—a wood-paneled room with two card tables pushed together in the center, surrounded by a motley crew of chairs, a fish bowl, a television set and a natural-gas stove. On the walls were photographs of Myra's extended family, leaflets announcing auction sales and a local steam threshing jamboree, and pseudo-sassy signs that opined things like: COFFEE, CHOCOLATE AND MEN. SOME THINGS ARE BETTER WHEN THEY ARE RICH.

Myra was originally from Watertown, a city of twenty thousand some thirty miles east. In 1962, she married a Cluts, Gordon Cluts from Vienna, and moved to the south part of town. Gordon died twenty years ago, but Myra still lives in the same house and still farms the same 360 acres, with help from her son-in-law. "Time goes fast," she said, joining me at a table. "When I think I've been here forty years . . . it doesn't feel that way."

For the past seventeen years, she has run the post office, which doubles as a coffee shop offering free food and beverage, donations accepted. Myra serves homemade cookies and ice cream and soda pop for the kids. She uses words like "super-duper," and does so in that accent, peculiar to the upper Midwest, that makes just about any utterance sound like apple pie. She is, it seemed to me, something of a town grandmother.

"This is a contract post office, so I'm not a postmistress or anything," she explained, pronouncing it *poost*-mistress. "I imagine they would shut it down if I said I was going to quit. But I feel that I owe it to my community, as long as I am able, to not make any waves." She laughed. "People say, 'Are you the mayor of Vienna?' And I say, 'No, I just think I am.' "

Myra can usually be found there for a couple of hours in the morning and a couple more in the afternoon. She happened to be the only one there when I walked in, which isn't often the case. "There's always somebody who shows up," she said. "We've got several bachelors who don't have any wives, so they come in. Stan Bruha. John Borseth. Elwood Multhauf. Basil Englert . . ."

"Sounds like a men's club."

"We have Joyce Anderson, who lives in a house down there," she continued. "And we have Mark Proudy and his father LeMoyne Proudy. They come in. They live out in the country," she added, as if Vienna were an urban jungle.

"What's the conversation about?"

"Oh, anything . . . how a few horses were electrocuted in De Smet during last week's storm . . . or who's running with somebody . . . Oh, did you see his pickup down at so-and-so's house? And she's divorced and takin' her name back. . . . We get blamed for a lot of gossip, but we don't like to call it gossip. Basil Englert calls it our therapy time."

She laughed again, and I noticed a couple of relevant signs on the wall. One stated: THERE'S NOT MUCH TO SEE IN A SMALL TOWN. BUT WHAT YOU HEAR SURE MAKES UP FOR IT. The other asked: IF WE WERE ALL PERFECT, WHAT WOULD PEOPLE TALK ABOUT?

We eventually got around to talking about the September 11th attacks, which Myra remembered with a sigh and a shudder. "I was standing in my kitchen. I had Watertown KWAT on. It's a talk show in the morning, probably an hour. And I was doing my baking for my shop here, and all of a sudden they broke in . . . I get goosebumps . . . that something had happened in New York." She wiped an imaginary crumb from the table, the same table around which the community gathered in disbelief. "We had the TV on here. You can't imagine such devastation! That's what we couldn't understand—why anybody would feel they had to do something so bad."

Like any good grandmother, Myra pulled out a photo album to stir fonder memories. She pointed to a photograph and to an empty chair. "That's Vernon Rasmussen. He used to sit right there. He's in Watertown now, but he lived two miles out on a farm. Never married. He had a stroke about four years ago. It wasn't real serious. It didn't affect his mind or his speech, but his mobility's not too good. . . ."

He was still rehabilitating two months after the stroke, on a warm Sunday in October, when it came time to harvest his corn and beans. "Everybody knew him. He's lived here all his life. So everybody passed the word. We're going to have a combine bee," Myra recalled. "His family brought him up from the nursing home. They took a picture of him standing and watching everything."

The Lutheran Brotherhood and some of the local ladies made lunch and took it to the fields. Sixteen combines harvested the grain, which was hauled to storage by five semis, eight tandem trucks, thirteen tractors and wagons and a couple of grain carts. Vernon's entire 260 acres were completed in four hours.

Myra straightened out the photo, shrugged and mumbled what might serve as middle America's interpretation of the Golden Rule, something fit for South Dakota's license plates: "It's just something you do."

Back on Main Street, the bar was closed and the sky was threatening, a storm creeping in like a blue gray tsunami. I headed out of town just as the rains came, and they came hard—fat raindrops falling with intent. A half-hour later, at Memorial Park Campground on the shore of Lake Kampeska, I sat, warm and dry, listening to the raindrops pelt Phileas and reading the local paper, the *Watertown Public Opinion*.

The above-the-fold headline: MEMORIAL PARK BEACH CLOSED. It seems the fecal coliform level in the water was above the allowable limit. More disturbing to me, however, was another headline in the same edition. It was an article about the investigation into the previous year's anthrax scare, focusing on a particular scientist. Twice the report admitted that law enforcement officials say he "is not a suspect, and no evidence links him to the anthrax letters last fall." But this was the headline: FORMER ARMY RESEARCHER IS AN-THRAX SUSPECT.

Just then a siren began wailing, rising to a crescendo, then falling, then rising, then falling again. Outside, in what was now a drizzle, I saw people stepping from their trailers and motorhomes and shuffling in the same direction. There seemed to be no hurry-up in their gait, but there was enough purpose to make me follow. Our destination was a storm shelter, a low square slab of a building painted yellow. The inside was gray cement with low fluorescent lighting and a radio tuned to an AM station. But instead of a weather update, it was playing music. Loud music. Country music. Bad country music. Which may be why everybody was milling around outside.

My companions in waiting were a cross-section of campers who might have made intriguing shelter mates, but not for long. There were teenagers on cell phones, whining children clinging to their mothers' legs, men with bad teeth spitting sunflower seeds, terrifically overweight women stuffed into spandex, even a blue-haired old lady with a parasol, wearing silver dress shoes and more makeup than your average circus clown. The mood was more giddy than fearful, and after forty minutes or so the crowd began to disperse. The kids went back to playing paddleball in the street. The men returned to fussing with their RVs. A handful of people, maybe a dozen, walked the hundred yards to the lakeshore and peered toward the south, over the lake, as if waiting for fireworks.

Minutes later, even they had gone back to their cabins and campsites, leaving only me and, a few dozen feet away, a couple of teens flirting with each other, skipping stones and chatting somewhat uncomfortably. Waves lapped against the boulders at water's edge. Buoys swayed back and forth a hundred feet out. The sky bruised black and purple. And I stared, wondering, *Where's that tornado?* I'm not sure why. It's just something you do.

POLKA DOT

PRAGUE, NEBRASKA

In Heaven there is no beer. That's why we drink it here.
— *"In Heaven There Is No Beer Polka"*

The musical poet Gordon Sumner once revealed something rather intriguing regarding the tricks of his trade. "Great music," he said, "is as much about the space between the notes as it is about the notes themselves." (Yes, he is better known as "Sting," but I just couldn't find the courage to write, "As Sting once said . . ."). His point is well taken, and relevant to my expedition. Think of the United States as a brilliant symphony—an orchestral piece emphasizing sounds like San Francisco's violin solo, Chicago's wailing saxophone and New York City's perpetual percussion. The little hamlets, forming my song of the open road, are the spaces between the notes.

What fascinates me is how these tiniest dots on the atlas go about attracting the attention of the wayward traveler. How does one turn up the volume in the empty spaces? Believe me, they find a way. The little town of Rockville, for instance, about a hundred miles west of Prague, bills itself as the Lobster Capital of Nebraska, which is a bit like being the "Bikini Capital of Saudi Arabia." Once each year, Rockville imports crustaceans all the way from Maine and manufactures a festival around it. The town of 111 folks becomes a gathering of thousands. Of course, it isn't cheap to fly lobsters into Nebraska. As one resident admitted to a newspaper reporter, "This is not a high-profit deal. It would be a lot easier to serve catfish."

Rockville is only slightly more creative than hundreds of other small towns, many of which engrave their imaginative appeals on highway welcome signs. In my travels, I have become a connoisseur of such efforts, collecting community slogans like so many refrigerator magnets and mentally dividing them into various categories—catchy cleverness (Garden City, Missouri: A TOUCH OF HEAVEN ON HIGHWAY SEVEN), cheekiness (Superior, Wisconsin: I'M A SUPERIOR LOVER), historical puffery (Seneca Falls, New York: BIRTHPLACE OF WOMEN'S RIGHTS), information (Britt, Iowa: FOUNDED BY RAIL, SUSTAINED BY THE PLOW) and self-deprecation (Gettysburg, South Dakota: WHERE THE BATTLE WASN'T).

Who can resist the swagger of small towns? When Beaver Dam, Wisconsin, urges passersby to MAKE YOURSELF AT HOME, I may not comply, but I still find myself smiling a mile later. When Jewell, Iowa, calls itself A GEM IN A FRIENDLY SETTING, I suspect that, indeed, it just may be a diamond in the rough. When Eaton Rapids, Michigan, shouts, WELCOME TO THE ONLY EATON RAPIDS ON EARTH, I applaud the research, if not the appeal. The options apparently are endless, but all slogans have one thing in common: They identify a community as a place of some significance, a destination worthy of consideration. It is as if the town is saying, "I boast, therefore I am."

Before hitting the road again, I reexamined my atlas and my next destination. Here was a diminutive hamlet in a rather nondescript region, very much in the space between the notes yet somewhat in the shadow of Nebraska's two-note chord, Omaha and Lincoln, and nearly lost in the crease of the United States map. This appeared to be a slogan-deviser's challenge.

It is roughly the same distance from South Dakota's Vienna to Nebraska's Prague—about 250 miles—as it is from the one in Austria to the other in the Czech Republic. South of Sioux City, I crossed the Missouri River again, as well as the state border. The terrain became grassy hillsides and packs of squat trees and boundless fields of corn, and the sign said, NE-BRASKA . . . THE GOOD LIFE.

Highway 77 took me farther south. For a mile or two, I enjoyed the semantic pleasure of piloting my Winnebago past Winnebago High School, Winnebago Hospital, the Winnebago Police Center and the Winnebago Travel Court in the town of Winnebago amid the Winnebago Indian Reservation. After pausing for an endless Burlington Northern freight train in Winslow—which is one way to get travelers to notice a town—I reached Fremont, with its tree-lined avenues, its auditorium hosting a RIGHT-TO-LIFE GARAGE SALE, and its auto parts store marquee: GOD BLESS THE U.S.A. On the southern end of town, just past a set of enormous concrete grain elevators, I rumbled over the Platte River, which was running low, exposing grassy islands and looking more like a gloomy bog than one of the nation's great waterways.

Nebraska is said to have more miles of river than any other state, but most all were parched. The newspapers were calling it the third-driest long-term spell in more than a century, a drought severe enough that the governor was asking that the entire state be declared a disaster area, the potential economic impact being upwards of one billion dollars. I had earlier passed through the town of Uehling, where an improvised sign said simply, KEEP PRAYING FOR RAIN. Ironically, at the same time, the other Prague, the European version, was suffering through its worst flood in five hundred years.

South to Highway 92, then east seven miles until I came upon a large billboard: WELCOME TO WAHOO! THERE'S ONLY ONE. And also: HOME OFFICE OF DAVID LETTERMAN. On the other side of town was another sign: WAHOO—HOME OF THE FAMOUS MEN. Apparently, one of these famous natives was turn-of-the-century baseball Hall of Famer Sam Crawford, who was known as "Wahoo Sam." I had always believed it to be a nickname derived from an exclamation of some sort, like Hughie "Ee-yah!" Jennings or The Say Hey Kid. Now I know better. Funny thing is, had he been born in another town about five miles north, he might have been known as "Colon Sam."

Wahoo is certainly not alone in trumpeting its celebrated natives. I have been startled from many a highway reverie upon learning that the Oklahoma hamlet of Yukon is the HOME OF GARTH BROOKS or that the South Dakota town of Doland is HOME OF HUBERT H. HUMPHREY. But often a hamlet's identity is less about people than place. As a general rule, if the town is on the edge of something, it is a gateway (Bolivar, Ohio: GATEWAY TO TUSCANAWAS COUNTY). If a town is at the confluence of roads or rivers or regions, it is either a magical meeting (Lowry City, Missouri: WHERE THE OZARKS MEET THE PLAINS) or it is a proud crossroads (Barstow, California: CROSSROADS OF OPPORTUNITY). Predictably, centrally located communities constitute the heart or the heartland. Rockwell City, Iowa, is THE GOLDEN BUCKLE OF THE CORN BELT. Blue River, Wisconsin, is the HEART OF THE LOWER WISCONSIN RIVER.

So where does that leave Prague, which I came upon seventeen miles later? GATEWAY TO WAHOO . . . IN THE HEART OF HIGHWAY 79 . . . WHERE A LONELY COUNTRY HIGHWAY MEETS A LONELIER RURAL ROAD . . . NOT TOO FAR FROM THE EXACT CENTER OF NORTHWESTERN SAUNDERS COUNTY.

Perhaps a less literal approach . . . Prague: PRIDE OF THE BOHEMIAN ALPS.

A man named Charles Culek is credited with being the first permanent Czech settler in Nebraska, arriving in 1856. A decade later, several Protestant families left Czechoslovakia and settled in what would become the Prague area. Czech immigration to the United States reached its height around 1880, and some fifty thousand newcomers, most of them from the Province of Bohemia, came to Nebraska. The majority settled in the eastern part of the state, particularly in a few counties on the outskirts of Lincoln, between the Platte River and the West Fork of the Big Blue River. The region became known, perhaps with a wry grin, as the Bohemian Alps.

The earliest settlers had names like Kastl, Hajek, Kaspar, Vavak and Cizek. Not long after they began their farming operations, they suffered their first setback—a horde of grasshoppers that invaded on August 12, 1874, destroying the crops in a matter of hours. The grasshoppers left two days later, but they also left eggs, which hatched and caused more damage the following year. Two decades later, it was hot, dry weather that caused complete crop failure. The year after that, it was hail. But the Czechs had come a long way to become Czech-Americans. Slowly but surely, they survived the weather and tamed the soil.

Like Vienna and Amsterdam, Prague owes its beginning to the arrival of the iron horse when the Omaha and North Platte Railroad chose the site as a location of a station along one of its branch lines. The Lincoln Land Company paid Joseph Kaspar $5,500 for 160 acres and sold lots in the spring of 1887—Nebraska's version of the Prague Spring. "Praha," the capital of Czechoslovakia, was the residents' original choice for a name, but they settled on the English equivalent. Of course, in these parts, they pronounce Prague to rhyme with "plague." Given the hail and hoppers of its early days, perhaps it is apt.

One of the first buildings in town was Joseph Sedlacek's saloon, which, as we shall see, is also fitting. In my research, I came across a sepia photo showing old Joe Sedlacek in his Sunday best, sitting with his legs crossed at the ankles, his mustache thick, his meaty hands poking out from the sleeves of his suit jacket. Joe's portly wife stands behind him with her hand resting uncomfortably on his shoulder. Both are wearing the serious expression expected in photographs of the time. They seem to want to look important. And so did Prague. The village boasted the usual barbershops and harness shops and blacksmiths, but there was also the Prague Hotel and the cigar factory and the county's first hospital.

But like so many other country hamlets, Prague's eminence began to fade as the automobile supplanted the railroad

and metropolitan options replaced rural America's depen-
dence on local businesses. The village reached its peak just before the Depression, the 1930 census recording 421 residents.
By the time I arrived, it had been more than sixty years since
passenger service along the rail line was abandoned and two
decades since the last shipments rode the rails out of Prague.
There was a subdued sign at the edge of town: PRAGUE: POP.
282, and the one-block business district was populated mostly
by grasshoppers.

Evening was already approaching, and I was tired, so I decided to grab a quick dinner at what appeared to be a promising local option—the Czechland Inn. The entrance looked
like a back exit, one of those nondescript doorways meant for
those in the know. It was a multipurpose gathering place—
pool tables, pinball machines, a long L-shaped bar, a large-
screen television, a dining area. Above the bar were baseball,
softball and darts trophies. The walls were festooned with University of Nebraska memorabilia, the red and white of Cornhusker Nation. I noticed two flags, too—one American, the
other Czech, separated only by some mounted deer antlers.

The dining area, open on weekends, was papered with
scores of photographs and newspaper clippings chronicling
Prague's past—a series of pictures depicting the demolition of
the old grain elevator, a rendering of the long-gone Kellner
butcher shop, a clipping from when the Fendrick house was
destroyed by fire. My favorite was a photo of the 1930 Prague
High School basketball team—eight young men with their
hair parted on the side, wearing tight shorts and drooping
socks—which got me imagining an old-school fast break of
Kucera to Vlasak to Svoboda.

I took a seat at the bar, ordering an artery-hardening meal

and an I'll-have-what-they're-having drink favored by the locals around me. It was a goblet of beer mixed with tomato juice, a traditional Czech cocktail known as a red *bulacek*. I struck up a conversation with a couple of middle-aged women, Yvonne and Carolyn, who regaled me—or at least distracted me—with tales of Prague, stories that had very much a 1950s quality to them. Yvonne had just returned from a demolition derby in Wahoo, still the hottest ticket at the county fair, featuring a few of her friends from Prague. "We just went there to watch. . . . And drink beer," she said.

Carolyn reminisced about some of the iconic scenes of her childhood—the free outdoor movies they used to show at the Prague National Hall down the street, and the circuses and carnivals that used to come through town. She recalled a place

DOWNTOWN PRAGUE

known as Candy Bar's Meadow, where the local kids used to tap kegs. "It had two driveways into it," she explained, "so if the cops came you could zoom out the other way." And then there was Vampire's Row about two miles outside of town, Prague's version of Lover's Lane. "I think a lot of people went there and drank also."

It may be relevant for me to note here that the Czech Republic is the greatest per capita consumer of beer in the world, greater even than Ireland, which chugs in at number two, and more prolific than the United States and Canada combined. So it comes as no surprise that in Prague, Nebraska, there were two saloons before there was a post office. And in this dwindled town, there were still two drinking establishments. Bud's Bar and Keno was just across the street.

This being a small town, after all, Candy Bar, himself, soon walked in. He was a farmer in his fifties. Kenny was what they called him before he was saddled with a nickname from childhood. "I grew up in this bar," he told me. "When I got old enough to drink and even before. There aren't very many places to hang out in a small town."

I asked him about the evolution of Prague.

"What's left is doing alright," he said, noncommittally. "I'm probably going to say something I shouldn't, but the inter-relationship between each nationality . . . it's been broadening out the area and that just discontinues the . . ."

"You mean, the different ethnicities have been intermarrying?"

"Yeah, that's what I'm trying to say," he nodded. "It wasn't fifteen years ago that you'd come here any day of the week and there'd be tables full of people speaking mostly Czech. Now, you never hear it."

Carolyn echoed a similar sentiment. "Very rarely do you find anyone speaking Czech like they used to."

"Do you?" I asked her.

She shrugged. "Pivo. That's beer."

As the Sunday evening moved on, the tavern really began to bustle, but it was growing late, and another red *bulacek* would have left me stumbling toward Phileas and fumbling in the dark for a campsite. I drove one mile north to a free campground in the 192-acre Czechland Lake Recreation Area, where I was the only overnight camper. At first, this was a pleasant notion. I sat on a picnic table atop a hill overlooking the lake and watched a couple of anglers drift across the water as the sun disappeared and the sky deepened. Then night came, and I was utterly alone, the world around me black as ink. Which might have been fine until the mysterious car arrived, rumbling slowly around the campsite loop and then speeding away and then rumbling around once more. I grew anxious in the darkness. Are they roaming? Are they lost? Or are they scouting out the best place to dump my body? But the car never returned. Soon, I was alone again, accompanied only by thousands of gnats clinging to my windows, a chorus of chattering crickets and heat lightning bouncing around the horizon. I drifted off to sleep.

It rained that night, an answer to those prayers, and the next morning, under an aluminum sky, I revisited Prague. Four decades earlier, when John Steinbeck chronicled his *Travels with Charley*, he recalled an earlier visit to that other Prague, the one in what was then called Czechoslovakia. He had been accompanied by a friend, who spent his time meeting with city officials and reading reports. Meanwhile, Steinbeck, as he put it, "roved about with actors, gypsies and vagabonds." They flew home together and discovered that each had taken home an entirely different Prague. "We brought home two cities, two truths," Steinbeck wrote.

I was certain that such a dichotomy would present itself more readily in a sprawling metropolis, where every intersection offers tangents and every tangent offers the possibility of a unique subculture and a divergent point of view. But in this Prague, so small that it was a satellite of Wahoo for goodness sake, there weren't tangents as much as alternate routes to the same perspective. It was what it was, the question being: What exactly was it?

Best I could tell, it was Czech-American to the bone, a truly hyphenated place. On the one hand, it exuded Americana. There were baseball and football fields on the edge of town, neat little houses rimmed by sprawling hayfields, boys riding dirt bikes past a lonely grain elevator, a couple of teenagers cruising the near empty streets in pseudo sports cars, a polished white Presbyterian Church, a brick K-through-12 school that the locals had fought hard to save, hand-drawn flyers posted throughout the village that shouted, "Happy Birthday Jimmy Kubik" and more U.S. flags per capita than any town I have explored.

The sign in front of the village hall announced: CONGRATS GIRLS 18-AND-UNDER SOFTBALL, CLASS C STATE RUNNERS-UP. Such contemporary successes are commonly writ large on the outskirts of American towns—the self-congratulatory form of self-promotion. Angola, Indiana, celebrates its STATE BAND CHAMPIONS. Three Oaks, Michigan, brags, THREE OAKS ELE-MENTARY SCHOOL GOLDEN APPLE AWARD WINNER. And Fond Du Lac, Wisconsin, calls itself WINNER'S CHOICE, having produced a Miss Wisconsin, a Dairyman of the Year, an Olympic medalist, two champion windsurfers and three major lottery winners.

Prague, too, could boast lottery winners—an older couple who had used family birthdays for numbers on a Powerball ticket, winning $8 million in 1995. They promptly left town, but they seem to have descended from one of the original settlers. Perhaps he escaped the arbitrary autocracy of the Hapsburg regime and built a farm in the Heartland. His descendants became millionaires. It doesn't get more American than that.

On the other hand, although the village was no longer 99 percent Czech, it was still very much a Czech community. The streets were named Elba, Waldstein, Lusatia, Danube. The school was at the corner of Moldau and Moravia. The village board of trustees had names like Polacek, Odvody and Kuncl.

Old men gathered at the Czechland Inn to drink *bulaceks* and play *taroky*, a Czech card game. The backdrop on the stage in the Prague National Hall featured Czech dancers and a large Czech salutation: VITAME VAS. Posters around town promoted next month's Prague Czech Heritage Day, featuring a polka dance, an appearance by Nebraska's Czech queens and some music by the Prague Czech Brass Band. The Kolac Korner Café, across the street from the Czechland Inn, would be serving their "famous roast pork and duck dinners with dumplings, sauerkraut and all the trimmings."

Somewhere in Prague's progression, the fading ethnic bonds and the growing American roots seem to have met in the middle. The village was comfortably balanced, with a foot in each world. In order for a small town to promote itself, it first has to define itself. Prague may have offered two truths, indeed.

I strolled across the street to the Kolac Korner Café, scattering a half-dozen grasshoppers with every other step while noticing that the restaurant wasn't on the corner at all.

"People say, 'Well, you call it Kolac Korner, and it's in the middle of the block,'" grinned Mark Nemec, a big, strapping Nebraska farm boy, as blonde as hay, who joined me at a table by the kitchen. "I say, 'Hey, we're Bohemian. Give us some credit!'"

The *kolac*, or the Americanized *kolach*, is a flat sweet yeast bun with a depression in the center filled with anything from fruit pulp to cottage cheese. In the Bohemian Alps, the recipes were often handed down for generations, each varying according to family preferences, settlement traditions or the regions in the homeland from which ancestors came. The Kolac Korner Café offered a dozen different flavors. I opted for a traditional poppy seed *kolach*, along with a "famous" roast pork and sauerkraut sandwich.

The café's décor was fervently Czech with a dash of American. I sat at a square table covered in a red-and-white-checked tablecloth and a vase of fake flowers—one red, one white, one blue—as well as a tiny U.S. flag. Polka music was playing softly. There was a Czech flag on the wall, along with a city map of the Czech capital and a little Ziggy comic of obvious relevance. It showed Ziggy in a car, asking directions from a farmer leaning over a fence. "I'm afraid I can't help you, mister," said the farmer. "I got lost on this very road myself 'bout twenty years back and ended up just settlin' down here."

Mark's roots went quite a bit deeper. I had noticed a newspaper clipping in the Czechland Inn about his great-grandfather,

Thomas Nemec, who was born in Deutsch, Moravia, in 1848. Twenty-seven years later, he found his way to Saunders County with his wife, grandmother and two children, purchasing eighty acres for about $200. He had enough money left over to buy a stove and four hens. It was two years before they could afford a wagon and a pair of oxen. Mr. Nemec led the oxen; Mrs. Nemec held the plow. Their first house was made of sod, but before that they lived in a neighbor's granary and slept in a hole dug out of a large straw pile. Over the years, Thomas Nemec's holdings grew to 560 acres, which he distributed among his offspring. He was the iconic immigrant patriarch, the kind of a man who, when one of his horses died, simply walked the twenty-seven miles into Wahoo one day and bought another one. That happened in 1920, when he was seventy-two years old.

MARK NEMEC

The thirty-eight-year-old man sitting in front of me, Thomas's great-grandson, had an earnest, innocent, almost childlike quality to him. He wore a red University of Nebraska cap and a T-shirt celebrating WILBER, NEBRASKA—CZECH CAPITAL OF THE U.S.A. This seems to be the most common means by which a community forges an identity, by calling itself the Something Capital of Someplace. The Something can be anything from cranberry pie, cheese curds and artichokes to snowshoe baseball, sturgeon and trolls. The Someplace depends only on ambition. Consider three towns in slogan-happy Wisconsin: Sauk City is the COW CHIP THROWING CAPITAL OF WISCONSIN and Reedsburg is the BUTTER CAPITAL OF AMERICA. But Green Bay is the TOILET PAPER CAPITAL OF THE WORLD.

Wilber's self-proclaimed status meant Prague still had to shop for a slogan. But Mark's cap and T-shirt reflected the origins of his restaurant, spawned a decade and a half earlier by the perfect hybrid for Nebraska's Bohemian Alps—a blend of Czech cuisine and American football.

"This started as a family project for Cornhusker games," Mark explained. "Our farm is four miles north of town, about a quarter mile off the highway. Nebraska fans were going to Lincoln, taking Highway 79, and we offered them free coffee on the corner. And then we would sell homemade *kolaches.*"

The Kolac Korner.

"The mailman would stop and the highway patrolmen and all the Nebraska fans. At its peak, it was every bit of a couple hundred people every Saturday," he continued. "We took something that was our ethnicity and we attached it to something that was statewide."

"So you were selling a little bit of . . ."

"Of our heritage. Definitely."

Mark didn't play football, himself, explaining, "With nine kids and a farm and everything else, other things were a little more important than sports—like getting good grades and the livestock and the chores, running the farm, watching the budget." For a while, Mark was a general agriculture major in Lincoln, trying to work his way through college with various jobs in food service. But funds were in short supply, and he left school to take a position at the agricultural services agency in Wahoo. When his family opened the restaurant in 1992, Mark was hired to be, as he put it, "cook and chief bottle washer." He is now the head chef and manager.

"Business picked up right away, I think due to the fact that we catered to the Czech culture," he recalled. "On Friday nights, we have a fish fry and live polka music. I think people appreciate that, an avenue to get out and celebrate their heritage."

Mark seemed to possess a reverence for his roots that is uncommon in his generation, my generation. He was hoping to continue the tradition, explaining his bachelor status with an embarrassed laugh. "I'm holding out for that Czech girl!" His was a respect for history, really, which is also increasingly unusual these days, when folks tend to dismiss as irrelevant anything that occurred before they were born. As Billy Crystal once said about a younger woman, "I asked her where she was when Kennedy was shot, and she said, 'Ted Kennedy was shot?' Mark was president of the Nebraska Czechs of Prague, a local chapter of a statewide organization established, before he was born, in an effort "to preserve and promote the Czech culture, customs, heritage and traditions."

"I realize this is America, and it's a melting pot. But I still think it's very important to know your roots, where you come from. I truly believe if you understand your ancestry and who they were, it helps you know more about yourself in the here and now," he said, leaning forward on the edge of his seat. "Some of the immigrants, when they came to America, they wanted to sever their European ties because they wanted to be recognized as Americans. They didn't want to go through any type of discrimination. They didn't want to suffer any more hardship than they had ahead of them already, coming to a country with next to nothing. I think those who wanted to be more Americanized, with a new start, those are the families that just tossed it aside. And those who wanted to hang on to their heritage and keep those ties, they enforced that within their families. I truly believe it would be a very sad day when you hear no more Czech music or Czech singing or even the language in and of itself, which is very beautiful."

Although Mark claimed to speak only a little Czech, there were several times throughout our conversation when he offered the Czech translation of various words, and I thought I could still detect, three generations later, a hint of his ancestors' home country in his speech. "My father speaks it very fluently," he said, "and when people from the Czech Republic stop in to visit, we usually call him. If we can catch him at home, he'll come into town and sit down and speak with them for a couple of hours."

But here, in the space between the notes, Mark's father, Adolph, passed his heritage on to his children through the language of music. He had joined a band right after graduating from Prague High in 1941, courting his wife, Gladys, while they traveled from one polka dance to another in an old Flexible Bus. Later, for years, he directed the Adolph Nemec Orchestra, playing polka fests throughout the region. When his children were old enough, they joined him. Mark was the drummer. Jim played the bass horn, and Cindy the French horn. Connie and Joe were adept at various instruments. Virginia took up the trombone. Laura opted for the baritone. Debbie and Kristina played the trumpet. They traveled, as one big polka-playing clan, to places like Cincinnati and Detroit, Oklahoma and West Texas. It was like the Partridge Family, only the electric keyboard was replaced by an accordion.

Nowadays, Mark is a member of the Prague Czech Brass Band. "They say every Czech song that was written was about an incident that really happened," he said, handing me a cassette of the band's recordings, songs with names like "Grinders Polka" and "Pilsener Waltz," each with the Czech translation in parentheses. "Czech people are very passionate about their music and about life, very emotional. I'm probably a prime example of that."

This was evident a bit later, when Mark mentioned that he had once been to New York, to the top of the World Trade Center. He recalled his memories of the day the towers fell, how he was working in the restaurant's kitchen that morning when he received a phone call from one of his employees telling him he had to turn on the TV, the one on top of the refrigerator, used mostly for Nebraska football games.

"I saw it, and I couldn't believe it." His voice quivered, and he paused for a moment, struggling to keep his composure. "I was mad. Yeah, I was mad." Tears formed in the corners of his eyes, and then he caught himself and shook his head. "You don't do that to Americans."

Every town needs a drummer like Mark Nemec, keeping a steady beat, making sure the others don't lag behind. "These are Czech people, and they're very stubborn. They're very opinionated and headstrong. When something needs to be done, they come together. But they all have their own way of doing things." He chuckled. "Sometimes, living in the community, you wonder: Why do I stick around here? Outsiders visit and say, 'What a neat place! You guys have such a lovely town, and the people are so nice. . . .' But a friend and I have a running joke: Well, you ought to see them after you leave."

He laughed again, somewhat giddily, and added, "But these are good people. I think Prague has its heart in the right place. I don't know don't about its mind, but its heart is okay."

This may explain Prague's contribution to the record of municipal marketing. Perhaps the village had run out of options. The city of Wilber, nearly five times as populous, was already Nebraska's Czech Capital. Prague wasn't much of a gateway or a crossroads. Its most illustrious natives weren't famous enough for highway signs. Nothing of general interest had been invented or initiated there. It couldn't rely on historical claims or regional boasts or wordplay. But alas, there seems to be a promotional tool of last resort—small-town bigness.

Darwin, Minnesota boasts the world's largest ball of twine. Sparta, Wisconsin touts possession of the world's largest highwheeler bicycle. The world's largest globe is in Yarmouth, Maine. One town alone—Vining, Minnesota (population 100)—claims to have the world's largest coffee cup, clothespin, doorknob, extension cord and square knot.

Well, the people of Prague seem to have wanted to create something tangible, something memorable and, apparently, something edible. In 1987, during Prague's centennial, the chairman of the village board introduced an out-of-the-blue proposal that appeared to offer just the right mix of heritage and hyperbole: *Let's get ourselves in the Guinness Book of World Records. Let's make the world's largest* kolach.

I suppose there was something understandable about the idea. In Prague, polkas were prevalent, but the Czech heritage seemed to be most plentiful in the food. In fact, on the occasion of Mark Nemec's one and only trip to the Czech Republic, he had been struck by how much it reminded him of home. Not the 500-year-old churches and the 1,200-year-old castle ruins, of course, but rather the sliced up fried rolls with scrambled eggs for breakfast, the tea made from a linden tree, the alderberry wine.

So Prague's citizens went to work. They trucked in 250 gallons of cherry pie filling and 700 pounds of dough. They constructed a huge platform to bake it on and a big metal shed to bake it in. When it was done, the giant pastry measured nearly fifteen feet in diameter and weighed more than 2,600 pounds. When the folks at Guinness informed them that, unfortunately, there was nothing with which to compare the feat, they simply cooked up another, slightly larger one five years later. So now there are signs on either side of town: *Welcome to Prague: Home of the World's Largest* Kolach.

You could look it up.

XANDER, FUN
AND THE ONE-ARMED MAN

LONDON, WISCONSIN

I leave when the pub closes.
—WINSTON CHURCHILL

Driving under cotton-ball clouds, humming along with the Allman Brothers, I passed over the Mississippi River and into Wisconsin. Always, as I cross the so-called Father of Waters, I find myself grinning rather stupidly, affixing significance to the experience that seems disproportionate to the sixty seconds or so it takes to complete it. I suppose I'm marveling at the magnitude of the river's impact on the country—geologically, geographically, psychologically, historically. But I've done it every time—when I've crossed at Lake Itasca, at Winona, at Moline and Muscatine, at St. Paul and St. Louis, at Memphis, at Vicksburg, at Baton Rouge.

Now, having just cruised through Iowa's gut, I could add musty, old Dubuque to the list.

I had about 130 miles ahead of me. There are a few ways in which one can survey the distance. You can do it in linear fashion, a straightforward succession of dotted yellow lines. In that case, I followed State Highway 11 to County Route A to Route M to KK to K to 18 to 134 to O. Along with Missouri, Wisconsin is an anomaly among the states in that it insists on describing county roads alphabetically and repetitively. County Route A, for instance, can be found in more than a dozen different counties. It is as if somebody spilled some Alphabits while printing the atlas. This led my thoughts to my older son, all of twenty months old at the time, who knew the entire alphabet, except that he called every letter *d*. But ask the folks in the Wisconsin hamlets of Eastman or West Bend or Big Patch or Whitehall or Modena or Spirit or Range or Poplar or Kohlsville or Bloom City or Irvington or Cedar Falls or Boyd or Owen or Blaine, and they will all claim residence along a County Route D.

Or you can travel in staccato bursts of billboards and marquees, a choppy tin-and-fiberglass narrative of place. Thus I learned that the town of Shullsburg offers A STROLL BACK IN TIME. County Highway OK is just past Monroe. It's 77 degrees at 1:13 P.M. at the Bank of Brodhead. Ty Bollerud is running for governor. Albrecht Taxidermy is open for business. South Side Beverage Mart is offering a Coors thirty-pack for $15.29. Ed Thompson is running for governor, too. The Sports Boosters Chicken Barbecue is next week. It's 86 degrees at 1:56 P.M. at Black Hawk Credit Union in Jaynesville. O'Leary is running for Rock County Treasurer. Fresh eggs are seventy-five cents a dozen. Billy Ray Cyrus is coming to the Jefferson County Fair.

And you can get two chili dogs for two bucks at Jim's Burger Corner in Jefferson.

There is a third way to pass the time, by finding poetry in the miles—an iambic odometer, if you will. So my journey was all rolling hills and road kill, John Deere and "Pray here," vegetable stands and Packer fans, hay bales and beer sales, sweet corn and "Save the Unborn," Holsteins and trampolines, blackbirds and cheese curds, Methodist churches and maples and birches. So goes the sonnet of southern Wisconsin.

My route to London took me through Cambridge, population 1,101, a pleasant enough place, despite the fact that it now refers to itself as "the salt-glazed pottery capital of the world." From its origins in 1847 as a dam on the north loop of the Koshkonong River, the settlement, about thirty miles from Madison, evolved into a resort community of sorts due to its proximity to Lake Ripley. Indeed, a pair of famous residents of Ripley's shores—Ole Evenrude and Arthur Davidson—made significant contributions to the life of leisure. Evenrude invented the outboard motor; Davidson made motorcycles with a fellow named Harley.

By July 4, 1848, there were perhaps three hundred residents of the new community, and a large celebration was held at a hotel called the Onion House, during which the village was formally named. Said one orator, "England had her Cambridge, Massachusetts has her Cambridge . . . so shall Wisconsin have hers."

London came later, by railroad. Cambridge missed the train.

In the early 1880s, the Chicago & Northwestern Railroad constructed a new line from Milwaukee to Madison. But while Cambridge's citizens were sedentary in the certainty that the railway would be coming through town, the eager residents of nearby Lake Mills managed to attract the tracks there instead. The line did find its way through some sheep farms a few miles from Cambridge, however, on land owned by an Irishman named Archie and a Scot named Angus. One wonders why either of them would be willing to settle on London as a name for the boomtown that emerged, but there is a simple anecdotal story about its origin. Supposedly, the auctioneer surveyed the big crowd during the land auction in 1882 and commented, "My goodness, when I look out here, it looks just like London." Sarcastic or not, apocryphal or not, London it became.

A community sprang up around the London railroad depot. At one time or another, it boasted three hotels, four taverns, a grain elevator, a creamery, several tobacco warehouses, a cigar factory, a movie house showing silent films, even its own newspaper. For a couple of decades at the turn of the twentieth century, a small train—a second-hand engine known as the Cannonball—operated on a spur of the railroad line constructed between London and Cambridge. The Chicago & Lake Superior Railroad, as it was called, never grew beyond the three-mile route, making it the shortest in the state.

Today, the tracks are gone, removed a couple of decades ago and replaced by a bike trail. I couldn't reach London via the shortest railroad line in the state, so I took the shortest state highway instead. The explanation I heard is that, since the federal mail arrived in London and had to be shipped to Cambridge, federal law required it to be transported along a state or federal road. So County Route O masquerades as state Highway 134 for a couple of miles just until you make it to London.

I arrived to find an unincorporated rural hamlet heading toward what smelled like a suburban future. The older houses were clustered near the center of town, along with the few commercial enterprises that still had a pulse—a lumber yard, a fertilizer plant, a heating contractor. But on the fringes were modern houses on treeless land, a subdivision of a barely divisible place. There were SUVs, mothers driving kids to swim practice, towheaded boys pedaling their bicycles in circles. Where once there were dairy cows, there was now a wiffleball field. What was once the fine brick K-through-8 schoolhouse was now a community center and London Bridges Pre-School. Madison was perhaps two dozen miles away. London was evolving from boomtown to bedroom community.

I chatted with Chad, a thirty-two-year-old bricklayer with a wife, two daughters, a basset hound named Buford and a black Labrador named Layla. He grew up "on the other side of town," which meant about three blocks west, with his six younger brothers, five of whom still live in London. In flat vowels and shrugs, he told me how they used to play football in the fields, fish for bullhead in the creek and milk cows on the local dairy farms that have since disappeared in favor of larger, more distant operations.

I met a middle-aged engineer for a company that makes food processing equipment, a fellow named Greg, whose wife had responded to the September 11th attacks by planting little American flags along their walkway leading to a big Ol' Glory on their front door. "I think everybody in America felt connected to it," he mused. "Regardless of how vast this country is, it felt like it happened in your own backyard." Of course, nobody ever asks the folks of London, Wisconsin, about the state of the union. But when Charles and Diana got married,

Madison TV crews were quick to send a smirking reporter here to broadcast London's opinion of the state of the Union Jack.

And I sat down with seventy-eight-year-old Lois, alongside old issues of *Lap Quilting* and *Birds & Blooms*, in the tiny house she and her late husband Herbert had purchased for $1,500 back in 1947. She dusted off framed photos of the London of yore, recalling the hotel, the post office, the barbershop, the cheese factory. "It used to be," she said, "that most everybody who lived here was related to somebody else who lived here."

London was a fine idea. Norman Rockwell might have set up an easel. But I found myself growing discouraged. It was all so . . . predictable. I was uninspired.

In *The Innocents Abroad,* Mark Twain mused on such a feeling in Italy, in another setting nicer than most: "How the fatigues and annoyances of travel fill one with bitter prejudices sometimes! I might enter Florence under happier auspices a month hence and find it all beautiful, all attractive. But I do not care to think of it now at all. . . ." It was still relatively early in my journey, but the fatigues of travel were translating to impatience. I longed for something unique, something unexpected, perhaps an imperfection in the diamond, a werewolf in London.

There was potential in the London Depot. Not the railroad depot—that was long gone—but rather a tavern at the corner of Main Street and O, an antidote to suburban notions. Which was as it should be, not only because this was a London pub, but because this was Wisconsin. They like their beer in Wisconsin.

Forgive the generalization, but the facts rise to the surface like the head on a mug of Heineken. Or Old Milwaukee. Or Milwaukee's Best, the latter being a staple of my college days, even though I was schooled in New York. Never mind that it tastes like fermented socks; cheap beer is cheap beer. You can visit the Pabst Mansion in Milwaukee, too. And you can tour the Miller Brewing Company's plant. In fact, legend has it that when a national magazine published a story about beer drinking on college campuses, it had to leave the University of Wisconsin at Milwaukee off the charts because its students' remarkable rate of beer consumption irreparably skewed the statistics.

Before it was closed in 1999, the Heileman brewery, on the western edge of the state in La Crosse, boasted the World's Largest Six-Pack—a set of six storage tanks, each several stories high and painted to resemble Old Style beer cans. A sign in front explained that the massive sextet could hold enough beer to fill 7,340,796 cans, providing one person a six-pack a day for 3,351 years. Across the street, one could pay homage to the statue of Gambrinus, a fifth-century duke credited with supporting farmers in growing hops—and thus elevated through the centuries to a loftier position: King of Beer.

When nationwide numbers are crunched, Wisconsin generally rivals Nevada in per capita beer intake. And let's face it, any state that consists primarily of desert and free casino drinks shouldn't really count. In Wisconsin, there are more than two hundred new alcohol drinkers every day and more than twelve thousand drinking establishments. The Tavern League of Wisconsin estimates the total economic contribution of the alcohol industry to be in excess of $7 billion, providing more than 130,000 jobs and rivaling agriculture and tourism as the state's top industry.

So, yes, they like their beer in Wisconsin.

There were once four taverns in London, all within about a hundred-foot radius, and this in a town that has never counted more than a couple hundred residents. The London Depot, formerly known as Jim Behm's Tavern after a long dead owner who pronounced his name just like the whiskey, was the only drinking establishment still on tap. I stepped in, figuring people visit bars for two reasons—either to find comfort in the familiar or exhilaration in the possibility of random encounters. I crossed my fingers that, even on a slow Wednesday in Wisconsin, the latter possibility remained.

The setting was typical—dim lights and dart boards, pool and pinball and Packers banners, a menu of pork sandwiches and sweet corn, a jukebox offering everything from Prince to B.B. King. At first blush, I was once again resigned to normalcy. But the woman behind the bar had an edge to her. This was Gina, the owner, somewhat menacing in a black T-shirt bearing the Rolling Stones' tongue-and-lips "Tattoo You" logo. She handed me a bottle of local swill from a cooler covered in bumper-stickered irreverence: I'M NOT DEAF. I'M IG-NORING YOU . . . PETA—PEOPLE EATING TASTY ANIMALS . . . IF I GAVE A SHIT, YOU'D BE THE FIRST PERSON I'D GIVE IT TO. . . .

When I told Gina I was looking for someone *different*, she allowed a half-grin and nodded toward the rear of the establishment. "Well, you can try my friends out there. I think they're pitching horseshoes."

Well, they weren't. I'm no Hercule Poirot, but when you barge conspicuously through a back door to find an unwashed gang of hippies standing on a porch, smoke wafting, the air ripe with a particularly pungent odor, and then they scatter like pigeons at the sight of you, you can surmise with some certainty that they weren't passing around a horseshoe.

LONDON'S PUB

Only one of them stood his ground, a comparatively clean-cut chap who turned out to be Gina's brother from Denver, a serious but friendly sort who was in town before heading to his best friend's wedding in Minnesota. We talked. I explained the intrusion. Indeed, I explained my whole reason for visiting London, as if this were an inspection station and I were the one with the contraband. He tilted his head for a moment, and then this: "I'm going on faith. I figure if you are indeed a writer, the names will be changed to protect the innocent." As it turns out, there was no need. After some cajoling, the three flighty pigeons returned and introduced themselves, with giddy irreverence, as Xander, Fun and the One-Armed Man.

The One-Armed Man was big, burly and a bit wild-eyed, with a goatee, a ponytail and two fully functioning arms. Fun was baby-faced with hair like kelp. He wore a hemp necklace over a tie-dye and carried three crystals in his pocket. As I was later informed, one was supposed to ward off negative energy. Another was to help keep him grounded. A third, he said, was for mental clarity.

And then there was Xander. He had long dreadlocks and a kudzu beard. His septum was pierced, and hanging from it was a miniature horseshoe. His eyes were bloodshot slits. He wore a long shirt splattered in so much paint that it almost obscured the saying, attributed to Gandhi, stitched across the chest: THERE'S MORE TO LIFE THAN INCREASING YOUR VELOCITY.

"I've got many names," Xander began. "Some people call me Chaos. Some people call me Slander. Some people call me the Beer Nazi." He was a transient, temporarily earning $14 an hour in the Madison area as a painter, which explained his wardrobe. And he lived in his van—or lately, crashed wherever there was an open porch because, you see, he gave his van away to a stranger.

"The guy was in an imminent ill state. I was real fucked up," he explained in a scratchy, smoke-stripped voice. "This kid walks up to me and goes, 'Hey man, are you going to New York?' And I said, 'No, you are.' I wrote him out a bill of sale right there."

The jukebox inside the London Depot shouted a Grateful Dead tune, "*I'm not runnin' but I take my time. . . . A friend of the devil is a friend of mine. . . .*" I had heard the moribund band was staging a reunion concert in Alpine Valley, Wisconsin, that week, and I suspected perhaps Xander and Co. were part of the group's renowned traveling circus. Fourteen years earlier, I had attended my one and only Dead show in Alpine

Valley. It didn't go quite as planned, the plan being that a friend and I were to meet two others for a preconcert barbecue in the parking lot. Meet us, they said, at our white Volkswagen van.

You can guess the rest. This being a caravan of counterculture, there were dozens upon dozens of Volkswagen vans. So we wandered aimlessly, toting a bag full of hot dogs and buns through the summer heat, wading through a gauntlet of blissed-out humanity, until a friendly couple selling bratwurst and acid was kind enough to lend us a corner of their grill. The concert was an afterthought. It was a surreal experience, albeit a sober one. I was nineteen and innocent enough. Admittedly, that day, everyone looked like Xander to me.

Xander shook his head and packed his pipe. "I went to a few Dead shows, as much as I could take. But I got burned out. You go to six, seven, eight shows and you're like a walking zombie, dude. You can't take the drugs anymore. You need a fuckin' dose of the woods—relaxation." Xander spread his arms out like a hippie Jesus and added, with a sort of sardonic verbal wink, "This is a respite, man. This is a great little town—the gem of America."

About five centuries earlier in London, England, xenophobic Britons outlawed the recently imported "wicked weed" of hops because they were fearful of an insidious foreign influence. As I watched Xander and friends sit at a backyard picnic table, passing around their own weed, I could rather understand the apprehension. They were clearly temporary visitors here, twenty-first-century nomads, hedonistic (if essentially harmless) trespassers in bucolic London. Then again, perhaps so was I.

We were random variables introduced to the usually predictable rural tavern, where a collection of retired farmers play cribbage in the morning, where hunters stop in the afternoon to register for the turkey chase or rehash it afterward, and where locals pop in before dinner for some small talk and swill. Heck, on Fridays, a bunch of folks gather for the weekly meat raffle, spinning a roulette wheel and hoping to go home with a dozen pounds of pork chops.

But on this Wednesday night in London, a foreign influence had come to party. So be it. My expedition was about discovering the exotic in the American outback. There were no rules as to residency. The fact that both Xander and I were essentially just passing through in one way or another doesn't minimize the encounter. It wasn't only a smidgen of place I was exploring; it was a slice of time, too.

There would be others in the bar that night—Dan, a local who looked a bit like poet Allen Ginsberg, but who was actually a pinball wizard of howling proportions; five-foot-tall Jenn, an amiable union floor coverer, who was just coming out of a three-year relationship in which her girlfriend left her for a women's professional football player; and another fellow, whose name I didn't catch, who merely seemed to lurch around the tavern with open-mouthed exuberance.

Fun and the One-Armed Man, both initially wary, would eventually warm up to me, finally accepting that fact that I wasn't a Fed or a Narc or any other monosyllabic adversary. They held a Budweiser in one hand and a fistful of wild theories in the other, most of them accusing the current resident of 1600 Pennsylvania Avenue of planning the September 11th tragedy for political gain. I found myself in the unfamiliar position of defending Dubya, but really all I could think of was how much I would like to lock the One-Armed Man in a room with Pam White from Rome to see which one survived with philosophies intact. "I'm not like the rest of America. Instead of voting for the right guy, they want to vote for the winner," announced the One-Armed Man. "So I did a write-in vote. I voted for Bugs Bunny. I thought we'd be better off."

My money was on Pam.

So the bar was lively with character. But something about Xander proved both captivating and discomforting. His speech was machine-gun fast, a sort of Kerouacian stream of consciousness. Indeed, he was likely what Jack Kerouac envisioned when he wrote, "The only people for me are the mad ones, the ones who are mad to live, mad to talk, mad to be saved. . . . The ones who never yawn or say a commonplace thing but burn, burn, burn like fabulous yellow roman candles."

Trying to anticipate Xander's train of thought was like trying to predict the bounce of a football. But as he spoke, and as I noticed the others watching him speak, I sensed that he had found a world where his disdain for mainstream society was a source of strength, as if he were some sort of Gen-X neo-hippie guru to a nonviolent Manson family in the heartland. Here follows Xander's story—an American tale, like it or not:

"When I read Kerouac, he totally freaked me out, dude. I was sixteen years old, and I wanted to steal cars and run away from home, man. Then I read *The Electric Kool-Aid Acid Test*, and those two books pretty much were the themes that fuckin' set me on fire. I've been traveling for the last ten years, since I dropped out of college in Chicago. First semester, dude. I was out of there. Wrote my English teacher a poem about being a bum, and she liked it. I was already ready to drop out, but that was, like, the straw that broke the camel's back. I went to Boulder, Colorado, and I worked at a virtual reality arcade, which was really intense. I did LSD and everything at work. I was buggin'. We annexed our space from the Boulder Theater, so we had all these cool shows—Bo Diddley, Bob Weir, Ricky Lee Jones. I met all these really cool people. I taught Bob Weir and some of the other Grateful Dead how to play virtual reality against these three drunk women. Then I got his autograph on a BHIP—Boulder Hemp Initiative Project—flyer. It had all these facts about, like, marijuana legalization and how long it's been used and everything. Pro-legalization stuff, man."

On the jukebox, Led Zeppelin: *"The sea was red and the sky was gray. . . . Wonder how tomorrow could ever follow today. . . ."*

"Then I got caught," Xander continued. "I had a wireless mike that I spoke through to instruct the people how to play, and I got caught by the owner, Dick, who never paid his taxes. He thinks I'm recording a show, which is like a five-thousand-dollar fine from the FCC. I'm only listening. I'm not recording. Still, I get suspended for a month. But it was cool. The snow was dumping back in ninety-three. So I went to Utah, and I skied. For like a month, man. Then I bought ten grams of crystal mescaline from Ward and tripped my ass off. Ward is a cool town. It's an artist community, and they've outlawed flush toilets there because they don't want people to fuckin' move there, man. And there's like one store that's been randomly owned, and you can go there and pick up your tie-dye and your fuckin' groceries or whatever you need. The sheriff and deputy switch jobs every year. Like, the deputy is the sheriff one year, and the sheriff is the deputy, and they trade every year. I've been at the sheriff's house with his sons smokin' pot, plants growing in the window and shit. It's a cool town. After that, I hitchhiked for my first time around the United States— I was nineteen years old. I did my first Rainbow Gathering in Dale, Oregon."

"What," I asked, "is a Rainbow Gathering?"

"Oh, my God!" he replied, as he sucked smoke into his lungs. "How many hours do you have?" He blew a trail into the Wisconsin night. "In 1972, these hippies got together with Vietnam veterans, and they decided to pray for peace. . . ."

The Rainbow Family of Living Light likes to describe itself as the largest nonorganization of nonmembers in the world. It began about thirty years and one month before Xander and I crossed paths, with the first Rainbow Gathering of the Tribes. The Gathering is now driven by word of mouth, but the original invitation read as follows:

We, who are brothers & sisters, children of God, families of life on earth, friends of nature & of all people, children of humankind calling ourselves Rainbow Family Tribe, humbly invite: All races, peoples, tribes, communes, men, women, children, individuals—out of love. . . . All nations & national leaders—out of respect. . . . All religions & religious leaders—out of faith. . . . All politicians—out of charity . . . to join with us in gathering together for the purpose of expressing our sincere desire that there shall be peace on earth, harmony among all people. This gathering to take place beginning July 1, 1972, near Aspen, Colorado-or between Aspen & the Hopi & Navaho lands-on 3,000 acres of land that we hope to purchase or ac-quire for this gathering—& to hold open worship, prayer, chanting or whatever is the want or desire of the people, for three days, but upon the fourth day of July at noon to ask that there be a meditative, contemplative silence wherein we, the invited people of the world may consider & give honor & respect to anyone or anything that has aided in the positive evolution of humankind & nature upon this, our most beloved & beautiful world—asking blessing upon we people of this world & hope that we people can effectively proceed to evolve, expand, & live in harmony & peace. . . .

The three thousand acres proved too much of a challenge, but the gathering took place on private land offered for the occasion. It wasn't intended as an annual affair, but it became that. The Gathering is Out There, in every sense of the term. Every year, during the first ten days of July, thousands—sometimes tens of thousands—converge on an ever-changing, secluded location in a national forest. Participants bring their own camping equipment, their own utensils and, increasingly as the decades have passed, their own reasons for arriving. They come to meditate for peace . . . or to celebrate anarchy . . . or to gain support for a cause . . . or to dabble in alternative lifestyles . . . or to perform workshops . . . or to go back to the land . . . or to stick it to authority . . . or to run naked in the woods . . . or to prophesize . . . or to proselytize . . . or to immerse themselves in all things psychedelic. It has been called a finishing school for hippies.

There is no formal organizational structure, and there are no membership criteria (as one Rainbow once put it, "All that's required is a bellybutton, brother"). The only fees or dues are the ones that find their way into the Magic Hat passed around at meals, the donations going toward things like bulk food, first aid supplies and plywood covers for the latrines. The Rainbows develop their own water supply, reseed the land afterward and aim to leave the site cleaner than it was when they arrived. Still, they invariably lock horns with local authorities, most often the U.S. Forest Service, which has no stomach for what they perceive as twenty thousand longhairs smoking dope in the trees. Thus various arrests and lawsuits tend to accompany each Gathering, involving folks who call themselves Zoe Love, Butterfly Bill, Granola Jay, Stone Turtle, Question Mark, Living Freely, Strider, Plunker, Starrchild. . . .

Xander, Fun and the One-Armed Man had recently returned from a Gathering in Michigan's Upper Peninsula. The year before that, it was Idaho. Before that, Montana, Pennsylvania, Arizona, Oregon, Missouri, New Mexico, Alabama . . . "Next year, it's probably in Utah," Xander announced. "Supposedly, it's based on consensus. There are scouts who go out and gather information and present it to a council. And the council comes to a consensus on where to go. But the truth of the matter is, with a bunch of hippies smoking pot and drinking coffee, the only thing that works is tyranny. And so there are actually a bunch of people who picked the place long ago, and they get people so worked up. And they don't tell us where it is. And they don't tell us. And they don't tell us. And they don't tell us. And finally people are so fed up, and it's close to the time of the actual Gathering, finally they tell us where we can go. And we go there.

"It's an illegal gathering when there's more than seventy-four people, and there's a chaos element. Alcohol is allowed only in the parking lot. You have to walk a mile to the Gathering part. And there are many, many kitchens and stages and

XANDER AND FRIENDS

theaters and parades and drum circles and trumpets and horns. I mean, it's intense. It's crazy. I used to work on the back of an ambulance, and I got busted with a half a sheet of acid. So now the only place I can work as an EMT is at the Gathering. I work at the Center for Alternative Living Medicine (CALM, I noticed), which is like a M*A*S*H unit that sets up and deals with all the cuts, scrapes, boo-boos, psych trips, serious trauma, broken legs, fuckin' people falling out of trees, whatever. I can do it tripping. I can do it stoned. I can do it for seventy fuckin' hours. It's fun, man."

As Queen shouted from the jukebox, Fun and the One-Armed Man tried to talk me into traveling with them, writing a book about the experience and then funneling the royalties their way. "Think of the most bizarre thing you can possibly imagine, magnify it by about ten, and that's what you'll experience, man," said the One-Armed Man, as he and his compatriots passed the pipe in an infinite loop. I told him maybe in my next life, which he seemed to take at face value, and I asked Xander to finish the story of his long, strange trip.

He kneaded his fingers through his beard. "Geez, man, that was ten years ago!" He laid his hands on the table, palms down, and tried to focus. "So I went to the Gathering, then to the coast of Oregon and Washington. Then I went home. I settled down. I got my EMT license, and I got a job in a nursing home in southern Illinois. Centralia. You gotta do ninety days of volunteer time to get hired on by the ambulance service, and I got busted with a half a sheet of acid. I got a six-year sentence with a prison boot-camp option. That was in 1994, when there was all that flooding going on in southern Illinois, and I did sandbagging and all kinds of crazy work shit. I did four months of boot camp, then three months of house arrest, then a year and eight months of parole. But before I could finish my parole in '96, I absconded and went to Oregon because I was, like, smoking crack and selling coke and shit. I couldn't take it anymore. I had to change my people, places and things. So I went to Oregon and just ate mushrooms for a month."

From the bar, the Grateful Dead again: "*Busted . . . down on Bourbon Street . . . Set up . . . like a bowling pin . . .*"

"And then, I'm on the lam," Xander continued. "I'm leaving the state, right? And I get pulled over for having a loud muffler. And these fucking cops . . . I pull over for one reason and one reason only—that's just to roll two joints. I don't even get out of my van at the gas station. So I roll the joints and drive out. I get out on the road and light one up. I'm going down the Interstate. I smoke almost a whole joint. I'm down to my fuckin' roach, and I look in the fuckin' rearview mirror and there's blueberries and cherries. And I pull over, and it's reekin' like dope, dude. And the cop is asking me for consent to search, and I don't give him consent. And he runs a dog out. And the dog jumps up on the door and barks. And I'm like, fuck. And he asks me to get out. The dog finds my coke grinder in my backpack, which has a tenth of a gram of residue on it. The dog finds it! And then they find a half-ounce of pot and a bag of roaches. I came up with this bullshit story that my fuckin' aunt has to be picked up to go to my uncle's funeral, who just died. They let me drive to the police station, and I gave them a sob story and cried, and they let me go. They dropped the felony coke possession charge and just charged me with two misdemeanors—the pot and the coke paraphernalia—if I returned in a week. But fuck that! I bolted. I went straight to Oregon, man. I ran on that charge for two years and eight months and then faced it in '99. I pled guilty to the pot and got acquitted of the coke charge anyway. Did thirteen days and then promptly violated my probation, which I'm still on the lam from. But it's a bench warrant, man. I ain't fuckin' worried about it."

Xander pointed a finger at me through the haze. "You know, ignorance of the law is no excuse. But not knowing that you're breaking the law is an excuse. If I don't knowingly possess it . . . if you guys put coke in my car, and I didn't know it, and I get caught with it, I didn't know that coke was in there. That's an excuse. You can get out of fuckin' shit like that." With a tone of mock innocence, he declared, "I did not know I was breaking the law. I wouldn't break the law. I'm a law-abiding citizen."

He grinned and let the sarcasm settle over us. "So you beat the rap," I said.

"Except for the pot," he shrugged. "I went to a bench trial for that with a public defender. I didn't have a jury or nothing, dude. I saved them money. I was nice. And you know what? The officers lied in fuckin' court. The testimony that I gave sounded just like this: 'I just pulled off to roll a joint, your honor. Then I smoked a whole joint. I must have been six miles down the fucking Interstate. I wasn't at the top of the exit ramp, like the officer said in the pretrial. . . .'"

It was like interrupting Hamlet's soliloquy, but I had to jump in. "Wait a second . . . So your defense hinged on how long it takes to smoke a joint?"

"Yeah, basically, 'cuz they were lying. I said, 'It was a roach, your honor, when they pulled me over. . . .'" He grinned again. "I'm a misdemeanor kid, man. I don't do no felonies or nothing anymore."

Just up the road a ways stood the 113-year-old London Moravian Church, a denomination that is said to be unencumbered by written doctrine, preferring a simple statement, known as "the ground of the Unity," which reads, in part, "In the light of divine grace, we recognize ourselves to be a Church of sinners." I watched this collection of modern-day countercultural standard bearers, belching hallucinogens into the night and reveling in antiestablishment episodes, and I thought: Sinners, indeed.

Xander went on with his tale. "I couldn't take probation anymore because I pissed dirty methamphetamines and pot for two months because all my friends in southern Illinois are, like, meth cooks, man. And I can't stay away from the shit. It's bad stuff. Horrible, dude. And all cheap and free and everywhere. So I pissed dirty for two months. Then I went and joined the carnival, dude. I ended up being a carnie for five months, man. I worked for these fuckin' shady, low-life motherfuckers and tried to lose my conscience. I worked for Italian fuckin' mobsters, people who carried guns and wads of money. I made like two thousand bucks in a weekend, and I only got about twenty percent of the cut. I went from Minnesota down through Texas, over to New Orleans, then wintered in Florida with them until I left a Miami show. By this point, my boss had accumulated six hundred bucks that he owed me and wasn't paying me. Every time, he'd always be shy a few bucks, and it started to add up. And then at some point he just cuts you loose. He's laundering all this cash, anyway, and keeping it off the books. So at the last minute, we had set the rides up at the Orange Bowl, and he went to the airport to pick up some kids who worked for him, and I just bailed on him. I said, fuck you. I'm gonna cut my losses right now. So I left and I hitchhiked for six days to go up north in Florida. I went to a Rainbow Gathering in Ocala in February 2000. . . . I haven't brushed my hair or shaved my beard since, man."

Chaos theory, at its most elementary level, is the notion that it is possible to get completely random results from normal equations. It's about unforeseen variables affecting the point of origin, a phenomenon known as the butterfly effect because the difference can be so small it is comparable to a butterfly flapping its wings. The idea is that a butterfly in, say, Australia in April can affect a tiny change in atmospheric conditions, which creates more unforeseen variables, which eventually cause a profoundly divergent weather result in, say, Bangladesh in June. So what might have been merely high winds becomes in-

stead a killer typhoon. Mathematicians call it sensitive depen-
dence on initial conditions. An imperceptible alteration at the
start can have profound long-term consequences.

I mention this because, as it turns out, Xander grew up a
couple of towns over from me along Chicago's North Shore.
He was a few years younger, of different heritage and able to
avoid brushing his hair for entirely different reasons from
mine. But all things considered, we came from the same
ecosystem. Xander had his own thoughts on his suburban initial conditions:

"That's white bread, man. I go back there now and look
around and think, wow, there ain't no Mexicans, ain't no black
people. I grew up in a place where every fourth house was the
same." By now, we had made our way back into the bar. Xander rested his beer on the pinball machine. Mick Jagger
shouted about honky-tonk women. "My parents moved here
from Denmark," said Xander. "In fact, I'm the third person in
my family to be born in this country. I spoke Danish before I
spoke English, man. I can still speak it. English is my second
language. My Danish relatives, when they have seriously trau-
matic experiences—an aneurysm or bone cancer or whatever—and they're near the end and all drugged up, they'll
speak Danish. They'll forget English. So maybe at some point,
if I get high enough, I'll forget English."

I wanted to tell him: Well, if it hasn't happened yet . . .

"My parents were both teachers. My dad put himself
through school and became a CPA. Later on, he decided to go
to law school, but my mom had an aneurysm, so he dropped
out. She's okay, a ninety-nine percent recovery. Except when
she drinks a lot, she kind of blacks out. And she lost her sense
of humor."

"Over you?" I asked.

"She never had a sense of humor about me. I used to just try to freak her out, man, but not anymore. I freaked them out enough already to where they're sort of numb to it. I used to lie to them all the time, man, in high school and stuff. They didn't know where I was, where I was going, who I was with or anything. So when they sit there and think about who their son was, it was a complete dream world, an illusion that I made up for them. Then after I got busted for LSD, I decided there was no point in lying to them anymore. So I told them everything. That kind of started a trend. I've been through rehab for crack and everything. And I just talk to them about it. I tell them everything. My parents could tell you three ways to cook crack, and they've never smoked a hit of crack in their life. When I'm fucked up and I need their help, I know they're there, man. They've showed me total, unconditional love.

"Scandinavians will often get married and fight it out to the bitter end, and they'll never give up on their children, no matter how much they hate each other," he concluded. "We're fighters, dude. My grandmother was wanted by the fuckin' Nazi police because she was a Danish citizen who was part of an underground system that snuck prisoners of war out of prison camps and into Sweden. She was cool, man. But Danish people have a fuckin' grudge against Swedish people because they were a neutral country, but they still bought German products, German gasolines, German filters, German shit on the shelves of their stores. My father was held in my uncle's arms in a basement off the streets of Denmark while bombs were raining overhead. I was named after that uncle. My real name's John."

With that, Xander wandered off to plan his next escapade,

score his next batch of something or other, take on his next alias—Chaos, Slander, the Misdemeanor Kid. I said my good-byes and shuffled outside, briefly releasing a Jimmy Page guitar solo into the streets of London until the door closed behind me, leaving me to silently stare at the Big Dipper hanging over the horizon.

The encounter was over, a random intersection of two travelers on two different roads. Just another conversation in a bar with a guy named John.

ALL YOU NEED IS LOUVRE

PARIS AND VERSAILLES, KENTUCKY

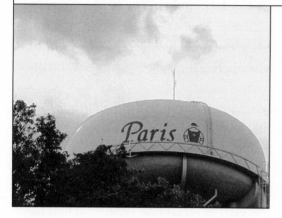

Imagination governs the world.
—NAPOLEON BONAPARTE

I f my expedition was a tonic for the soul, then the five days
I spent in Chicago, reunited with my family en route from
London to Paris, were a bandage for the heart. It had been
eighteen days since I had seen my wife and my two little boys.
My older son, still toddling, had no real understanding of the
situation beyond his three-word analysis: "Daddy. RV. Bye-
bye." His younger brother, just escaping the newborn stage,
was still grappling with the chore of physical existence, but I
worried that my face was fading from his recollection.

So far, much of my trip had suggested a journey through
the many faces of parenthood. I thought back to Rome and to
Pam and Jesse White's son, who chose to follow his parents
into the ranching life, despite its perils and frustrations. And

Carly Danhof-Bellach in Amsterdam, doing the same in the family's auto dealership, marveling at the accomplishments of a couple of generations. In Vienna, Scott Borg's teenaged son had joined him for an afternoon at the grain elevator. In Prague, Mark Nemec spoke reverently of his heritage as embodied by his father. Even Xander—irreverent, sardonic, screw-the-world Xander—cleared his head long enough in the London Depot to express appreciation for his parents' unconditional love.

As it turns out, the decision to relocate three-fourths of my family to my native Chicago for the summer had proved to be reassuringly sensible. Loving grandparents, playful cousins and old friends had made up for my absence, introducing my boys to the wonders of extended family, filling in the void the way water fills gaps. Still, one likes to claim one's space. When the two-month-old vomited on me in the middle of my first night home, I felt mine had been somewhat reclaimed.

Leaving again was difficult, and the weather reflected my frame of mind. For most of the dreary drive from Chicago through Indianapolis and Louisville to the Lexington area, the sky was low and angry. Dark clouds gathered like warships, and the rain came in shouts and murmurs, moving in frantic rivulets across my windshield. But Phileas and I splashed our way toward a reserved spot at Lexington's Kentucky Horse Park, where evening came early. The meteorologist on the 11:00 news suggested we might have seen the worst of the weather. His name was T. G. Shuck, which I placed in my mental file of favorite news names, alongside the weatherman in LA who called himself Dallas Rains.

Early the next day, I drove another twenty miles east, past antebellum mansions and picturesque horse farms, into Paris.

Its location shouts hedonism (it is nestled against the Stoner Fork of the Licking River in Bourbon County). But the *H*'s on the welcome sign were HORSES, HISTORY AND HOSPITALITY. Paris is the seat of Bourbon County, and with a population exceeding nine thousand it seemed a veritable metropolis in the scheme of my journey. It was chartered in 1789 and originally called Hopewell, which had been its founder's hometown in New Jersey, but it was renamed Paris the following year. Both the town and the county were named in appreciation for French aid during the American Revolution—one for the capital of France and the other for the French royal house.

A long-standing myth about the region trumpeted how ironic it was that Bourbon County was dry. On the contrary, the county claims to have given its name to the famous blended whiskey, first distilled there, they say, by one of the early settlers. And there is a three-story, twenty-room building in Paris called the Duncan Tavern, which has been in continuous use since 1788. The oldest building in town and the first in the state built of stone, it was a favorite of several American icons. Henry Clay stayed the night. Daniel Boone was a frequent guest. George Washington slept there.

The Duncan Tavern was closed for restoration (which rather put an end to its "continuous use" boast), as were many of the buildings lining the square around the grand county courthouse. Paris was a tired, old town opting for a bit of a makeover, a chin tuck here, a shot of Botox there. I wandered along Main Street for a while, peeking in storefronts, looking for the Bluegrass version of a Paris café. It wasn't quite a stroll down the Champs-Elysées, but it satisfied.

The sign at the Bourbonton Inn announced, SINCE 1954. The waitress, ancient and adorned in horn-rimmed glasses, seemed to say the same thing. The menu offered fried okra, breaded catfish, chicken livers, buttered beets. But my California stomach was protesting its recent fate, so I ordered a BLT and spent the hour listening to assorted conversations, which is just a fancy way of saying I was eavesdropping.

It was all drawled gossip and twangy small talk. The half-dozen patrons covered topics ranging from the difficulties of emphysema and the memories of that last half-pack of cigarettes (this was tobacco country, after all) to how so-and-so used to be a good-looking guy and his wife had the prettiest skin ya ever saw. I liked the way folks talked in the Bluegrass. They seemed to be generous with their syllables, as if savoring the taste of a word. "Well" was "way-ell," and "one" was "woo-un" and "where" was "hoo-way-ah." They offered up phrases like "Well, Garlene, how's the world doin'?" One lady turned to a chatty man at a table next to hers and whispered, "Yo' lunch is gettin' cold, darlin'." A waitress finished up her shift by shouting toward the kitchen, "Johnny, I'm gone! Gotta go git mah perm!" It was soothing and somewhat contagious.

Although Lexington is closer to Detroit than it is to Atlanta, there was no question that I had entered the South. Kentucky may qualify as the northernmost southern state. Or perhaps the southernmost northern state. It stayed loyal to the Union during the Civil War, but it was a border state in both setting and sentiment. Both Abe Lincoln and Jefferson Davis were Kentuckians by birth. In fact, not far from the Confederate War Memorial (the tallest structure in the Paris Cemetery) is the grave of a Union general.

But apparently the dichotomy of allegiance was even more intimate here. Before the rift, two brothers, Washington and Joseph Fithian, shared a medical office on Pleasant Street in

Paris. But when the conflict began, Wash, who had married a southern girl, donned a gray uniform. Joseph, married to a northerner, wore Union blue. When the fighting was over, the doctors returned to Paris and their shared medical practice, supposedly never speaking of the war again.

The great American writer Henry Miller was not a particularly great American enthusiast. He abandoned the States for Paris, France, returning only to bash his native land in a book he called *The Air-Conditioned Nightmare*. His American journey in 1939 and mine 63 years later were both undertaken amid the shadow of a depressed economy and the rumblings of war. But Miller's reads like a ride on the Vitriol Express. Boston was "a vast jumbled waste created by pre-human or sub-human monsters in a delirium of greed." St. Louis was "a foul, stinking corpse rising up from the plain." New York, his birth-place, was "the most horrible place on God's earth." Miller was disgusted by what he perceived as the veneer of optimism that pervaded his godforsaken mother country. He then admitted, "I, on the other hand, always expect the angels to pee in my beer."

I cannot marshal the same disdain. Cynicism? Occasionally. Disappointment? Often. Bemusement? Always. But for the most part, I travel with buoyant expectations, and it suits the open road. So Paris, Kentucky, is not the City of Light. Big deal. Perhaps it is at least the City of Light Lite. Napoleon's contention that imagination governs the world is relevant here, where a little creative accounting suggests that, per capita, the seat of Bourbon County offers as many exotic attractions as the capital of France.

In the Hopewell Museum, the local repository of all things

Bourbon, I had noticed a display of children's artwork, as supervised by one Jennifer Zingg. "America is no place for an artist," Miller also claimed. "To be an artist is to be a moral leper, an economic misfit, a social liability." Naturally, I expected to find just the opposite.

I found her, a couple of phone calls and a couple of miles later, stripping paint off the bottom of a sailboat in the parking lot of Crockett's Colonial Motel. She was a fresh-faced woman, her blonde hair mostly hidden by a blue bandanna. She had been raised on a farm along the Ohio River in the southern Indiana hamlet of Rome, and in her twenty-nine years she had made it all the way to Paris.

"I have been creative, artistic all my life," she began, as we found chairs in a cluttered back room of her house, which was in front of the motel. "While the other kids were out playing tag, I was drawing. If we were outside and they were swimming in the creek, I was making pots out of mud from the bank or weaving baskets out of honeysuckle vines. I've always done that, and I think I've always known that it's a part of me. It's who I am."

She was an artist of opportunity, using what she could find—which might explain how she came to arrive in what might be called her Gourd Period.

"If you pick them and cure them correctly, they harden. They make a great medium for artwork. I tell people I'm a gourd artist and they roll their eyes, but I try to take it to a different level that I've never seen done before," said Jennifer, who majored in art at Kentucky Wesleyan. "It's very much like pottery, and most people think it is until they pick it up, and then they're surprised because it's very lightweight."

In six months of gourd artistry, she had created fifty-six designs, most of which integrated various mediums—carving, staining, wood burning, oil painting—and usually some embellishments such as glass, wire and rope. Jennifer picked up one example, a striking creation called *Blues Singer*—a handsome gourd on which were painted various bluesy instruments. The words to Billie Holliday's "Summertime" were engraved throughout, accentuated by colored glass beads. Another gourd had been turned into a beautiful lampshade. Others, selling for about $200 each, had been fashioned into goldfish, beetles, circus elephants.

"What I love, personally, are painting and sculpture combined," she explained. "I like to incorporate both because I can never make up my mind which I like better. And I think that's why I like the gourds I'm doing so much because they're very sculptural, vessel-like. And then I'm able to carve and paint on them. So I'm kind of getting two-dimensional art and three-dimensional art all in one."

Two years ago, Jennifer and her husband, Jeff Crockett, had moved from the big city, Lexington, and purchased the Colonial Motel, a working-class establishment along the Paris Pike. They had been received warmly, both as business people and as a welcome dose of creative energy. Jennifer's veterinarian grew her gourds. Her masterpieces were on sale at a gallery on Main Street. And she had taken it upon herself to organize a guild of local artists, recruiting thirty people who, in two weeks time, would be displaying their artwork at the first-ever Bourbon County Local Artists Show.

"There's a lot of talent here," Jennifer insisted. "They may not have college degrees, but Kentucky is like that. It's very rich in fine craftsmanship and fine art and even craft turned into art. We'd like to market them and show them and also use it as a tourist draw for Paris. It really can't hurt."

Although she is a fan of Manet and Cézanne and Toulouse-Lautrec, Jennifer has never been to Paris, France. But someday she will, and she knows exactly how she plans to get there. That sailboat she had been stripping as I pulled up was a second-hand vessel they had purchased a week earlier in upstate New York. It was to be their means of expanding their canvas.

"Our dream is to retire to the ocean, so this is our practice boat. It was a great bargain, and we wanted a fixer-upper because we wanted to know what we're doing." She shrugged and smiled slightly. "We've never sailed in our lives. We've only read books about it. But you can't learn if you don't try."

"Are you going to paint it?"

"Yellow," she nodded. "Bright yellow." Then she let out a deep breath and a dream. "Hopefully, we'll sail away one day, and we'll make it to the Mediterranean, to the south of France."

Meanwhile, she turns gourds into gold in Paris. One could do worse.

Like the streets radiating from the Arc de Triomphe, quiet roads fan out in all directions from Paris, winding their way through the countryside, past stately trees and verdant pastures. What one notices most, however, are the fences, miles and miles of them, made of wood or stone, undulating with the hills. These are the world-famous horse farms of the Bluegrass, and none is more renowned than the three-thousand-acre spread a mile south of town, over the railroad tracks, just past the local version of the Eiffel Tower (a giant water tower that shouts "Paris").

I parked Phileas at the end of a quiet lane and made the acquaintance of twenty-four-year-old Wes Purcell, my guide for a personal tour of Claiborne Farm, which has been called the closest thing to a living Hall of Fame. Here is where one pays homage to the luminaries of thoroughbred racing. Having proved themselves on the racetrack, the horses are now demonstrating their prowess in the breeding shed, which is where the competition really begins.

Wes grew up on the farm. His father has worked there for thirty years and is now the brood mare foreman, meaning he is in charge of the two-hundred-or-so mares on the premises, as well as their foals. As a stallion foreman, Wes takes care of the fourteen spoiled-rotten studs whose sole purpose is to have their way with the mares.

"The mares have to come to this farm. No artificial insemination is allowed," he explained, as I followed him up a pathway beneath majestic sycamore trees. When Arthur Hancock launched the farm nearly a century ago, he had purchased nearly one thousand sycamores at a quarter apiece. They had grown nearly a foot per year, providing just the right amount of regality for the assorted racing royalty in their shade.

"These guys have contracts," Wes said, pointing toward the stallion barn. "It could be fifty-five mares in a season, or it could be one hundred. It depends on their demand, their age, their fertility. They could get five thousand dollars per mare or as high as a quarter of a million per mare. It depends on what their babies have been doing on the racetrack."

Then he tossed out this number: $70 million. That's how much the stallions earn, in clients' breeding fees each year. "It's a big business," said Wes, "a rich man's hobby, they call it."

He led me into the stallion barn, where each stall bore nameplates honoring the current or former occupants. The first stall on the left boasted four of the most celebrated names in racing: Bold Ruler, Secretariat, Easy Goer and Unbridled. It is akin to a clubhouse locker used by Lou Gehrig, then Joe DiMaggio, then Mickey Mantle, then Reggie Jackson, and it was empty due to high standards.

"Nobody occupies it now because we lost Unbridled in September," said Wes. "Eventually, somebody's going to fill the void, but they gotta be a little extra special."

"So it's like table number one at a restaurant."

"That's right. That's right," he nodded. "This is reserved only right here."

Wes made his way to another stall. "Let me walk in here and bring out Monarchos . . . ," he said, and just like that, I was standing before the previous year's Kentucky Derby winner. "You've gotta be cautious with these guys 'cuz they're 'proximately thirteen hun'red pounds. They like to bite and nip a little bit. We try our best not to stress the horses."

You have to be cautious, too, because this horse, his coat gray with just a hint of red, was valued at about $10 million. The second-fastest Derby winner in history, behind only the incomparable Secretariat, Monarchos would still have been racing had he not suffered a hairline fracture in his right front leg and started his breeding career early. His contract is the common "live foal guarantee" variety, meaning the client doesn't pay until his mare has a baby that stands and nurses from its mother. "Since he's the youngest guy on our roster, he bred the most mares of any of the horses," said Wes, "which was right at eighty-five mares."

Monarchos gets $25,000 per mare, which is still far from a superstar salary. Wes showed me Pulpit, a grandson of Seattle Slew, who has sired about twenty-five winners in two years and earns $60,000 per mare. And then he pointed out another, Seeking the Gold, who lived up to his name by earning $2.3 million on the racetrack and bringing in about $22 million in each breeding season. His fee: $250,000 per mare, with no guarantee. That is, you pay the money up front, and you have the whole four-and-a-half-month season (February to July) to breed your horse. A quarter of a million dollars just for the *possibility* of conception.

"We'll walk you down here, and show you Danzig," said Wes, and with that he brought out a bay horse, shorter than some of the others, blind in one eye, with a calcified knot in his left front knee the size of a baseball. "This horse here," he said, "is the number one active stallion in the world. He's valued at about twenty-five million."

Danzig, a son of 1964 Kentucky Derby winner Northern Dancer, raced three times and won all three. In preparation for his fourth race, he injured that knee and was retired from the track. That was in 1979. In nearly a quarter-century in the breeding shed, his offspring have earned nearly $90 million. At age twenty-five, which is about the usual life span of a thoroughbred, he still earns $250,000 per mare, no guarantees. "Let's let him get a drink," said Wes, as Danzig slurped from a trough. "Old man deserves a drink." Were I nearing the end of my life span, half-blind, with the pressure of copulating in front of a crowd for a fee of $250,000, I think I might need a drink, too.

These stallions are spoiled, of course. They are fed red clover hay and sweet feed, which consists of corn, oats, protein pellets and molasses for flavor. Once every hour in the stall, a spray mists them to keep away the flies. The soft walkway to the breeding shed consists of recycled tires, about $500,000 worth of material, so the stallions won't bruise or chip a hoof while making sudden moves. Each horse grazes seventeen hours a day in a private paddock about an acre in size.

In all, there are fifty miles of blacktop road and seventy-five miles of fencing on the farm. But really, it all comes down to what happens in a thirty-by-thirty-foot room with yellow padded walls, a mulch floor and a few doors for safety. Even having grown up on the farm, or perhaps because he grew up on the farm, Wes seemed to gaze on the breeding shed with awe.

"You don't pasture breed because it takes longer," he enlightened me. "In this process, we can breed eight to twelve horses in an hour."

"That fast?"

"That fast."

"So Danzig," I quickly calculated, "is earning about fifteen thousand dollars a second."

"Danzig is actually one of our quicker stallions. It takes him longer to walk here than it does to breed the mare."

Fully one-fourth of the twenty 2002 Kentucky Derby horses had been conceived at Claiborne's breeding shed. Twenty-four Derby champions in all have been bred there, and twenty Preakness Stakes winners, and twenty Belmont Stakes winners. In 128 years, there have been a total of eleven Triple Crown winners. Six of them—Gallant Fox, Omaha, Whirlaway, Count Fleet, Secretariat and Seattle Slew—were conceived at Claiborne Farm.

"That," said Wes, "may be one of the most overwhelming statistics in sports."

If statistics satisfy, consider these: Secretariat, buried in Claiborne's cemetery along with other icons like Mr. Prospector, Riva Ridge and Swale, won sixteen races in twenty-one starts. He was the first-ever two-year-old Horse of the Year. He was the first horse to break the two-minute barrier in the Kentucky Derby, performing the unprecedented feat of running each quarter faster than the preceding one. He nearly broke the track record two weeks later in the Preakness, winning by more than two lengths. And in the Belmont, Big Red set a world record for a mile and a half and finished thirty-one lengths ahead, becoming the first Triple Crown winner in a quarter-century. Charles Hatton, the dean of American turf writers and the guy who coined the term Triple Crown, called Secretariat "the most perfect racehorse I have ever seen."

Four of the horses in Claiborne's cemetery were buried in pine caskets eight feet by eight feet by six feet deep. A fifth was buried in oak. "Secretariat, being a premier horse, gets the premier wood," Wes explained, as we stood amid the gravestones. "The traditional method of burial is head, heart and hooves. Head for vision. Heart to get the blood pumpin'. Feet to make 'em run. That's what makes 'em a racehorse." Indeed, upon Secretariat's death, the doctor who performed the necropsy discovered that his heart was about a third larger than any horse pump he had ever encountered.

The tour over, Wes walked me back toward Phileas and pointed up. "About three years ago, there was a giant cherry tree growing right here, as big as these sycamores." Its absence is perhaps a lesson that even the most coddled creatures in the world can be undone by nature's lowliest living things.

In the late spring of 2001, the Kentucky horse-breeding industry experienced its worst crisis in at least two decades, taking a hit of hundreds of millions of dollars as pregnant mares throughout the Bluegrass experienced unexplained stillborns and aborted pregnancies at seven times the normal rate. Farms were losing two, three, four foals a day. Claiborne, not as hard hit as some, still lost one late-term and fifteen early pregnancies. Researchers at the University of Kentucky Gluck Equine Center hypothesized various causes—bacteria, viruses, toxic molds—before finally settling on a remarkable theory: Blame the Eastern tent caterpillar.

Apparently, black cherry trees contain substances that produce cyanide under certain conditions. The caterpillars ate the trees' wilted leaves, absorbing the cyanide but not being affected by it. Warm temperatures allowed the caterpillars to multiply, then a cold snap sent them marching across pastures, migrating for food. The mares consumed the caterpillars in large numbers, and the cyanide killed the fetuses. So Claiborne Farm chopped down all its cherry trees.

Far-fetched, I know. But I cannot tell a lie.

The afternoon wind began to pick up a bit as I made my way along Route 68, on the northern edge of town, and took a right turn into 1955. The Bourbon Drive-In theater, in continuous operation for nearly half a century, was decorated with the kind of exaggerated features—sloping roofs, slanted windows—that once conjured up futuristic notions, but now only suggested charming obsoleteness.

The theater is open on weekends from early spring to early autumn, $4.50 for a double feature, no charge for kids under nine. But it was a Thursday, and there were three-hundred-plus vacant parking stations. The upright speakers stood silently before an enormous steel and fiberglass screen like some sort of postapocalyptic troop review. I squeezed Phileas into a space and headed for the concession stand, where the proprietress and I chatted while standing on either side of a horseshoe-shaped counter, surrounded by posters touting the latest Mel Gibson and Harrison Ford flicks. She was a bubbly red-haired lady with an accent that was pure Bluegrass. Her name was . . .

"Trish Earlywine—early in the mornin', wine you drink . . ."

Something about rural America leads folks to do this, to turn their names into playful puns and mnemonic devices. One fellow I met announced, "I'm Bill, I come to your house on the first 'n fifteenth of every month." Another explained, "Name's Pitt, like a big ol' hole in the ground." The effort was consistently endearing.

Trish had grown up one county over, living with her parents above the little Texaco service station they owned in Blue Licks. At the Fourth of July Blackberry Festival in 1967, she met her husband, Lanny, a rather reticent fellow who served as a drill sergeant during the Vietnam War. Trish and Lanny had been the mom and pop behind the Bourbon Drive-In, itself a vanishing icon of mom-and-pop businesses, for eight years. They purchased it from Lanny's father, who had run the place for thirty-eight years.

The Bourbon Drive-In still utilized a straw dispenser from the 1940s, a popcorn machine from 1953, a projection system so old that it was used equipment when the theater began. So it was rather curious when Trish declared, "You have to change with the times. You have to!" She was talking about the menu, which offered everything from corndogs and shrimp baskets to fried pickles and pork tenderloin, along with a full spread of candies. "I carry two particular brands of candy bar here just because one customer wanted one and one wanted the other," Trish chortled. "It's a hoot!"

If catering to individual customers isn't enough of a throwback, consider that Trish also answers her phone, sometimes standing in her kitchen, when people dial up the movie theater's number. "They can't believe there's an actual person on the line. I give 'em movie times or directions to the thee-ate-er," said Trish. "And then we'll git to talkin'. I'll ask 'em, Hey, whaddya wanna see? What movies do you like?"

There are certain movies the Earlywines won't show—the films they deem wholly inappropriate to the drive-in's core family audience, especially the ones where the language is so foul even a Bluegrass lilt wouldn't purify it.

"I'd be lyin' to you if I said I never played a movie like that 'cuz even a good movie will throw in some bad words. But if they have a lot of the . . ." and here she whispered . . . "F-word, I don't like that at all."

(Note to self: Do not introduce Trish to Xander.)

"But you're not going to git away from that," she continued. "Right or wrong, the youth in America rules. Maybe too much. Maybe we've given 'em too much power. It's all about money. . . . And, you know, movies reflect society. It's not the other way around. They're giving the people what they want. They're giving the people what they are."

Lanny and Trish have been associated with the drive-in long enough that over the decades they have seen children become adults, move away and then return with their own kids. "They want their children to experience what they experienced. That's how the cycle goes," Trish mused. "I find that the older you git, the more you want to git back to your roots."

So the people come and pull out their lawn chairs or turn their pickups backwards and let their legs dangle. Their children bring pillows and blankets, maybe even the pet dog. Boys and girls from four different counties mill around in separate packs. Occasional couples hint at a coupling behind tinted windows. And everyone tries to catch the dialogue over the sound of the occasional freight train roaring down the bordering railroad tracks.

Once in a while, a night at the drive-in becomes a collective community experience. People still approach Trish at the supermarket and tell her they'll never forget the time, for instance, when the lot was full and the movie was *Twister* and nature itself vied for best supporting actor in the form of an ominous sky and a lightning frenzy in the distance. "God gave us special effects that night," Trish recalled, and then she shook her head. "That's one thing, you know, as the years go by, the storm'll get bigger. Until one day the story'll be that the screen blew away."

THE EARLYWINES

(Apparently, part of the Bourbon Drive-In screen actually did collapse during a storm once, back in the early days. As Mel Gibson is my witness, Lanny Earlywine claims the movie playing that night was *Gone with the Wind*.)

Any drive-in loses business when it rains, but the Earlywines aren't, as one might assume, the only folks in the area who don't pray for wet weather. After all, if the farmers don't have spending money, they don't spend it on movies. "Just a little soft rain at two o'clock in the mornin' is fine." Trish grinned. "Doesn't hurt the farm, and it doesn't hurt the drive-in."

Not that one makes much money anyway, which is likely why Trish described herself and her husband as dinosaurs. In the early 1930s, Richard Hollingshead hung a screen between two trees in his New Jersey driveway and showed a second-run movie called *Wife Beware*, inventing the drive-in theater by combining America's two most precious commodities— movies and cars. Nearly three decades later, at its peak, Kentucky boasted some one hundred drive-ins. Today, there are barely a dozen.

During the week, Trish does the paperwork for the theater, while husband Lanny finds work as a stone mason. "If you own a drive-in theater, you always have to work two jobs," Trish explained. "You're only open six months out of the year and you don't make money when you open, you don't make money when you close. You got maybe ten good weekends."

She handed me a Dr Pepper and a straw. "This has been the best season for movies that I've ever seen. It won't happen again next year."

In the aftermath of the September 11th attacks, much fuss was made about two aspects of the movies—attendance and content. The former soared, and state-the-obvious analysts attributed it to a need for escapism like never before. But content was a problematic issue. Could movies hit too close to home? Would we never be as desensitized to big-screen violence as we had been before we saw the towers crumble and the Pentagon blaze? Movies like *Die Hard, Air Force One* and *Independence Day* were dismissed as relics of an age of innocence. One filmmaker even returned to the editing room and removed images of the World Trade Center from his movie.

There was a similar reaction in the sports world. I recall a *Sports Illustrated* essay, a few days after the attacks, that welcomed the certain demise of the violent sports metaphor. No more "aerial attacks" in football, the essay declared. Certainly, no more dual NBA seven-footers described as Twin Towers. But within the year, terrorist movies were being greenlighted. *Headline News* was once again whimsically showing condemned buildings imploding. And not six months after the attacks, a *Sports Illustrated* basketball preview dubbed a couple of seven-foot teammates Twin Towers, with no sense of irony—or, apparently, memory—whatsoever.

So entertainment hasn't changed. But according to Trish, everything else had.

"I turned on the TV that day, just as the second plane went in. I was standing there in the living room, and my first instinct was: The world as I knew it just ended. I felt devastated. I felt heartbroken. I cried. For some reason, I felt like I knew those people who died. Because they didn't just kill them. They struck everybody. It was an attack against America—no different than if you knew every one of them by name. I saw it on TV when Reagan was shot. And I saw the *Challenger*, too. There's been a lot of tragedy, and I grew up in the sixties, with

Kennedy and Martin Luther King and Bobby and all those. But with this . . . I thought the world as I knew it ended. And it did. You're never gonna have the security you had before that day."

The wind began to whip through the empty speaker stations at the Bourbon Drive-In. Trish glanced up at the clouds moving in. "There's a lot of innocence lost in the world anymore. But I still have to believe that the majority of people and things in the world are still good. They have to be. If they're not, then God's gonna come back. 'Cuz he told us that . . ."

The Cathedral of Notre Dame, in Paris, France, is an example of significance conveyed through decoration. At the time of its construction—a job that took just under two centuries—it was the largest and tallest French building by far, the first cathedral built on a monumental scale. This Gothic masterpiece—with its fourteenth-century flying buttresses, rose windows, ornate doorways and delicately carved pinnacles, balustrades, gables and gargoyles—was built as a symbol of prosperity. It was a paragon of the architectural aims of the day—light and excess.

In contrast, there is another religious and architectural icon in Paris, Kentucky—completed rather quickly in 1791, about the time much of Notre Dame was being despoiled during the French Revolution. This one, just northeast of Paris, offers a rather dark interior and a somewhat featureless and functional design. If anything, it stands as a symbol of antiopulence, a simple gathering place amid the impoverished American frontier. But significance needs no ornamentation.

The Cane Ridge Meeting House was constructed by settlers who had been led to the region by Daniel Boone. They constructed a thirty-by-fifty-foot church from blue ash logs, but in an effort to protect it from the elements a limestone superstructure was built to enclose the meeting house in 1957. This is what I found beyond rolling hills and leafy tobacco fields on the outskirts of Paris.

Betty Allman, an enthusiastic little woman who served as a part-time docent of sorts, met me at the building's entrance after watching me drive in. She lived about seven miles down the road and owned a small tobacco farm. "Right now I'm a windshield farmer," she said. "I'm a widow, and I drive around in my pickup and look through the windshield and tell the young men what needs to be done."

She led me inside, where there were more than a dozen stained-glass windows on all sides of the stone superstructure, a modern attempt at ornamentation that told various aspects of the Cane Ridge story. But I let Betty do most of the telling, as we stepped a few feet into the meeting house and a couple of centuries back in time.

"This," Betty announced, "is the largest one-room log structure in the United States."

It was, of course, perilously close to being a manufactured superlative, akin to promoting the nation's widest two-lane road or the largest miniature horse. A few miles away, on the corner of Eighth and Main in Paris, there stands an otherwise unexceptional edifice described in the town's promotional literature as "the world's tallest three-story building." This had the same absurd ring to it, but there are a couple of important distinctions: The Cane Ridge Meeting House is older than Kentucky, and its architectural uniqueness is only a footnote in light of its theological significance.

In early August 1801, as many as twenty thousand people gathered there for the Great Revival, an epochal happening that has been called the most important religious event in American history. It was the largest, rowdiest and most publicized episode within a broader movement that transformed the nation's culture of worship.

"For eight days, they preached, day and night—from wagon beds, stumps, platforms," Betty explained. "They were Methodist, Presbyterian, Baptist, rich and poor, black and white. There would be six or seven preachers preaching at one time."

Never before had so many people given themselves over to such brazen religious abandon—a mass lamentation of sins. Apparently, there was a whole lot of wailing, convulsing, twitching, jerking and uncontrollable laughing. Lots of barking, fainting, rolling on the ground, speaking in tongues. And there were a good many screams of ecstasy, some cries of anguish and a handful of catatonic stupors for good measure. "The noise was like the roar of Niagara. At one time I saw at least five hundred swept down in a moment as if a battery of a thousand guns had opened fire on them. . . . Immediately followed by shrieks and shouts that rent the very heavens," an eyewitness later recalled.

As we walked through a few rows of nineteenth-century pews, Betty continued her story, in a sing-songy voice used almost exclusively by people who enjoy what they are saying. "Everybody had an answer as to why it happened. Some were scoffers and said it was all a put on. Others said it was the hand of God—that God thought the frontier needed a shock to wake them up to their need for the church again. There was a lot of lawlessness on the frontier. This sort of brought them out of that wildness. They suddenly realized that they had let God fall by the wayside, and they needed him in order to survive, as well."

But this was also a seminal event in the social culture of a state just beginning to emerge from those chaotic frontier days. The temporary city that sprang up around Cane Ridge was the first great public gathering in Kentucky, the preachers and preachees being joined by various horse traders, whiskey peddlers and inquisitive observers of all stripes. For lonely Kentucky farmers, it proved to be especially fruitful, as evidenced by the bevy of babies born nine months later. The wild revival had the curious effect of facilitating a more settled society.

Betty pointed toward a painting hung on a wall near the pulpit. "Now this is Barton Stone. He was the third minister on the ridge. When he came here he was a Presbyterian. . . ."

Reverend Barton W. Stone had organized the Great Revival, and apparently the frenzy didn't sit well with the more formal Presbyterians of the time. Three years later, Stone broke with the Presbyterians completely, starting the Christian Church movement, an effort to replace denominationalism with independent churches.

"It was the first new religion in America," said Betty, as if heralding the arrival of the Whig party or Technicolor movies or hip-hop.

Ironically, what began as an independence movement became a de facto denomination itself. In the twentieth century, it split into three more movements—the Disciples of Christ, the Church of Christ and the Independent Christian Church. Indeed, millions of Americans—be they Revivalist Baptists or Pentecostals or Billy Graham believers—can trace much of their form of religious expression to these Kentucky hills.

Some six thousand people a year visit the meeting house. It isn't quite the ten million pilgrims a year that Notre Dame receives, but it generates enough donations and contributions to maintain the building in its original form. You can get married there. You can stage a family reunion there. You can purchase Cane Ridge T-shirts, visors, mugs, key rings, line drawings and souvenir booklets. But Betty was adamant about making one point in particular: It is not a shrine; it is a church.

"We have services here most Sundays between the first of April and the last of October. If you come here as a church group, you bring your minister with you. Any church, any congregation is welcome, as long as they remember it is not just an old log structure. It's a place of worship."

Betty said her farewells, and left me to wander about the pews, leaf through the Chalice Hymnals and sneak up to the pulpit like an employee testing out the boss's desk. Admittedly, I am not a frequenter of places of worship. But as I stood up there, next to a 122-year-old pump organ, laying my hands on a 166-year-old Bible, staring up at the 211-year-old balcony, I felt a power surging through my veins. It was only the sway of history, I think—the ghosts of frontier farmers speaking in tongues.

When Mark Twain traveled the world more than a century ago, he brought his distinctly American point of view to the great palace at Versailles. Twain was usually unimpressed by over-the-top opulence and monuments constructed out of ego and entitlement, but he was unapologetically astounded by what Louis XIV had created. "Your brain grows giddy, stupefied by the world around you," he wrote, "and you half believe you are the dupe of an exquisite dream."

Perhaps his sarcastic wit would have preferred a visit to Versailles, Kentucky. Less than thirty miles from Paris, on the western fringe of Lexington, Versailles is the seat of Woodford County. A bustling little city of nearly eight thousand, it was established in 1792 on eighty acres belonging to a child named Hezekiah Briscoe. Young Briscoe had a guardian, Marquis Calmes, who served on General Lafayette's staff during the Revolutionary War and is said to have named the town after Lafayette's birthplace. But my research says Lafayette was born in Auvergne.

No matter, this being Kentucky and not France, the locals pronounce it "ver-SALES." So they were probably better off staying away from Auvergne.

Remarkably, as I drove past a strip of fast-food franchises on Versailles Road (otherwise known as U.S. 60), I was startled to come upon an honest-to-goodness castle, a gray, incongruous edifice that appeared unexpectedly atop a hill along the busy highway. A dozen turrets. Four corner towers. Twelve-foot walls. No access for the curious. The palace of Versailles.

This attempt at blue-bloodedness in the Bluegrass was the brainchild of a mysterious man named Rex Martin, who achieved his wealth through real estate and ownership of eastern Kentucky coal mines. He was rich and good-looking. His wife, Caroline, was beautiful. They had a precious son, Rex Jr. When husband and wife spent a vacation in Europe, she fell in love with castles, and he vowed to build one for her, purchasing fifty-three acres and breaking ground in 1969.

During the other, more famous castle's construction in the other, more famous Versailles, tens of thousands of laborers toiled in conditions so unhealthy that legend has it the dead were hauled off by the cartload every night. Rex Martin's citadel was more modest, but still quite excessive. He built a thirty-two-room, 10,400-square-foot residence inside the stone walls.

By 1975, the castle wasn't quite finished, but the marriage was. The house remains unfurnished. There are working lights, central air-conditioning and a fully functioning heating system, but nobody has ever lived there. It is a sight both whimsical and forbidding, conspicuous and vacant.

Martin retired to Florida and never returned phone calls. For years, there was a FOR SALE sign on the castle's locked iron gate fronting the highway, but he never seemed inclined to sell it. A lot of wackos called. He tired of the nonsense. Now, as I maneuvered Phileas to the side of the road and walked up to an equally uninviting side gate, the only sign shouted KEEP OUT! WARRANTS WILL BE ISSUED AGAINST OWNERS AND/OR LICENSE NUMBERS OF TRESPASSING VEHICLES . . . NO EXCEPTIONS!

I sat there for a few minutes, watching the drizzle plink against the windshield and feeling a bit like a disloyal knight banished from the kingdom, when suddenly a pickup truck drove up to the gate and a woman in her early twenties unlocked it.

I hopped out of Phileas and approached her. "Do you live here?"

She tried her darnedest not to make eye contact with me, as if I were either a menacing autograph-seeker or an IRS surprise. "Take care of it," she drawled. Then, without another word, she climbed back into the pickup, drove through the gate, climbed out, locked it again and rumbled toward the castle and out of sight.

I stood there for a few more minutes, weighing the risk-

THE CASTLE IN VERSAILLES

reward of trespassing, until I saw the same pickup coming back down the hill toward the gate. This time, a man in his late fifties was at the wheel, the woman's father, as it turns out. He stopped a dozen feet away and kept the motor running. One arm hung out the window; the other gripped the steering wheel. I cajoled him into a garbled conversation through the iron bars. It offered the fleetingness of a toll-booth chat and the futility of a prison visit, but I felt like the one locked down.

The driver's name was Bill, he revealed. He was the care-taker and had been for decades. He had known Mr. Martin since before the castle was a gleam in his eye. Yes, he allowed, that's his double-wide trailer just outside the castle walls, like a serf's humble dwelling outside the lord's palace. He cares for the grounds, keeps the residence clean, sees Mr. Martin about once a year when the man of mystery—said to prefer all black ensembles and a large hat—comes to town to pay his taxes.

"I've tried to get 'im to turn it into a bed and breakfast. I guar-on-tee you he'd net five hundred a night," said Bill. He shook his head. Thousands of dollars have been offered by locals who hope to borrow it for weddings, receptions, New Year's parties. Movie stars have inquired about the castle. Locals have proposed various museum possibilities. Always, the answer is no. It just sits there, empty and rife with rumor, the subject of more speculation than any other building in the Bluegrass.

"Are there trespassers often?" I asked, this coming right after Bill refused a small bribe to take me on a personal tour.

"Yep."

"Are there arrests made?"

"Yep." He pointed toward the gate and prepared to head back in the direction of the castle. "See that sign right there? If they git caught, they get fined two-hundred-fifty dollars, and they can't get outta jail for twenty-four hours."

Suddenly, I was startled again, this time by something furry nuzzling against my ankle. It was a tiny kitten, skinny and alone, weaving its way in and out of the iron bars, in marked contrast to the regal lions glaring from the meaningless knockers on the black gate. My new friend could have had the run of the castle, an imperial cat, Feline Monarch of the Bluegrass. Instead, he stayed with me, lapping at some milk I poured onto a plate, releasing an occasional heartbreaking meow. Evidently, unlike Mr. Martin, he preferred the solace of human contact.

It was only later, long after my trip was completed, that I came across a brief article printed in the Louisville newspaper.

Martin had died. His castle had finally been sold—to a lawyer from Miami for nearly $1.8 million. The man had big plans. He hoped to turn the castle into "the pride not only of Woodford County but the state." He would renovate it, upgrade the property around it and live in it for a while "to get the feel of it and enjoy it." Then, he said, he would use the place for charitable events.

It seems as if the lonely castle has a future of usefulness, of good karma, if you will. However, from my perspective, behind the iron gates and beneath a graying sky, it oozed an ominous air. So I stood at the side of the road a little while longer, staring at it and half wondering, as Twain wrote, if I was indeed "the dupe of an exquisite dream." Certainly, it was a dream unfulfilled, a moral of some sort that no king's castle is complete without a queen. After the French Revolution, Louis XIV's Versailles was never again used as a royal residence. But in this Kentucky palace, it had been an insurgency of affection, a love poem wrought in stone that remained unfinished because the love ended before the poem did.

THE NAKED TRUTH

ATHENS, NEW YORK

No great genius has ever existed without some touch of madness.
—ARISTOTLE

I steered Phileas along the concrete arteries of West Virginia, then sliced my way through Maryland's panhandle and eastern Pennsylvania, before finally arriving in the heart of New York's Hudson River Valley. Although it was a pleasant drive through great forested mounds of Appalachia, I was captivated not by the scenery but the signs.

Along I-68 in West Virginia, there was an exit billboard announcing Fairchance Road at Cheat Lake. As I have discovered in my wanderings, this is not an uncommon sort of incongruity in America. Occasionally, these merely result from semantic coincidence. For instance, in Montgomery, Alabama, the first capital of the Confederacy, you can place your money in the Union Federal Savings Bank. In St. Louis, where the Gateway Arch was constructed over thirty months at a cost of $11 million, there is a business called the Arch Wrecking Co. And in Mark Twain's hometown of Hannibal, Missouri, the Huck Finn Shopping Center is named after a penniless protagonist.

Sometimes, whimsy is the culprit, such as the existence of Santa Claus Lane in the California hamlet of Summerland or Mrs. O'Leary's Restaurant in Chicago, where Mrs. O'Leary's cow started the famous fire of 1871. And I have to assume that—because Richard Nixon grew up in Whittier, California, and his dirty tricks unit was known as the "plumbers"—the owner of Whittier-based Nixon Plumbing is grinning at his cleverness.

I can go on. There isn't a single public school in Learned, Mississippi, not one place of worship within the town limits of Pray, Montana, nary a golf course in Divot, Texas, nor a baseball diamond in Ballplay, Alabama. The thermometer has reached 115 degrees in Cool, Texas. Conservative political candidates are far more popular than their opponents in the vicinity of Liberal, Kansas. And the town of Bottom, North Carolina, is located at the top of the state.

I suppose all of this could simply be dismissed as an innocent byproduct of creative naming, and I might be persuaded that, in a sense, bizarre juxtapositions are the aim—the adjacent squares of America's patchwork quilt. Maybe it keeps us on our toes. After all, the Michigan hamlet of Hell is only twenty miles east of Eden. We all have to watch where we're going.

So I pay attention to the signs. In Frostburg, Maryland, next to a forty-foot-high collection of girders at odd angles, there was an announcement: NOAH'S ARK BEING REBUILT HERE. In eastern Pennsylvania, just past the Poconos, I came across a misspelled sales pitch: MAPLE SIRUP FOR SALE. In southern New York, arrows directed me toward the Seussian twin cities of Cripplebush and Crumbville. Finally, as the Hudson River came into view, I breezed past a notice shouting: DAN HOOKER FOR ASSEMBLY. But only two of the four words were emphasized on the roadside poster, causing the inattentive traveler to think he just passed a sign shouting HOOKER ASSEMBLY. It turns out that the last name of another candidate for state assembly was Cherry. I am curious who earned more votes.

On the southern edge of Athens, a drowsy town of four thousand on the west bank of the Hudson, I encountered a hand-drawn billboard: STOP THE ATHENS GENERATING PLANT: WRITE GOVERNOR PATAKI. But draped over the sign, obscuring much of it, was a makeshift banner, its intentions suspicious, that said simply: Welcome. The dueling signs tell all about the latest battle of Athens.

THE PRESERVATIONIST

Much of the land on which Athens is located was purchased from some local Indians in 1665 by a handful of Dutch settlers. Within a few decades, most of it belonged to a fellow named Jan Van Loon. This came to be called Loonenburgh. A nearby tract of land was purchased in 1794 by a group of speculators who fantasized about its becoming the capital of New York. They called their dream city Esperanza, which is Spanish for "hope." But hard times befell them, and their holdings were partitioned only a few years later, soon being incorporated with Loonenburgh into the village of Athens.

So Hope failed. About two centuries later in Athens, you could say it did again.

Carrie Feder was the first of a trio of Athens philosophers I encountered, each living their lives according to very different belief systems. She lived in a nearly two-hundred-year-old house in the center of town, just a few blocks up the hill from the river. There were posters in the windows: STOP ATHENS GEN. In her late forties, with long curly brown hair, she was dressed in black and white, which is, philosophically, pretty much how she saw things. Carrie and her husband had moved from Brooklyn to Athens in the late 1980s, starting a historic-home restoration business.

"We moved up here because we thought it was such an amazing town that had so much potential," she said, as we settled in a back room of her house. "And it's beautiful. They're cleaning up the river. It's taken us several generations to get to the point where it is now. You can actually swim out here, whereas before it was almost a cesspool."

Although the Hudson is only 315 miles long from its source high in the Adirondacks to its mouth at the southern tip of Manhattan, no river in North America offers more diversity. Its lower half, along which Athens is located, is not really a river at all, but rather a tidal estuary, an arm of the sea in which freshwater fish like trout and bass share the waters with sea horses, dolphins and seals. But by the 1960s, the river was so polluted that it was read its last rights.

It had been a slow poisoning by greed and indifference— sewage plants polluting the water, landfills destroying wetlands, pipes from prisons and factories belching toxins into the river, funeral homes draining blood and formaldehyde, gun clubs discharging lead, oil tankers chugging fifty miles upriver just to rinse their holds within spitting distance of municipal drinking-water intakes. Legend has it that fishermen plying their trade around a General Motors assembly plant could simply examine the river and tell what color the cars were being painted. Along the Hudson in Manhattan, the horror stories of filth floating up included tires, condoms, excrement, even a grand piano and a dead giraffe.

But the river also spawned activists, who formed environmental groups and battled polluters vigilantly, diligently, litigiously, turning the Hudson into arguably the modern environmental era's most critical legal battleground. Perhaps the most notable organization is Riverkeeper, whose chief prosecuting attorney is Robert F. Kennedy, Jr. The organization and its army of indignant citizens have prosecuted more than one hundred polluters (they call them "environmental lawbreakers"), reclaiming the river, dump by dump, pipe by pipe, battle by battle, bend by bend.

Carrie Feder saw the same potential for revival in the buildings alongside the Hudson. "The architecture is really what attracted us to Athens," she began, handing me a glass of lemonade and sitting upright in a chair across from me. "There are two hundred seventy houses on the national historic register. It's like a compilation of all the historic styles of American architecture. As you walk up and down the street here, you can see all the different periods. There aren't that many towns that have that collection intact. And the reason it is here is because we're right on the river. Different styles could get up here quickly because Athens was basically on the interstate."

En route to Athens, alongside an interstate of the paved variety, I had made an unscheduled stop at an attraction that I just couldn't resist. It was called Roadside America and advertised as an ENCHANTED MINIATURE LAND OF YESTERDAY &

TODAY. Over the course of some sixty years, a man named Laurence Gieringer had turned his hobby of carving miniatures into a creation of paradoxically epic proportions, luring passersby in Pennsylvania by offering a synopsized America in eight thousand square feet. He carved mountains, rivers, waterfalls, baseball fields, coal mines, oil wells, churches, outhouses, covered bridges, bus terminals, swooping airplanes, hustling trolleys, a dance hall, a circus, even a tiny fountain bubbling in a miniature zoo. Brochures ballyhooed the presentation of various types of American architecture, as if the only place in which to view such a collection was a dim air-conditioned room alongside a superhighway.

But Athens was the real thing. Admittedly, every other residence begged for Carrie's restorative powers. The houses looked tired and worn, making Athens pleasant yet imperfect, like a fashion model with a crooked smile. But it was also a monument to civilization's evolution along one of America's great waterways, and, unlike the kitschy attraction in Shartlesville, Pennsylvania, admittance was free.

Another feature at Roadside America occurred every hour or so. The lights dimmed until the miniature village was bathed in dusk. Then a brief light and slide show, dominated by images of Jesus Christ and the Statue of Liberty, took visitors through a night and the next morning in America. So it wasn't only condensed space, it was also encapsulated time. But again, Athens' environs offered the real thing, in particular a spot just across the river at a place called Olana.

An exotic Persian villa set on a 250-acre estate, Olana was the carefully constructed home of Frederic Church, one of the most successful American artists of the nineteenth century. The building, now owned by the state, happened to be closed

to the public on the day that I arrived. But I had come for the
scenery anyway. Most everyone did. In fact, I noticed that a
couple of women had set up easels to capture a slice of the estate's 360-degree view of the river valley. This is much the
same thing a twenty-four-year-old pioneering painter named
Thomas Cole had done in 1825, camping in the valley for several days while sketching the scenery. Generations of artists
followed suit, drawn by the grandeur of the sweeping river valley backed by the Catskill Mountains, and they formed the
first native painting movement in America, which came to be
called the Hudson River School.

More than mere landscape paintings, the art of the Hudson
River School was essentially an oil-on-canvas translation of
the nineteenth-century American transcendental movement,
championed by writers like Emerson and Thoreau. It was an
homage to nature in an increasingly industrial age, the first
great appreciation of American beauty and a suggestion that
spiritual enlightenment came out of a reverent sense of place.
Ironically—or perhaps revealingly—the paintings often found
their way into the collections of the industrial robber barons
who were growing rich by exploiting the land.

Frederic Church was Thomas Cole's most illustrious pupil.
Annually, his Olana estate draws three hundred thousand visitors and infuses the local economy with more than $9 million.
So while the Hudson River is famous for its history—its role as
the topographical centerpiece of Revolutionary War strategies,
as the site of the first practical demonstration of the steamboat
and the first railroad incorporated in the United States, as the
transit route (via the Erie Canal) between Midwestern farms
and New York City's port—this particular stretch of the Hudson is also famous as a landscape. People make pilgrimages to

Olana so they may witness the valley through the eyes of the Hudson River School painters, a vista invaded by civilization but not yet destroyed by it.

Which is why so many people, Carrie Feder among them, were so stunned a few years ago when PG&E National Energy Group announced plans for the Athens Generating Project, a 1,080-megawatt natural-gas-fired power plant in Athens. It was to occupy twenty acres two miles west of the river, including three 180-foot smokestacks, a 90-foot-high housing complex with cooling towers and a four-million-gallon oil storage tank. And it would be visible from Frederic Church's studio.

"Most people's reactions were the same as mine," said Carrie. "You really weren't that concerned when you first heard about it because it was so ridiculous. You couldn't believe that

CARRIE FEDER

they were going to site the biggest power plant of its kind on the Hudson River within the viewshed of Olana, an area with fifteen hundred houses on the National Register. You couldn't believe it. But things happen, and they just start rolling on their own, and you can't stop it."

She tried. Carrie took more than a year off work to fight the corporate giant. She and a handful of likeminded neighbors formed a local advocacy group called STOPP (Stand Together Oppose Power Plant). They circulated a petition, planned rallies, lobbied state officials and sued the Army Corps of Engineers, alleging a failure to properly investigate the plant's impact.

"What we did, more than anything," said Carrie, "was try to get people in this town and in the surrounding area to join in the protest, make people motivated to participate."

As it turned out, this was no easy task. Carrie and her cohorts ran into a series of hurdles as a result of the town's location, its size, its economy and its roots.

"It became completely obvious that the Pataki administration was behind this plant, but Athens is so close to Albany that a lot of people have some connection to state government, on whatever level. So a lot of people were afraid to come out against this," she explained. "I grew up mostly in New York City. You have a certain anonymity when you live in a huge metropolis. But when you live in a small town, every movement is watched. And people here are connected to each other. So it was very hard to get people to protest or sign their name or anything. It became sort of a class lines thing—the city people versus the people who have lived here their whole lives. People who move here tend to see the beauty and potential. People who have always lived here see the fact that there aren't enough jobs."

Athens remains a somewhat depressed economic area, the kind of situation corporate invaders prefer because the prospect of new work and new money smells that much sweeter. However, a large percentage of the six hundred workers employed during the power plant's two-year construction were from outside the area, and only thirty full-time jobs would be available once Athens Generating was up and running. Thirty jobs. You could build a bowling alley and a diner and have virtually the same payroll.

"I've learned that if you get into environmental fights anywhere, you find the same elements. They usually take place where the opposition is not going to be that bad because the people don't have the money or the time or the education," said Carrie. In fact, PG&E was so confident that it started construction on the plant eight months before the project was even approved by the Army Corps of Engineers.

"There was a very defeatist attitude here. This multibillion-dollar corporation came in, and we were told by everyone that there's nothing we could do, almost as if it was eminent domain. Basically, you end up studying the laws, you see that it can't be possible, and then you see the government circumvent the laws. You'd go into a state legislator, and they'd look at you very patronizingly, and they would say, 'You know, I wouldn't want it in my backyard either. I'm sorry, but we need this for the greater good.' Well, maybe it doesn't sound believable, but this is sort of the backyard of the United States. There are certain places that have special meaning to the country. I mean, I get very disgusted because you hear all this patriotic talk all the time, but when there's something people should be patriotic about . . ." She let her words drift off, like the current around a river bend.

It might seem a pipe dream, a handful of Athens activists
going up against an energy giant, but the Hudson is where
river-patrolling Davids have been going toe-to-toe with polluting Goliaths for decades. Whereas environmentalism was tra-
ditionally a somewhat blue-blooded pursuit, the Hudson's
hopefuls helped to make it blue-collar, a grassroots phenomenon focusing on protecting lives and livelihoods.

The Hudson River Fishermen's Association, for example,
was founded in the 1960s by a motley crew that included an
airline pilot, an orthodontist and a prison guard. Its first president was a gravedigger by trade. The organization evolved into
Riverkeeper, which has spawned more than seventy associated
Keeper programs patrolling waterways from Alaska to Maine.
Its budget, originally fifty dollars a week, is now measured in
millions, and Riverkeeper enjoys the services of a law clinic at
Pace University Law School, where a dozen students and pro-
fessors do nothing but prosecute Hudson River polluters.
These law students have faced off successfully against highly
paid attorneys representing some of the most imposing institu-
tions in the country, including Con Edison, Exxon Oil, the
U.S. Army, New York State and, its most frequent defendant,
New York City.

Hudson River environmentalism has been a manifestation
of the phrase "Think globally, but act locally." It has emerged
as an ecological neighborhood watch program, a battle to save
the planet from one backyard polluter at a time. Carrie Feder
never considered herself an environmentalist before Athens
Generating arrived. She still doesn't. Sure, she is the kind of
Athens liberal scorned by the Oregon ranchers I met in conservative Rome, but in many respects she represents the kind
of leave-us-alone logic demanded by Pam White along the

Owyhee 2,500 miles away—someone *on the river* who knows best how to protect it.

Goliath won in Athens. Or maybe David did. It all depends on expectations. The motion to halt construction of the power plant was dismissed. The judge referred to a compromise of sorts that was already in place between the Army Corps and the plant. Remarkably, the agreement stated that PG&E could build its smokestacks if it agreed to paint them green. Most of the parties were simply paid off. Athens Generating announced its pride at becoming the largest taxpayer in Greene County. Most of the money, however, would go to the school district of Catskill, the already more revitalized town adjacent to Athens. As for Athens, itself, the local government settled for $3 million.

"Three million over twenty years," said Carrie, shaking her head, "for a plant that is going to be valued at over one billion dollars."

On the other hand, environmentalists could claim a small victory. Each year, power plants across the country cool their turbines by sucking in trillions of gallons of water, destroying billions of fish in the process. After fighting tooth and nail, Athens Generating conceded to use a more expensive dry cooling method, reducing the daily intake from several million gallons to about 180,000. Still, *The New York Times* examined the issue and deemed it "The Right Plant in the Wrong Place."

"We succeeded in that we improved the plant from what was initially proposed. But it still doesn't belong here. And it is still a total failure of the system," Carrie sighed. She meant a system that passes the National Environmental Policy Act, the Clean Water Act and the Safe Drinking Water Act, but still operates under a matrix of greedy businessmen, compliant government officials and impotent environmental agencies; a system in which Olana is designated a National Historic Landmark and the Athens environs constitute a National Heritage Area, but against industrial assaults such designations preserve nothing.

"The way I look at it," Carrie concluded, "we're two hours and fifteen minutes from one of the biggest cities in the world, and here we are on the Hudson River, looking at essentially the same view that painters in the nineteenth century saw. If you have something like that, why not hold on to it while you can? Maybe it's not so bad to have one plant, but it's going to open the door to a lot of other things."

Indeed, the floodgates may have been opened on the Hudson. As the Athens venture gained momentum and a parade of other schemes appeared on the horizon (including another half-dozen power plants), the National Trust thought enough of the threat to list the Hudson River Valley as one of America's Most Endangered Historic Places. In fact, as I drove through the town of Hudson, just across the river, the protest signs in the windows shouted things like GREEN, NOT GREED: STOP SLC. The St. Lawrence Cement factory was a coming behemoth, promising to be more than twice the size of the PG&E eyesore with twenty-story warehouses, a forty-acre coal-burning complex and a four-hundred-foot smokestack belching a six-mile-long plume of steam.

At a public hearing, the cement factory's attorney simply pointed toward Athens and its new power plant under construction, and he said, in effect, what's one more?

THE MODERNIST

I descended the hill to the river, which flowed lazily under a blazing midday sun. There, staring out toward the 128-year-old Hudson-Athens Lighthouse, stood a man with longish silver hair and a somewhat unapproachable demeanor. Naturally, I approached him.

"Hi, do you live here?"

He eyed me cautiously. "Well, I own this place," he said, pointing to the Stewart House, a bed-and-breakfast a few dozen feet away.

I asked him his name, and the caution quickly became circumspection. There was an uncomfortable pause. "Owen Lipstein."

The circumspection became suspicion when I said, perhaps a bit too eagerly, "I know that name."

After some explaining and cajoling, I breached his defenses, and we escaped the sun for a corner table inside the Stewart House. Over the course of the next hour, I found Owen Lipstein to be enigmatic—blunt yet guarded, confident yet self-deprecating, outspoken yet indecipherable. He talked in a deep-voiced monotone, sounding like a man with a perpetual hangover. But he spoke eloquently, as if he always expected his words to be captured for the record.

"I think, as a body of water, rivers to me are the most interesting. They have movement, direction. In this case, it's tidal, meaning it literally has the ebbs and flows of the planets," he said, nodding toward the Hudson rolling past the window. "To me, the best two books in the English language—*Heart of Darkness* and *Huckleberry Finn*—were written about the river. And if you're going to ask me if I identify with those characters, the answer is yes. I don't know if I identify more with Jim or with Huck, whether I'm running from slavery or I'm an innocent abroad. And to my group of friends in the city, I'm certainly like Kurtz in *Heart of Darkness*. They lost me. I'm out of radio contact with the publishing world."

He was once the toast of that world, a magazine impresario, helping set a nation's pop culture agenda by tapping into trends. But it was a ride like the tide, full of ebbs and flows. He founded *American Health* magazine just as the self-health boom arrived in the early '80s, then became part owner and editor-in-chief of *Mother Earth News* and *Psychology Today*. He spent the rest of the 1980s as a poster boy for success and excess, an unfettered Duke of New York, but when he overextended himself financially and the inevitable crash came, it came hard. His declaration of bankruptcy was welcome fodder for pedestal-topplers at various national publications, and for a couple of years he didn't much want to get out of bed. But he soon rose from the dead, resuscitating old projects and pursuing new ones. At one point, he was editor-in-chief, simultaneously, of *Psychology Today*, *Mother Earth News* and *Spy*. The *Wall Street Journal* called him a publishing wunderkind. *Cosmopolitan* tabbed him as its "Bachelor of the Month." It was Owen Lipstein, Act 2, and his magazines were a reflection of himself.

"When I was doing *American Health*, I was very into health and fitness. And when I was doing *Psychology Today*, I used it as an opportunity to explore my own curiosities about human nature. And *Spy* was a magazine for the smart adolescent state of mind, which I identified with extremely well. It was a glorious time because it coincided with me being suspect of the status quo. I came to work everyday and made fun of assholes and pomposity and hypocrisy. It was fun to do."

Then, in 1996, while still only in his late forties, he abruptly left the publishing world, retiring, in a manner of speaking, to a one-hundred-acre tract of land along the river in Athens—a dramatic change of scenery for life's third act. Sitting in the bed-and-breakfast in the bucolic town one hundred miles and a million light years from Manhattan, Owen reflected on his pre-Athens past and described it, somewhat ashamedly it seemed, as an existence full of drama. Then he added, "I was preparing for a life on the stage."

It turns out there was another side to Owen Lipstein, another passion he hadn't yet tapped. He had well utilized his MBA from Columbia, but back in the late 1970s he had also earned a Master's degree in literature from Sussex University in England. It was there that he fell under the spell of William Shakespeare, who, as Owen was eager to point out, was both a dramatist and a capitalist.

"Shakespeare's inspiration was he decided once and for all that if you wanted to stay in control of your creative material, you had to own the theater. If you were creative, no one had ever thought you had to own the fuckin' stage. We know about Shakespeare the poet, but we don't often focus on Shakespeare the entrepreneur. And he was a very successful entrepreneur. So he built the Globe Theater, and he built it by a river."

Such was Owen's inspiration, too. He purchased the Stewart House, envisioning a corridor of sorts between the Athens inn and a theater on the outskirts of town. On his property, he built a private residence, a swimming pool and pool house, a two-bedroom log cabin and an Actor's Lodge reserved for performers during the summer. An outdoor stage, at the bottom of a natural amphitheater, with seating for 250 and black walnut trees and the blue Hudson as a natural backdrop, was the focal point for Owen Lipstein's latest start-up—Shakespeare-on-the-Hudson.

During its first two brief summer seasons, Shakespeare-on-the-Hudson staged the Bard's plays conservatively—standard settings and character interpretation, Elizabethan costumes, strict adherence to the text. Owen found it uninspiring, so he took the reigns for the second show of the third summer and fearlessly tweaked *The Tempest*, placing it in the modern era, a story about contemporary and universal dilemmas. Instead of a man at life's end, brooding about impending death, Owen reimagined Prospero brooding about the future, a man confronted with a crisis of direction.

"I saw him as a man in midlife, honestly choosing between commerce and art, a man who developed extraordinary power over a little island and was tempted to go back into the big world."

The parallel was too obvious to ignore. I cocked an eyebrow at the play's director. "Now, is that you?"

He didn't hesitate, but offered a wry grin. "Don't worry. I don't think I'm Prospero. But in my mind, his issues were my issues. And I worked through my issues through the lens of what Prospero said—my experience of leaving magazine publishing and coming to a small town and living in almost this divine paradise full of people, some who I like and some who I don't. Prospero's issue was: Do I go back and assert myself as king of the land I was exiled from, or do I hang out where I can . . . and make music?" Owen swiveled his drink and watched the ice settle. "Prospero breaks his wand, if you will, metaphorically, and returns home. It turns out I had a different opinion about what I wanted to do with the rest of my life."

He directs every production now, and every production directs the audience toward a fresh interpretation and illumination. So *Macbeth* was set in Depression-era Alabama. *Much Ado About Nothing* was moved from Messina, Italy to Messina, Texas, in 1885—Shakespeare as a shoot-'em-up western. *King Henry V* took place during World War II, and the French became the Germans. In Owen's latest elucidation, *A Midsummer Night's Dream*, the context was 1969 and a long, strange trip through New York, from Athens to Woodstock. In this version, Puck's "magic flowers" were replaced by a few tabs of LSD. As for Hamlet, which is on Owen's agenda, he thinks the story lends itself well to a country music theme.

"I can just see Ophelia singing, 'Crazy, I'm crazy for feeling so lonely. . . .' "

The aim isn't to mock Shakespeare. On the contrary, the goal is to breathe new life into four-hundred-year-old words, to translate them into relevance and stage them as timeless truths.

"I think works of extraordinary genius that are at once particular and universal are easily adaptable," Owen explained. "Shakespeare happens to be the smartest, the best, the brightest, the most adaptable, but most people think of it as something bad that happened to them when they were kids. I try to make it more accessible to a modern audience."

The lesson, of course, is that Shakespeare's themes, first produced alongside the Thames four centuries ago, are applicable along the Hudson in the twenty-first century. All of us lead Shakespearean lives, whether we represent questioning heroes or liberated heroines, whether we grapple with dysfunctional families or gender confusion or love triangles or death or greed or vengeance. Everyone's lives are filled with comedy and tragedy, and it ebbs and flows.

For Owen Lipstein, another ebb arrived a few months before I did, when he awoke with a start in the middle of the night, ran downstairs to his living room and found his pool house consumed by fire. More than a year later, his entire compound was still condemned. We drove there, in his black 1970 Cadillac convertible with the fuzzy dice hanging from the mirror, and strolled the grounds, or what was left of them. The psychedelic set from A *Midsummer Night's Dream* was still standing, surrounded by burned-out hulks and dead leaves. It all looked like a bad acid trip.

"It's really hard for me to come here," he said, as we surveyed the damage. "Fire burns history."

It was a demoralizing setback, but not a devastating one. Providing the insurance company comes through as expected, Owen planned to rebuild the compound, maybe even redesign it. He talked about distancing his private home from the theater itself, separating his life a bit more from the drama—which might suggest another lesson in the reinterpretation of four-hundred-year-old sonnets: We can learn from the past.

THE NUDISTS

One of Shakespeare's least known and least applauded works is a play called *Timon of Athens*, a rarely staged tragedy of sorts. The writing is so uneven, riddled with inconsistencies in rhyme and character and prose, that most critics are certain much of the writing wasn't Shakespeare's at all. One critic declared it "the sparsest, nastiest, most repellent play in the canon . . . an ugly play that seems to have been written by a tired, angry old man."

Its theme is this: Does money buy friendship? Can affection be separated from materialism? Timon is a wealthy man
in Athens whose unchecked generosity is his downfall. Surrounded by sycophants, flatterers and whores, he takes great
pleasure in giving gifts to his friends, to such an extent that he
takes out loans from the very people he rewards. When he is
forced to mortgage all his holdings and declare bankruptcy, his
friends abandon him. Timon, who has always walked the line
between naïve idealist and gullible fool, becomes a bitter mis-
anthrope, cursing mankind in a particularly bile-filled tirade,
calling on all Athenians to suffer strokes and fevers and itches
and general leprosy.

"Nothing I'll bear from thee but nakedness, thou detestable
town!" he shouts, and he goes off to live naked in the woods.

Which is funny, because so did I. At the top of the hill sloping up from the river in Athens was the Schoharie Turnpike,
which led inland a few miles toward a campground set off
from the road. Juniper Woods was a pleasant retreat offering
sixty-five wooded acres, several dozen campsites, a couple of
lakes, a swimming pool and one very significant feature—it
was clothing-optional.

Now, I have something of a reputation for inhibition. I
don't dance unless forced to, and usually only at weddings. I
have an unnatural fear of karaoke machines. I had been to exactly one nude beach in my life, and I had remained fully
clothed and half traumatized. So when a middle-aged man
and woman drove up in a golf cart, as I stood at the entrance
to Juniper Woods, and I noticed they were wearing exactly one
article of clothing between them, I maintained a poker face
developed only through many years of marginally successful
seven-card stud.

Peggy was forty-nine, with short-cropped red hair. Jimmy was ten years older, bearded and burly and buck naked. Suffice it to say I could describe him in much more detail. They were strongly accented natives of the Boston area and had been an unmarried couple for twenty years. For nearly half that span, they had also been enthusiastic nudists. Peggy and Jimmy had purchased the campground the previous year, after her mother died and she lost her job and they realized it might be time to buy that business they had always dreamed of owning. Of course, they had usually discussed owning, say, a restaurant or a flower shop. But a nudist campground? That was too good to pass up. So they bought it, spending April through November in Athens and then returning to seasonal jobs (and several layers of clothing) in Massachusetts during the winter.

They led me to a site right in the center of things, a few dozen feet from the pool. Only a few minutes later, an older woman in a towel knocked on my door. Barbara was her name. Her husband was Walter, who, as I witnessed several times over the weekend, liked to say, "I'm Walter. This is my wife Barbara. We're the Barbara-Walters!" The Barbara-Walters were hosting a little barbecue at their trailer. Peggy and Jimmy and a few others would be there. I was more than welcome to join them.

Here arrived a dilemma of mind and body. Clothing optional, said the brochure. But few seemed to be opting for clothing. Do I conform to their nonconformist lifestyle, shedding my clothes and my inhibitions? I disentangled myself from the predicament only through some twisted logic. Supposing that, in general, my inhibitions stemmed from a desire to fly under the radar, the only way I was going to remain somewhat anonymous at Juniper Woods was by joining the naked horde. Furthermore, I rationalized, if I was going to explore America in all its glory and myriad forms, I couldn't sneak my way into a subculture while distancing myself from the same. It takes one to know one, I figured. And besides, I didn't know a soul.

So I stripped down, took a deep breath and stepped out of Phileas into the bright sunlight of public nudity. And you know what? I felt liberated, if vulnerable. It was something different, essentially harmless, somewhat goofy, barely rebellious, like facing backwards in an elevator or wearing white after Labor Day.

In ancient Athens, nudity was a widespread phenomenon, of course. The Greeks viewed it as one of the fundamental differences between their culture and that of their barbarian neighbors. Athletes in ancient Olympiads competed unencumbered by clothes. In fact, the word gymnasium comes from the Greek "gymnos," meaning naked. In that Athens, it seems to have been nudism spurred by if-you've-got-it-flaunt-it sensibilities, the physical aspect of the Greek "Ideal." In this Athens, it was more of an if-you've-got-it-accept-it perspective. Or better yet, ignore it.

I was told that the rule of thumb (and other body parts) was: Look, but don't stare. In theory, that was fine. In practice, it was like yelling up to a tightrope walker, "Don't look down!" So I couldn't help but find the experience exceedingly weird at times, offering sporadic surreal moments, the first being that barbecue, where I was surrounded primarily by nude old men sticking forks into a plateful of knockwurst, trying to ignore the phallic violence of it all.

Later that night, I put on a pair of shorts and strolled over to the pavilion, where a large group had gathered for Jimmy's birthday party. A fortyish man, as naked as the day he was born, was strumming a guitar. Another fellow, equally unclothed, was playing an electric keyboard, and they were singing. "Don't you know that you're . . . some kind of wonderful . . ."

A French-speaking couple was struggling to line dance. An obese woman did the twist. A woman with one leg sat on a bench and bounced to the music, as her toy poodle hopped around frantically.

"Can I get a wit-ness . . . Can I get a wit-ness. . . ."

Everyone was giddy and nude; everything was hanging and bouncing and swinging and jiggling. And there was fifty-nine-year-old Jimmy, the birthday boy, in the middle of the dance floor, doing the Macarena, wearing only a smile.

And I thought to myself: I have crossed a continent for this?

Of course, I was as interested in the journey to nudism as the nudity itself, and I was able to gain some insight a short while later, after the music had stopped and the crowd began to disperse. There must have been a million stories in the naked city. I found two in the form of Robin, a real estate broker from Manhattan, and Bryon, a chemical engineer from the Chicago area. They had just arrived, so they were still fully clothed. We sat down at a table in the pavilion and embarked on some intelligent discourse amid the advancing quiet of the nudist campground, which, tempting as the analogy might seem, is not the same as subscribing to *Playboy* magazine for the articles.

Robin had dark, curly hair and a smart, serious demeanor, somehow making her Brooklyn accent sound almost professorial. Surprisingly, given where her life path had taken her in her thirty-nine years, Robin had been raised as an Orthodox Jew.

"I was uptight and Orthodox and married and divorced," she said, neatly summing up her past life. "I was a Sabbath observer, kosher—not anymore, but I was. I married an Orthodox guy, a computer programmer. I've been divorced now for ten years, and those ten years have been a period of a lot of personal growth and evolving. It's been a long, strange trip."

There is a line in *Timon of Athens*, spoken by a churlish and cynical philosopher, in which he marvels at Timon's abrupt transformation, telling him, "The middle of humanity thou never knewest, but the extremity of both ends." Robin's spiritual makeover was nearly as dramatic. How does one evolve from Orthodox Judaism to dabbling in organized nudism? She had an answer at the ready.

"Burning Man changed my life."

Burning Man is an annual end-of-summer jamboree dedicated to radical self-expression and self-reliance in Nevada's Black Rock Desert. The thousands of participants congregate in theme camps, each more bizarre than the next. One of Robin's friends—whom she described as a "fellow Yeshiva girl gone bad"—had coaxed her into attending. This was a year before terrorism struck Robin's hometown, before she joined the thousands of shell-shocked New Yorkers walking briskly northward from the devastation on a beautiful summer day, before she went to give blood and was told that sadly there was no need, before she was evacuated from her building on several subsequent occasions, each phony bomb scare as terrifying as the last. But maybe she had anticipated a need for profound self-examination. Regardless, she got it.

"We were the Echo Shower camp, and we had a water system that recycled itself, and we would shower people. Thousands of naked people would come running in and out of our camp all day long. The stuff that I saw there, the things that I learned . . . I learned terms that I had never heard of before in my life. I saw a lot of polyamory, people hooking up with different people all the time, a lot of free love, S&M, a lot of blatant sexuality all over the place. You could be walking along and there's a couple out there having sex in public, doing their thing. Or I'd walk into my camp in the morning and someone would be flogging someone just for the hell of it. Everything was out there. It totally floored me."

"Until then, you were a pretty straight arrow?"

"Yeah, pretty much," she shrugged. "Well, I don't know. I was always a seeker, so I always had it in me. But this definitely pushed the envelope for me."

"Did you participate . . ."

"No, I didn't. I was so shocked, so freaked. Two-thirds of the people out there were walking around in costume, very flagrant about their sexuality. And I was so freaked that I was wearing, you know, leggings and T-shirts and a hat and sunglasses. But it was a double whammy for me because there I was in this environment, the Burning Man, and I was also in this theme camp with a bunch of people who had all been through a series of workshops together with the overriding topic of love, intimacy and sexuality. So they all sort of spoke this language that I didn't really understand. It sounded almost like a secret code, but I could sort of catch the wave of what was going on underneath. So when I left Burning Man, I thought I could do one of two things. I could either go back home and say those guys are wacko and I don't want anything to do with them. Or I could check this out for myself. And that's what I did."

The Human Awareness Institute, founded in 1968 by a fellow named Stan Dale, offers a series of workshops examining "The Seven Levels of Love, Intimacy and Sexuality." They have titles like "Loving Yourself," "Integrating Sexuality and Spirituality" and "The Dance Between Control and Surrender." They are clothing-optional classes.

I tend to be a skeptic and a pragmatist, disdainful of self-help quests that tend to amount to someone else pointing out the obvious. Just once, I would like a self-made, self-help millionaire to admit: "Best way to help yourself? Pretend to help others, and make a mint off of it." But Robin wasn't some lost soul searching for a guru. She was a bright woman with a compartmentalized life—friends who are Orthodox and married with kids, others who are single in the Manhattan scene and, yes, still others who are part of the spiritual-growth-let's-get-naked crowd—and she was simply trying to explore the latter more profoundly. She was still working her way through the seven-step program, evidenced perhaps by the fact that she wasn't yet a fully committed nudist, spending much of her time at Juniper Woods partially clothed. But she was smiling and grateful for the self-reflection. Who was I to judge? Hell, I had walked around bare-assed with barely an introspective pause. Which of us was the more rational, after all?

Robin had met Bryon at one of the workshops. But just as Shakespeare's sonnets lend themselves to myriad interpretations and environmentalists arrive at the battle scene through different sources of indignation, nudists are nudists for various reasons. Robin was seeking self-awareness; Bryon liked being nude.

"My grandfather was a Presbyterian minister. I actually lived in the church for the first nine years of my life. But I would say from birth, or at least from a very young age, I was a

BRYON AND ROBIN

nudist. My parents tell me how I used to run around nude. Living in New Jersey, I would run nude through the farmers' fields at night. I would take care of people's swimming pools when they went on vacation, so I could go skinny-dipping. I just knew that not having clothes on feels really good."

Byron claimed to be forty-seven, but could have passed for twenty years younger. He was thin and fit, with intelligent eyes, a beard that hadn't been trimmed in three years and a voice rather high-pitched and sing-songy. Over the course of the next day, as I saw him wandering the grounds, bearded and bare bodied, he looked like some sort of character out of Greek mythology. King of the wood nymphs.

"I mean, I drove from Chicago to here totally nude," he

continued with a chuckle. "I had a towel next to me so when I drove through a tollbooth or if there was a bus going by, I'd cover up. But to have the windows open, it's like a massage from the wind for 850 miles. So I'm nude wherever and whenever possible. I'm just not an in-your-face nudist."

Perhaps that was unfortunate phraseology. Then again, for a subculture that prefers to remain unencumbered, nudists spend a lot of time focusing on semantics. There is, for instance, the difference between naked and nude. "Nude means not having clothes," said Bryon. "Naked, to some people, means exposed, vulnerable. There's a distinction there."

Likewise, folks who aren't clothing obsessed can be called nudists or naturists, and there are preferences therein. "If you say you're nudist, some people think if you're naked in front of people from the opposite sex there must be something sexual happening. So nudist, for some people, is a very emotionally charged word. People assume a lot of things that it's not," said Bryon. "Naturist, besides being a nudist, tends to imply more a philosophy, a way of living life more in harmony with nature. But I tell people I'm a nudist because if you say you're a naturist, people think you're a birdwatcher."

More distinctions of nomenclature: Juniper Woods is a clothing-optional campground, as opposed to a nudist campground, the owners preferring to give campers a choice, a notion that causes disagreement among some, who figure either you are a nudist or you aren't. The nonnudist world is referred to as the textile world. Landed nudist clubs are groups who own a nudist facility. Nonlanded nudist clubs are nomadic organizations that meet in various places. Either way, whatever you do, don't call it a nudist colony. The phrase smacks of eccentricity and cultism. Nudists resent such implications.

The American Association for Nude Recreation (AANR), the oldest and largest organization of nudists in North America, boasts more than fifty thousand members and 250 private clubs, campgrounds and resorts. One may also enlist in organizations with names like the American Nudist Association and the Naturist Society, which has a nonprofit political adjunct that spends most of its time defending naturist freedoms against the venom and political muscle of religious conservatives.

Nudism is a serious business (some estimate it to be a $400 million industry), but nude advocates aren't without a sense of humor. In my research, I came across an annual report from the legislative chair of the Eastern Sunbathing Association in which he exhorted his fellow nudists to remain steadfast while battling ill-informed attacks against their lifestyle. "In times like this," he concluded, "I am reminded of a statement made by Benjamin Franklin in 1776 on the occasion of the signing of the Declaration of Independence: 'We must all hang together, or assuredly we shall all hang separately.' "

At least, I think he was kidding.

No federal U.S. law specifically allows or prohibits nudity. Still, the nonprofit Naturist Action Committee finds itself battling dozens of examples of state legislation at a time, all of which would stop or impede nude recreation. To nudism advocates, the fundamental problem with these laws is that they confuse nudity with sex.

"There are clubs that I know of that are swingers' clubs," Bryon admitted. "There's one club I know of where they won't say you can't bring kids, but they've got bungalows there, and if you leave the curtains open it's not just permission to watch, it's an invitation. This kind of thing upsets a lot of nudists.

They say that those aren't real nudists, that they give us a bad name."

Indeed, "Nude is not lewd" is a common refrain among naturist organizations. Among the rules posted at the campground in Athens was this: "Juniper Woods is a family-oriented resort and therefore no overt sexual behavior will be tolerated. Conduct is to be of the highest standards and appropriate for a family setting." There was, in fact, a certain asexual quality to the atmosphere there. Once again, this harkens back to *Timon of Athens*, whose main character's attitude toward sexuality evolves from indifference to a fierce animus against such indulgence. So, arguably, the playwright's most antisexual work is the one in which a fellow lives naked in the woods outside Athens.

"I was at a nudist resort in Indiana, where I'm a member. I've got a trailer out there, and I was out for a long weekend. There were probably seventy nude women running around the place, and I didn't have any sexual reaction the entire weekend," Bryon insisted. "Then I drive two miles down the street, and I'm pulling into the local gas station to tank up before heading home, and this woman wearing a pretty sheer dress steps out of a Chevy Blazer. And I'm like . . . boing! So being dressed, and how it's done, that's much more provocative."

He then told me something I would hear more than once at Juniper Woods. "You know, with couples, the person who wants to try it the first time is usually the guy. But when they try it, the one who wants to go back a second time is usually the woman. I know many women who say you will never catch them in a bathing suit. But they'll be nude all day long and very comfortable."

Robin nodded her head vigorously. "I won't wear a bikini! I will not wear a bikini—ever!" She laughed. "But when you're here, after about five minutes, you get desensitized. For the most part, people here are not model gorgeous. They're just not. It's people. When you're in a place like this, it levels the playing field."

By that I believe she meant the notion that a world without clothes has much the same effect, ironically, as a school dress code, removing the implications and affiliations of fashion. The result was diversity that, frankly, I hadn't expected. Not long ago, the American Association for Nude Recreation commissioned a study that found, to many people's surprise, that the typical nudist is a Republican executive from the suburbs. But as I sat by the pool the next afternoon, covering myself with a towel as much as I could without appearing to break the poolside no-clothes rule, I found it impossible to categorize the scene's participants. I watched as an overweight man, a middle-aged woman, a couple of grandfathers and two African-American preteens batted a beach ball around the water and laughed as if they had known each other for years. Sitting poolside were an interracial couple, a model-gorgeous blonde and her muscled boyfriend, a chubby black fellow and a man with a cane and a large scar across his hip.

It was actually an inspiring scene. But still, there remains a clothed and indignant opposition to nudism, its latest tactic being the accusation that family nudism is a form of child abuse. Regarding this, I must admit that I see an uncomfortable gray area. "Family unity, family nudity" is another nudist bromide, but some organizations seem to promote underage nudism to a rather creepy extent. For instance, the AANR sponsors youth camps in which children essentially graduate from a Juniors Camp to a Leadership Academy to something called Nude University. Apparently, there is a theme for the camps each year. In 2002, it was: "From the gulf stream waters to the redwood forests, this land was made nude and free."

Somewhere, Woody Guthrie is rolling his eyes.

Bryon made the point that an early desensitization to the titillations of nudity can translate into a mature perspective on body acceptance and attraction. There is a certain logic to the argument, but I wasn't sold. Perhaps I have grown more conservative while settling into parenthood, and I am just inhibited enough to think that, under certain circumstances, the occasional fig leaf is a fine idea. Maybe I just have trouble imagining a child responding to public nudism with the same intellectual detachment as the adults who promote the encounter. Whatever the reason, I still found something discomfiting about witnessing a nine-year-old girl running up to a naked forty-year-old man and hugging him hello. But then I heard the story of the nine-year-old and her eleven-year-old sister, and it was hard to argue against the results.

The girls were the daughters of Suzanna, the woman with one leg, a battle-hardened thirty-four-year-old who had experienced a series of devastations. The three of them were living in a trailer at Juniper Woods because the roof of their house had blown off during a windstorm only a few weeks earlier. A few years before that, Suzanna had lost her leg in a traffic accident less than a mile from the campground. Soon afterward, her husband decided to leave her, telling her she was half a woman, and she took the hateful comments to heart, hiding as best she could from the rest of the world, humiliated by her imperfection. Then she decided to become a nudist, joining a society where people walked around with surgical scars and saggy breasts and guts like inflatable rafts, and nobody stared because nobody cared. And she rediscovered self-esteem. Just as important, her daughters, who had survived the car accident physically but had become emotionally withdrawn afterward, found similar comfort in their new nudist family. They were sociable and friendly and happy and often nude.

"Our society is in trouble because we don't let people be who they are," Bryon later declared, as he sat naked on a grassy hillside, swatting at mosquitoes. "People without their clothes on tend to be more open, honest, loving and accepting of each other."

I saw nothing to disprove the theory. It could be that social nudism improves the quality of interactions by forcing eye contact, or that the increased vulnerability of nakedness displaces arrogance and aloofness, or simply that the kind of people who shed their garments shed their stress along with them. The folks at Juniper Woods were some of the friendliest people I encountered along my journey, clothed or not. I sensed nothing sinister in their motivations, and it can't be easy to hide the naked truth.

As I drove out of Athens and took one last look-but-don't-stare at the nude populace I was leaving behind, I suspected that it was likely the last time I would be immersed in such a society. That being the case, I wanted to take some sort of keepsake with me, something to remember it by. And I did.

Poison ivy.

SIBERIAN BLUES

MOSCOW AND SIBERIA, MAINE

The philosophers have only interpreted the world. . . .
The point, however, is to change it.
—KARL MARX

After rumbling through the Adirondacks, I spent an evening with my cousins and their four-month-old twin daughters in the tiny crossroads of Lincoln, Vermont, parking Phileas in the circle driveway of the nineteenth-century schoolhouse they had invaded—a lavender, bell-towered picture postcard of New England charm. From there, it was a hundred-mile pleasure cruise through the state capital, Montpelier, to the state's end at the Connecticut River.

To drive through Vermont in the summer is to roll through a series of iconic images, like driving through the opening credits of a movie: The sun reflecting off a slowly rippling river bend. An explosion of pink, purple and yellow roadside wildflowers. Black spruces rising to perfect arrowhead points. The soft, gray outline of the White Mountains brooding in the distance. A robin's egg sky. An occasional covered bridge, yawning a perfectly angled opening. Bright red barns, trimmed in white. Church steeples piercing clouds like holy bayonets. GOODRICH'S MAPLE FARM. SLEEPY HOLLOW BED & BREAKFAST. THE FARMER'S DAUGHTER WOODENWARE. THE VILLAGE ICE CREAM SHOPPE.

Then I reached New Hampshire. The first establishment I noticed, along the same winding Highway 2, was the Happy Star Chinese Restaurant, followed by a car dealership, a strip mall and a Dunkin' Donuts. A few miles later, these were replaced by sprawling children's playlands dropped in the middle of a national forest like bubblegum wrappers in a bouquet. Ride the Yule Log at Santa's Village. Tour the carriage museum at Six Gun City. Enjoy the bumper boats at Fort Splash Waterpark.

I hadn't seen a single highway billboard in Vermont, where there is said to be a statewide ban on such interruptions. The most memorable sign had been one that warned me of MOOSE NEXT 5,500 FEET. New Hampshire, just on the other side of the river, seemed like an international border crossing, which is exactly what residents of both states would contend.

Vermont and New Hampshire often share the same page of the atlas. Both are 98 percent white, lightly populated and within a few golf courses and corn fields of being the same size. Geographically, they are inverted mirror images of each other. But socially, politically, spiritually, they are stereotyped as opposites. Vermonters are sandal-wearing, Ben & Jerry's-eating liberals pushing for same-sex marriages and world peace. New Hampshire consists of conservatives in hunting caps who want to drive without seatbelts, pay fewer taxes and generally "Live Free or Die." Indeed, use your imagination. Paint New Hampshire black and Vermont white. Stretch and curve the top and bottom of each state. You have yin and yang—opposites, but cyclical opposites. You can't have one without the other, which may be why it is a mostly friendly state rivalry. They even agree on one thing: They both hate Massachusetts.

After just thirty-five miles of Living Free or Dying, I reached Maine, where the landscape began to flatten and mellow. If Vermont suggests a meticulously platted town, then Maine is an unincorporated community. If the former is a spiffy barbershop quartet, then the latter is four amiable drunks singing karaoke. Maine seemed a place in which to expect the unexpected. There were the usual antique stores, auto repair shops and campgrounds with names like Yonder Hill and Stony Brook. But wasn't that a head shop called Purple Haze in rural Dixfield? Did I spy a tattoo parlor in the town of Farmington? A rusting commuter train car on an abandoned stretch of track? An isolated strip club tucked into the woods?

Maine seemed to shrug off its incongruities, which is why I shouldn't have been surprised to spot three Wal-Marts along the way. Tom Wolfe calls them "the new landmarks of America," and indeed, as I noticed with increasing alarm during my journey, the late Sam Walton's empire is altering the cultural focus of small-town America with bull-in-a-china-shop subtlety. Superstores supplant town squares. One-stop shopping replaces a stroll through the business district. Traditional business communities are being discounted to death.

But it isn't the sociological and economic impact of Wal-Mart that disturbs me; it is the sheer size and success of it all. I tend to cheer for the underdog—the longshot filly, the backup

quarterback, the Jamaican bobsled team. So when I read that
Wal-Mart has become the most dominant force in American
retailing, the first service company to top the Fortune 500, the
largest in the world, with more than $200 billion in revenues
and more than one million employees, I find myself rooting
fervently for the corner drugstore. Wal-Mart stores in America
add up to a combined presence, not counting parking lots, of
nearly four hundred million square feet—close to fifteen
square miles. Or put another way, Wal-Mart is taking up space
equal to about one-third the size of San Francisco.

So perhaps my destination was appropriate. Under a cloud
of apprehension that capitalistic expansion is running amuck,
even in the Maine woods, I turned north onto Highway 201
and followed the Kennebec River into Moscow.

In 1783, a fellow named Joseph Baker trekked into Maine's
hinterlands, which were then actually Massachusetts' hinterlands. He set up camp with his wife and their six children on
the east bank of the Kennebec, in the shadow of what would
become known as Baker Mountain. A poem of the same
name, penned in 1964, explains how Joseph Baker's first log
cabin was washed away by the river, how he started anew at
the foot of the mountain, how he lived on ground nuts, fern
roots and bog onions when hunt and harvest wouldn't suffice.
And then, suddenly, there are these lines:

> *But Baker went crazy, that's what they say.*
> *So they kept him a prisoner to his dying day.*
> *In a large oaken cage he at last passed away.*

He died in 1816, the same year the town officially incorporated, and his neighbors tried to call their new hamlet Bakers-

town. The attempt speaks to part of the charm of the American landscape. You would be hard pressed to discover a town named after, say, John L. Sullivan or William Howard Taft or Alexander Graham Bell. But damn if there isn't one named after an early postmaster in Iowa or the daughter of a railroad president in Michigan or the first character to clear out some land in a West Virginia hollow. The Texas community of Ben Arnold was named after a three-year-old who traveled on the first train to arrive in town. In California, there is a town called Lee Vining, who bled to death in Nevada when he accidentally shot himself in the groin. There are hundreds of similar examples out there. But how many hundreds of millions of Americans have existed? And the names of only a tiny percentage grace the most basic element of U.S. civilization. So think about that the next time you snicker through Waldo, Kansas.

The residents were all set on the name until they discovered that there was already a Bakerstown to the south. As a second choice, the name Northfield was written on the first petition for incorporation, but it, too, was crossed out. There is a Northfield in eastern Maine. Finally, somebody offered a novel solution: Let's name the town after the Russian city burned by its citizens in 1812 in an attempt to dislodge French soldiers. So Moscow it became, an homage to martyrdom. Ironically, the other Bakerstown is now known as Poland.

I love leafing through the history of New England hamlets, mostly because the early names are straight out of Nathaniel Hawthorne. The men of Moscow were Asa and Abel, Hosea and Hiram, Levi and Laskey, Ezekial and Eusebius, Reufus and Reverius. The women either had names like Lucretia, Sophronia and Drusilla, or they were called Thankful and Content.

Maine's early Muscovites appear to have had little use for disrespectful behavior—and a fetish for cages. About eighty years after Joseph Baker's caged demise, another local Baker— his name was Sanford—invented something called the tramp chair, a contraption designed to rid jail-less towns of the publicly intoxicated. Also known as the rolling jail, it was essentially a wheeled cage just large enough to hold a body and shaped so as to barely enclose a prisoner sitting upright. There is a proud picture of it on page thirteen of the town's local history book, *Makers of Moscow*, along with a caption: "It is said that when news of the tramp chair was spread, tramps disappeared and drunken persons were less apparent on the streets." No doubt. It looked like something even Hannibal Lechter's chaperones would protest as too restraining.

But for all of Moscow's historical hardship, its modern-day existence is largely predicated on achievements that would have been unimaginable in Joseph Baker's day—conquering a mountain, taming a river, mastering the skies. Baker Mountain, the landmark that loomed so profoundly over the town's infancy, became the first tow-operated ski slope in Maine. In 1931, the rapids and eddies of the Kennebec River were turned into placid Wyman Lake by the Wyman Hydroelectric Station in Moscow, a 2,250-foot-long and 155-foot-high monstrosity of concrete and steel that powers much of central Maine. And did the U.S. Air Force hint at a sense of humor when it decided to construct a Cold War defense system—the $1.5 billion over-the-horizon-backscatter (OTH-B) air defense radar system—on Moscow soil?

I might have explored these Moscow superlatives. But I don't ski, especially in the summer (although the four seasons in Maine are said to be Tourist, Foliage, Ski and Mud). My attempt to clear security at the Moscow Air Force Station would have consisted of a quick flash of a library card. And my suspicion was that the town slogan—"Best Town by a Dam Site"— was the best thing about the dam.

Instead, I piloted Phileas past a cluster of houses, most of them as white as a Maine winter; past a school with missing letters (MOSC W ELEMENTARY S HOOL); past a town hall and its banner celebrating the town's "centeseptiquinary" (175th anniversary) in 1991; and past Trinity Baptist Church, where the highway crests a hill. I turned east onto Highway 16, veered left onto Messer Road and then another left down a grassy path into a clearing rimmed by a meadow and a line of trees. Behind a farmhouse—indeed, so close to it that one might have expected a jungle gym or a trampoline—was a graveyard. Short on time, I had been forced to prioritize my attentions, to seek the single most profound encounter in a town of some seven hundred people. I had chosen a dead man.

The cemetery had its origins in the demise of a thirty-two-year-old woman in 1813, the first recorded death in Moscow. The townsfolk had no place to bury her, so her brother offered a place in back of his home. In nearly two centuries since, she had been joined in this patch of eternity by several dozen others. I weaved my way through the granite slabs and the flowers hanging limp under the midafternoon sun, looking for one name in particular. I found it, not on a tombstone but on a small plaque topped by an American flag. The plaque had been placed there, over an apparently unmarked grave, by the Daughters of the American Revolution in 1899. I could barely make out the lettering: THE GRAVE OF DAVID DECKER, ONE OF THE BOSTON TEA PARTY.

It is one of those amorphous historical events, not quite

apocryphal, not quite definitive, but soaked in legend like . . . well . . . like a porous bag of chamomile. On December 16, 1773, a group of colonists boarded three ships in Boston Harbor and heaved 342 crates of tea into the murk. It was not a particularly clandestine affair (the histories speak of five thousand spectators cheering from the shore), yet not an especially festive event either (at the time, it was known as the "Destruction of the Tea in Boston Harbor," becoming a party only many years later). Nor was it universally applauded by Bostonians, only by the city's more radical factions.

This was unlike the creation of the Declaration of Independence, when the participants scribbled their names for posterity. Indeed, legend has it that John Hancock, himself, was seen throwing a crate overboard, but he left no signature. This was a mission veiled in secrecy. Many of these Sons of Liberty were highly placed in New England society, men with more deliciously colonial names: Amariah Learned . . . Ebeneezer Stevens . . . Nathaniel Frothingham . . . and some guy named Paul Revere. Any list of participants is inexact. How many were there? Fifty? One hundred fifty? They wore blankets and covered their faces in black soot, apparently pretending they were Mohawk Indians. Some never spoke openly of the affair, except among family.

One might wonder if history has idealized their motives. Maybe they were just a bunch of right-wing drunks dressing up as Indians and vandalizing some boats. Or perhaps it was nothing more than a response by some overcaffeinated colonists to a parliamentary act imposing restrictions on the purchase of tea. I prefer to think of it as one of our nation's most successful attempts at political theater, a protest bathed in, as John Adams later gushed, "a dignity, a majesty, a sublimity."

So here lay David Decker, one of the men who crafted this masterpiece of civil disobedience, which gave British hardliners reason to clamp down on the colonies, which led to an extreme reduction in colonial self-government, which further inflamed resentment and sparked resistance, which led to the formation of the First Continental Congress, which drafted the early framework of modern democracy, which transformed the world's philosophical and geopolitical landscape. For perhaps a century, this man's final resting place had apparently remained unnoticed, just an anonymous stiff in a backyard grave. Folks make pilgrimages to Jim Morrison's tomb; the least I could do was spend some time with David Decker.

So I stood there for quite a while, waving at a constant assault of black flies, watching butterflies flit from tombstone to tombstone, sipping a cold Snapple iced tea and contemplating the inequitable nature of just rewards. A tea party of my own in rural New England—that was my visit to Moscow. But I had to move on. I had to get to Siberia.

Ninety percent of Maine is covered by forest, the highest percentage in the nation. We tend to think of it as being a state governed by lobsters, but it might be more appropriate to think of Maine as wooden lobster traps. It is not the Lobster State; it is the Pine Tree State. The wood processing industry is the backbone of its economy, as was made abundantly clear to me during the next three hours.

I followed an easterly course along Highway 16 and then a northeasterly route up Highway 11, which took me along the fringe of the Maine wilds, the sparsely populated northwestern quadrant of the state with nearly as many lakes and lumber mills as people. The drive, like Maine itself, was 90 percent forest, a sixty-mile-per-hour trek through the woods, interrupted by an occasional meat market or gun shop. There were usually only hints at civilization along the way—a rusting black mailbox, a gravel driveway winding into the darkness, a sign for the town of Mayfield but no sign of the town, a plea scribbled on cardboard and hammered to a pine: BEAR PARTS WANTED.

It is ironic that the two places where I feel loneliest are the empty desert and the dense forest. In the former, visual cues in every direction convey a sense of isolation. With the latter, it is the intimidation of the unseen. Childhood's most troubling stories take place in the dark woods, surrounded by a massive array of the unknown. Hansel and Gretel drop breadcrumbs in the forest. Dorothy and friends tiptoe through lions and tigers and bears. You never read about Little Red Riding Hood reaching her grandmother's house by skipping through the sagebrush.

Of course, this is my personal bias, which likely stems from an incident when I was ten or eleven and trying only to ride my bicycle from a friend's house back to mine in my Illinois hometown. The route included a wide bike path through the woods, which I had traversed many times. But on this day following an overnight thunderstorm, the path was blocked by a puddle that had grown into a pond. I had no choice but to walk my bicycle through the trees, figuring I need only skirt the water for a few hundred feet before veering back toward the dry end of the bike path.

Well, one gets turned around in the forest. I lost my bearings somewhere between too far to turn back and not far enough to glimpse escape. I had lost my point of reference, and I moved farther and farther into the woods. The longer I spent in the trees, the more ominous they became. Finally, I took stock of my predicament and decided to pick one direction and run. I dropped my bike and started rushing forward, not unlike the parched desert traveler who strips off his backpack while stumbling toward a mirage.

I ducked leafy branches, tripped over logs, bushwhacked my way through the Midwestern jungle for what seemed an eternity until I finally saw what looked like a stranger's bicycle next to a clear path out of the woods. This was my mirage. As I moved closer, I realized the bike was mine. What I had interpreted as a path was a white fallen tree. I had made a complete circle. This is when panic gave way to hysteria. I grabbed my bicycle and crashed forward, charging through the trees as fast as I could, figuring forests aren't forever. I don't remember much of that last grasp at freedom except that, for some reason, I couldn't stop Gloria Gaynor's "I Will Survive" from blasting between my ears. It must have been 1979.

Obviously, I survived. But a crossing that should have lasted five minutes had taken about an hour. I wound up physically scraped, emotionally bruised and nearly a quarter mile from where I was supposed to be. I told no one and vowed never to let it happen again.

Well, I got lost a bit in Maine, too. At one point, I took an ill-advised turn and drove fifteen miles in the wrong direction, only realizing my mistake when the highway dead-ended into a cul-de-sac. This time, I didn't panic. Of course, this time I had Phileas for company and a pair of atlases. I always bring two atlases from two different mapmakers, just for this type of emergency, and I finally had the presence of mind to consult the second one, which was better marked in this particular region and righted me soon enough. Still, over ten thousand miles through half of the fifty states, the Maine woods would be the only place where I lost my bearings.

I continued through the trees, which crowded the pavement like spectators at a parade—second-growth pines, balsam firs, beeches, maples, spruce and intermittent stretches of white birch that, frankly, gave me the creeps. In their pale skin, they looked like zombie trees, and they seemed to be leaning *that much* closer to the road, as if grasping at passing life. I breezed past a few lakes, and even there the trees made their presence known, rising from the water like gnarled hands reaching from a grave.

I don't mean to make this leg of the journey sound gloomy and ill-omened. In fact, it was beautiful. But I never leave home without packing my neuroses. I only later came across a whimsical factoid that might have settled my stomach at the time: Maine manufactures more toothpicks than any other state, and these harmless little utensils are made from the white birch, my zombie tree.

Continuing north, farther into the heart of Timber Nation, I found myself gradually immersed in the infrastructure that made it so—heavily-laden trucks toting logs in the opposite direction, the Great Northern Paper Plant in Millinocket, lumber yards consisting of felled trees piled in tremendous heaps wider than a football field and three times as long. Many folks in northern Maine look at a tree and see only plywood, paper, a canoe paddle, a clothespin, a match. Of course, I write books. I want to sell as many as possible. You can't have books without paper. For me to scoff at the excesses of the timber industry is akin to being a vegetarian butcher. So I'll just remain silent on the subject, like the proverbial tree falling in the woods.

On Highway 11, I shadowed the East Branch of the Penobscot River, separated only by a thin row of trees. The sun was low in the sky, and its rays bounced off the river and sifted through the branches, creating a sort of stroboscopic effect on my travels, which lasted until the river strayed and the trees thickened and I found myself back in the clutch of the forest. At least from this point, I had been given specific directions. I encountered a cluster of houses, a sharp left curve, a sharp right curve and then a sign: SIBERIA ROAD. Left turn, past battalions of goldenrod. Nearly a mile, and then left again to a hayfield at the crest of a hill, where I finally let Phileas rest.

Below me, as the hill gradually descended, lay a modest brown barn, a corral crowded with grazing horses, a coop full of squawking and skittering chickens, a large garden and what appeared to be an insulated cellar but no house attached. And beyond these, in perfect view and towering above miles of uninterrupted timberland, stood Mount Katahdin, the northern terminus of the Appalachian Trail and the highest point in Maine. It was only a gray outline as dusk approached, but at 5,267 feet (almost exactly a mile high) its summit is one of the first places on the American mainland to catch the sun every morning.

Henry David Thoreau, who took four trips to this part of Maine 150 years ago and wrote about it extensively, once climbed Katahdin and mused, "The tops of mountains are among the unfinished parts of the globe, whither it is a slight insult to the gods to climb and pry into their secrets, and try their effect on our humanity." Here was a canvas for morning's first light, a residence—at a magical intersection of time and place—worthy of a pure spirit and an artistic soul.

A woman with shoulder-length auburn hair emerged from

the would-be cellar and offered a calloused hand. "I've always wanted to say this," said Donna Chase in a voice softened by shyness, and then she adopted a faux-Russian accent. "Vel-kahm to Siberia."

The story of how Siberia earned its name seems constructed of flimsy folk tale and supposition. Supposedly, some men were laying tracks for the Bangor and Aroostook Railroad during a particularly cold winter, and one of them commented that it was the coldest place on earth next to Siberia. End of story.

Russia's Siberia, which comes from the Mongolian word for "sleeping land," spans more than five million square miles. Indeed, the residents of Maine are closer to the Kremlin than the natives of Siberia's east coast. Maine's Siberia, on the other hand, is a tiny settlement of fewer than two dozen houses along Siberia Road. It is technically a "minor civil division" of Stacyville, which is a community near Patten, which is a small town of barely one thousand souls.

But the two Siberias actually share several characteristics— isolation, abundant forest and fur-bearing animals and excessive cold. This part of the country is so far north that for years both Canada and the United States claimed the region as their own. This is northeastern Maine, which is as northeastern as it gets—farther north than Montreal, farther east than all but a sliver of America. The first snow falls here as early as September and may not melt until May. It is a dry snow, and the winds are fierce, a combination that creates massive snow drifts. A winter trip from Siberia Farm to the store means a quarter-mile snowshoe to the paved road, a twenty-four-mile roundtrip drive to Patten and then a quarter-mile snowshoe return while trailing the groceries on a toboggan.

This kind of existence is why, despite Maine's pseudo-colonial pedigree, there were few settlements in this region until well into the nineteenth century. Long before there were any incorporated towns, the lumber industry thrived here. But in Siberia, it was the clearings that gained attention, as the area became known for growing seed potatoes. Farmers could use these to plant their crops because the remote location reduced the risk of cross-pollination, and the potatoes grew true to variety. It was the advantage of isolation.

In *Walden*, Thoreau wrote, "I went to the woods because I wished to live deliberately, to front only the essential facts of life, and see if I could not learn what it had to teach, and not, when I came to die, discover that I had not lived." He talked about driving life into a corner, living sturdily, reducing life to its lowest terms. Such was the philosophy of Donna Chase, living alone on the farm in distant Siberia, waking every day to a sunrise painted on a summit and reveling in the purity of self-sufficiency.

She lives in what is essentially a small basement notched into the hillside and originally planned to complement a house. During the first year that she and her husband lived in Siberia, their shelter was a simple tent, which made things interesting one day when Donna had an encounter with a black bear near her garden. It is one thing to come face to face with a bear; it is quite another to do it in your own backyard—and to have nowhere to run. Fortunately, the bear ran first.

When I arrived, there was no electricity at Siberia Farm. Donna lives by the light of gaslights. She drinks from a gravity-fed well and cans her own food, most of it coming from a garden, about 120 by 80 feet, that could feed a regiment—blueberries, raspberries, grapes, tomatoes, potatoes, apple trees, pear trees, plum trees. There has only been a phone at the farm for a few years. She has never owned a television. Indeed, on the day of the September 11th terrorist attacks, when the nation came to a standstill, it was hours before she was fully informed of the news.

Donna appeared younger than her fifty years, her magical youth elixir consisting of hard work. She scratches out a living in the North Woods by breeding Maine Coon cats, raising and training Welsh Cob ponies and selling postcards, posters, T-shirts and such bearing her dead-on drawings of Maine's abundant wildlife. Ironically, she relies on the Internet for her business pursuits, despite living in a region where a hard drive generally means a winter commute to town. For about a decade, she had been driving almost daily into Patten, where

DONNA CHASE

she rented a second-floor studio with a computer hookup. "I've been working with Windows 3.1," she said with a laugh and a shrug. She might as well have told me she was using an abacus and a megaphone.

But the building in Patten was scheduled to be torn down, so Donna has finally accepted the notion that it is time for electricity in her life. Of course, she will insist on underground cables at the farm. She might yield to the creep of technology, but she doesn't want to see it. And all of this comes on the heels of the recent unraveling of her seventeen-year marriage, her husband returning to southern Maine and leaving Donna to tend the twenty-seven acres on her own. It is an era of grudging change at Siberia Farm.

But Donna still has the company of her Maine Coons and her Welsh Cobs. They say people tend to look like their pets. In Donna's case, the animals she has chosen to raise reflect her philosophy and her will. Other breeds are more flamboyant and popular. Few are sturdier and more resolute.

There are many wild theories about the origins of the Maine Coon—that it evolved from a biologically impossible coupling of a semiwild cat and a raccoon, that it sprang from winter-tested felines brought over by the Vikings, even that its ancestors were a half-dozen cats sent to Maine by Marie Antoinette as she planned to escape the French Revolution. Most likely, it was simply a case of natural selection, survival of the fittest among the various breeds brought to Maine by seafarers from all over the world. Little by little, there developed a cat perfectly suited to endure New England winters. Its body was larger, so it maintained more heat. Its coat was heavy and water resistant. It had a long, bushy tail, furrier ears and big, round feet like snowshoes.

Donna has raised and sold several hundred Maine Coons over her nearly two decades as a breeder, usually keeping ten or twelve at a time. They have names like thoroughbred horses—Mystical Beginnings, Stone Soldier, and one particularly friendly feline called The Amazing Steve the Cat. There were no Fluffies here. When I arrived, most of them were to be found a few feet from her bed in a complex of wire mesh cages, each complete with a perching shelf, scratching post, snuggly beds. They were like little cat luxury apartments.

"They aren't in there all the time," she explained, as she showed me her sleeping, eating and cat-housing quarters. "Sometimes it's overwhelming for strangers to come in and see all these cats roaming around, so when I have company coming I tend to confine them a bit."

My thoughts turned to the lonely kitten I had encountered outside the castle in Versailles, Kentucky. I had considered taking him with me, but a suspected cat allergy was beginning to manifest itself insistently in Donna's house. A cross-country tour with a kitten riding shotgun would have amounted to one long sneeze.

"Are you wary of being thought of as eccentric?" I asked Donna, admittedly thinking just that.

She nodded. "I don't know why people attach that to cats in particular. You can't raise cats without having cats. They wouldn't think the same if it was goldfish or dairy cows or a stamp collection. This is a business. And it's a passion. And I'm doing something to save the breed." By that, she meant that many Maine Coons are currently having health problems as a result of too much inbreeding. Donna started a foundation line unrelated to the inbred varieties, a pure strain to save the gene pool.

Purity of breed is also a common refrain regarding Welsh Cob ponies, which are similarly hardy and sound, "a horse," said Donna, "that humans haven't meddled with." In the Middle Ages, Welsh Cobs were part of the essential string of mounts for British knights. Even into the twentieth century, the British War Office was using them to pull heavy guns through rugged mountains. At Siberia Farm, Donna requires that her horses only plow the garden occasionally or pull a log from the forest or drag a sleigh over the snow.

Or, once in a while, save a lumberjack. Donna told me a story about her very first pony, a now twenty-year-old horse named Windcrest Tiara, who was the offspring of the third Welsh Cob ever imported to the states. One evening, he kept grunting and tilting his head in the direction of the forest. Donna knows how to interpret every whinny and meow from her horses and cats the way parents know the cries of their children, and Windcrest Tiara was clearly trying to attract her attention. Donna stepped out her door, saw nothing, heard nothing and returned to the warmth inside. But he kept grunting and tilting, grunting and tilting. Donna stepped outside again. That's when the wind changed direction, and she heard faint human cries from the woods. A lumberjack had been pinned beneath a tree. Nobody had heard him but the pony. The descendant of knights' mounts came to the rescue.

Still, Donna admitted, in a tone of voice conveying both self-deprecation and a smidgen of pride, that her biggest claim to fame someday may not be her cats or her ponies, but rather her unique breed of chicken. "Years ago, somebody gave us a mixed flock of bantam chickens, and after a year or so every once in a while they would hatch out a chick that was pastel gray, which they called blue," she said. "They were so unusual and so pretty that I kept them. And for the past twelve or thirteen years, I've been trying to multiply this rare strain of blue chicken."

Donna's looked like birds from Mars. They were miniature with dark brown eyes, featherless legs and short combs because big elaborate ones would be more prone to frostbite. Their feathers, a blue gray color, are said to be sought after by those who tie flies for fly fishermen.

"Mine are pets," smiled Donna. "I call them Siberian Blues." In retrospect, I can think of no better name for Donna Chase's legacy.

Although Donna's New England accent was subtle, only every once in a while sneaking in a "yahd" or a "pahk," she has never lived anywhere but Maine. She was raised in the southeastern part of the state, living on the food her family produced by the hunt or the garden, surrounded by four siblings yet isolated from most social interaction by her strict mother and her rural residence. Donna was put to work early. Her first job, at age eleven, had her working in the apple orchards, placing fallen fruit into wooden boxes and dragging them to the edge of a road for pickup. For each box, which weighed more than she did when full, she received a nickel. Throughout the whole summer, she earned less than four dollars.

It was a sheltered existence, and Donna turned to art as an outlet. Her mother would cut brown paper grocery bags open and smooth them out for her to draw on. Donna drew animals. And she drew inspiration for her creative dreams from her grandmother, Otta Chase, who introduced her to poets and painters and anyone else she came across who made a living through the arts.

When Donna was ten, Otta gave her a small black-and-white print of *Horsefair*, by mid-nineteenth-century French painter Rosa Bonheur, which hung above Donna's bed for years. Today, a larger, color version of it hangs on her wall at Siberia Farm. It may be as much an homage to the artist as the art. At an early age, Bonheur was the only girl enrolled in a small private school for boys, only to be expelled for "tomboyish" behavior. She liked to dress in men's clothing. She became a sculptor, which was then considered man's work, and even dissected animals in an attempt to gain intimate knowledge of their bone and muscle structure. Dissatisfied by Paris society, she left in 1860 and settled in the Forest of Fontainebleau, where she surrounded herself with animals, both domestic and wild, until her death. Her spirit seems to have been reborn in Maine's North Woods.

Donna retrieved a recollection, as The Amazing Steve the Cat climbed into her lap. "When I was young, they asked me what I wanted to be when I grew up, and I said, 'A cowboy.' Because I liked horses," she explained. "Everybody laughed. They said, 'Oh no, you can't be a cowboy. You're a girl.' So a few years later they asked me again. 'What would you like to be?' So I said, 'A veterinarian.' And they laughed again. 'You can't be a veterinarian. You're a girl.' In between, in second grade I think, each child had to have a personal interview with the superintendent of schools. It may have been when they got the results from our IQ tests. He pointed to mine and said, 'See that, young lady? You can be anything you want to be. So what would you like to be?' And I said, 'A hermit.' "

It is safe to say she achieved each of her goals. Right out of high school, she settled in a little cabin on twelve wooded acres in a place known as Skunk Alley, where she had no electricity, of course. She worked at a veterinary hospital and found another job at a riding stable, where she met her future husband. She started describing to him a dream she had always harbored—to ride horseback across the country—and found that her aspirations meshed with his. So in 1981 they started off with a tent, sleeping bags, camera equipment and a few days' worth of food atop two horses, Ebony and Rooster. They traveled about twenty miles a day at a walking pace, finding food and shelter as they went along. Donna later admitted to me that she was probably born in the wrong century, that she should have been part of Lewis and Clark's adventure, the expedition's wildlife artist perhaps. "Or maybe," she winked, "they would have met me out there, riding a pinto pony." Alas, she was born into an era of jet planes and minivans and camcorders. So this was her modest Corps of Discovery. And they proceeded on.

They planned to make it to Oregon over the course of several months, but the ride came to a sudden halt thirty-nine days later in western New York when a nail punctured Ebony's hoof, a minor injury but enough to end the dream. Still, Donna grew animated as she relived the memory, which she treated not as a goal unfulfilled but rather as thirty-nine days of wonder. "I was completely impressed with the generosity of everybody we met," she declared. "And you know what? Nearly every single person said, 'Oh, I always wanted to . . .' And then they described a bicycle ride across the country or a horseback ride or a covered wagon or something. Everybody has had that dream."

I told her I understood. My visit to Siberia was part of a similarly life-affirming journey. Only my Ebony was named Phileas, and he came equipped with a spare tire.

The intrepid travelers were married a few years later, staying in southern Maine for the remainder of the decade but all the while scouring the state for the right place to set up stakes, a piece of open farmland where the horses could be set out to pasture and the only crowds were dense woods. So they moved to Siberia. But they never did get around to building a house. And maybe there wasn't a strong enough foundation in the first place. "Plans don't always work out the way you want them to," Donna shrugged. After more than a decade as part of a pair in Siberia, she found herself alone again, but not necessarily lonely.

Those who prefer a solitary existence tend to be drawn to this part of the country. In the local histories, there is the story of a man named Hunter Davis, who lived as a hermit on Shin Pond, about twenty miles north of Siberia. His also was a story of love gone astray, and he, too, found a sort of poetry in his privacy. Like so many other men with jackpot dreams, Davis made for California during the Gold Rush of 1849, leaving a sweetheart at home in Lincoln, a town about forty miles south of Siberia. He sent correspondence home to her, but her father was against the relationship, and he was the local postmaster. The letters never reached her, and she married someone else.

Davis returned home and headed north to Shin Pond in an effort to "mend a broken heart." He cleared land, built a tiny cabin, farmed, trapped, hunted and survived in the woods. He died around 1915, leaving a faded manuscript in his cabin containing poems about foxes and porcupines, dying swans and singing angels.

So isolation is a relative concept. There are times when even Donna feels a need to remove herself farther from civilization's stir, so she drives fifty miles north and twenty-seven miles inland on an unpaved logging road to St. Croix Pond, where there was once a logging village accessible only by railroad. The village has disappeared, and there are only a few camps left. Donna leases one of them. She swims, fishes, kayaks, paints, generally escapes from Siberia. There is a man there, an older fellow named Stan, who has lived in the woods by the pond for fifty years. On the rare occasions when friends take him into town, he calls it "going out to the clearing." He tells Donna that when he's ready to die, he is going to make his way even farther into the forest, deep into the trees, ostensibly falling lifeless where there is nobody there to hear it. There is always someplace more remote, a getaway even from the far away.

Donna had a younger brother, for whom escape was the tops of mountains. He went from being a champion high school gymnast to roaming the continent as a climber, approaching expert form by his twentieth birthday. "My brother and I were super close connected—I would say ESP," Donna reflected. "He would go off on climbing trips, hitchhiking. He might be gone three months, six months, eight months, and we wouldn't hear from him. Then one day, he would show up back home. I was working at the animal hospital at that time. Usually I would leave work and get in the car and think, Alan's home. I'd go home, and there he would be."

Donna shifted in her chair, as if anticipating discomfort. "He was invited to do a climb on Mount McKinley in Alaska, and ironically, that was the same year the volcano, Mount Saint Helens, erupted. We knew they were going to be out of contact for several months. They were supposed to come down in August. But sometime in July, I suddenly began obsessing about my brother. I felt drawn to sit down and paint a picture of him. When you paint, your mind goes to a different level if you're really concentrating. Some people say it's like meditating. But I definitely felt that there was something going on, something very bizarre, and I don't usually talk about it. I kept listening for him, and all I could hear was 'Light me home. Light me home. Light me home.' So I just concentrated on how much I love my brother, and before too many hours, I finished the little portrait, and I told my mom, 'I think something's wrong. I think Alan's in trouble.' She told me she had been having the same feeling."

They never heard from Alan again. It turns out that the eruption at Mount Saint Helens may have caused tremors that followed a fault line all the way up the coast to Mount McKinley, shaking loose an avalanche. Donna's brother and his three companions just disappeared. About a year later, a Japanese climbing team found an ice ax, which may have belonged to Alan Chase. His body was never found.

There is a sad irony to the connection Donna claimed to have with her brother because the bulk of her years have been spent trying to overcome a tendency to shrink from human contact, even as a child. "I definitely would not be talking to you if you visited ten or twenty years ago," she told me. "I was always much more comfortable around animals than around people. I had friends, but we didn't live in a village. There was only one other house nearby, and we weren't allowed to play with other children. We went to school and then came home. I would go a whole year and not speak in some classes. We didn't do any extracurricular activities. We were home doing chores. My mother didn't even want us going across the property line."

Like the seed potatoes that sprouted from Siberia, there was little threat of cross-pollination in the Chase family. Donna, who didn't go on her first date until she was twenty-four, long ago discovered that she needn't rely on constant human companionship. In fact, one thing she loves about her property, as much as the view, is the fact that the back of her farm abuts timber company land, meaning there may not be a single settlement or even a house from Siberia Farm to the Quebec border—one hundred miles theoretically devoid of human touch.

Donna rarely includes a human face in her artwork, preferring the curious head tilt of a red fox, the stiff posture of a white-tailed deer or the silent stare of a snowshoe hare. She doesn't even like to paint man-made objects. But recently, she has begun to dabble in the lines and shadows of humanity. Hanging in her home is a touching painting, recently chosen to be exhibited in the U.S. Capitol, of a boy looking at his reflection in a placid pond. One could argue that it reflects a change of attitude on the part of the painter, who has become more, as she put it, "socialized." Her shyness, once so dominant that it was crippling, is now only a barely noticeable limp. Ask her a reason for her recent transformation, and she points past her Maine Coons and her wildlife prints to the object of her latest passion—a fiddle.

Historically, the fiddle has been called the "devil's box" because it was thought by some to be an instrument of sin. Fiddles suggest a sort of musical abandon, knee-slapping, moonshine-swigging, mischievous merriment. It might have seemed an incompatible instrument for Donna, who has never been drunk in her life and seemed about as sinful as a newborn kitten. On the other hand, for an intelligent woman who radiated humility, it struck a perfect chord. What is a fiddle, after all, if not a violin without pretensions?

She had been playing for less than two years, but already she had progressed enough that she took her act on the road, such as it was in northern Maine. There are nearly three hundred snowmobile clubs throughout Maine, from Andover to Augusta and from Caribou to Cornish. They have names like minor league hockey teams: Bath River Runners, Blaine Belt-burners, Saco Pathfinders. Many of these clubs host musicians on a specific night each week, self-taught locals picking and strumming old-time country and bluegrass into the evening. On this Wednesday night, Donna invited me along to a gathering in nearby Island Falls. We climbed into her pickup and rumbled about twenty miles, even farther north and farther east.

The Big Valley Sno Club was housed in a modest wooden building overlooking Lake Mattawamkang. In the dim light, several dozen folks sat upright on benches and chairs. Near the entrance, a handful of wheelchair-bound youngsters with assorted disabilities had been wheeled in to lose themselves in the music, but most of the spectators were twice my age, and many, according to Donna, had known each other nearly all their lives. They grew up here before the Interstate made inroads into northern Maine a quarter-century ago. Homegrown entertainment was the rule in these isolated communities. Apparently, it still is. Donna and I settled in with some boiled hotdogs and root beer from a tiny back room, but most of the spectators just sat there, respectfully attentive to the musicians in front of them, clapping on cue, smiling and chatting occasionally, enjoying themselves in a restrained and habitual sort of way. A man with a deep voice like Tennessee Ernie Ford crooned what must have been a love song. "My hands are sweaty . . . my knees are weak . . . I can't eat . . . and I can't sleep. . . ."

The musicians were a semicircle of guitarists, some bass, a couple electric. There was a grinning fellow in shorts, white socks, black shoes and a camouflage cap; a tiny middle-aged woman cradling a black guitar bigger than she; a heavyset lady who wouldn't move an inch all night; an older gentleman missing a couple of fingers but not missing a chord on his guitar. That's George, Donna told me. She knew just about everyone. The woman with the black guitar was Rachel. The deep-voiced crooner was Roger. "These people," said Donna, "are my new family."

There was an etiquette of sorts to the arrangement. Each player in succession began a song, and the others picked it up. Occasionally, some audience members took it upon themselves to two-step or to shuffle up to the center of things and serenade their peers. In fact, while still finishing my hotdog, I looked up to find the woman who sold it to me holding a microphone and singing, "Silver thread . . . golden needles . . . cannot mend . . . this heart of mine. . . ." Her voice, indeed all the voices, seemed flat, off-key and perfect.

And then, a question from one of the guitarists: "Donna, did you bring your fiddle?" She nodded, smiled timidly and began tuning her instrument. A few minutes later, she walked up to the other musicians, huddled with them for a moment and then began playing—methodically, but quite admirably and with a slight smile on her face—a song called "Fated Love." Not only had she sought out the company of others; she had found the courage to take center stage. So if, indeed, the fiddle is the "devil's box," then let's give the devil his due.

PHILEAS AND FRIENDS

We stayed for another hour. Donna played once more. Then, with the twanged-up sounds of "Blue Suede Shoes" drifting through the doorway, we stepped back outside under a full moon over Maine. Back at the farm later that night, as her cats squeaked and scratched in the background, Donna shared with me some stories about the type of people who thrive in Maine's outback. The anecdotes conveyed a sense of whimsy about the wilds—how, for instance, folks around there like to canoe up to a moose swimming in a lake and hop on for a ride.

Generally, though, moose stories in northern Maine aren't all that funny. The animals can be nuisances to farmers because they walk through fencing like it's the tape at the end of a race. They tangle themselves in it, tear a quarter-mile of fencing out and drag it into the woods—over and over again. "One summer, we had a young bull moose and he traveled from one bog to another across our pasture. Probably three times a week, he would tear out the fences," Donna recalled. "Deer seem to learn to go under or over them, but moose seem to walk straight through." And they are more than nuisances to drivers; they can be downright dangerous. The moose are dark, so you can't see them at night, and they grow so tall that the front of the car knocks the legs out from under them, sending up to 1,200 pounds through the windshield. Donna has heard tales of roofs being peeled off like sardine cans.

And then there was the time her friend Freddy . . .

"Wait a minute. Shhh!" Donna whispered, and then she rushed to her front door, opening it and motioning me to follow. She placed her finger over her mouth and led me to her front stoop. We listened for several minutes, as at least a half-dozen coyotes, some of them sounding not a few hundred feet away, howled at the moon. It was an ominous noise, but Donna's explanation brightened it considerably. "They fall asleep during the day and then wake up at night looking for each other," she said. "They're just trying to make contact."

That mournful baying was the sound that put me to sleep that night, surrounded by hay rolls the size of oil drums, while Donna's Welsh Cobs clomped and snorted around Phileas, a four-wheeled intruder into their pasture. I slept surprisingly well. In the morning, before I made my way back toward the balance of civilization, I returned to the farm, where I was served a breakfast of homegrown potatoes, eggs from Donna's chickens, honey from her beehives spread on toast made from

Canadian potato bread, and a Maine delicacy called fiddle-heads, which are the young coiled leaves of the ostrich fern that grow wild in Siberia's woods. Smothered in vinegar, they tasted a bit like asparagus, a bit like artichoke. It was the most satisfying morning meal I have ever encountered.

I drove off with the sounds of a sweet fiddle filling my head, accompanied by a coyote howling the Siberian Blues.

CHANTS AND HOLLERS

CALCUTTA, WEST VIRGINIA

Without self-perception, there is no peace,
and without peace there can be no happiness.
— *FROM THE BHAGAVAD GITA*

The man who would become His Divine Grace A. C. Bhaktivedanta Swami Prabhupada was born in Calcutta, India, in 1896. He was raised in a family of Krishna devotees, adherents of a traditional Indian religion, with ancient texts written in Sanskrit, that emerged in its present form more than four hundred years ago. At the age of twenty-four, Prabhupada met his spiritual master, a guru called Srila Bhaktisiddhanta Saraswati, who assigned him a mission: "Go to the West and spread Krishna consciousness in the English language." It would be decades before Prabhupada was able to fully comply.

In 1944, he founded an English-language magazine about

Krishna consciousness called *Back to Godhead,* which he wrote and distributed in New Delhi. Fifteen years later, Prabhupada took the vow of *sannysan* or Hindu renunciation, jettisoning family and what had been a disinterested business career so that he could focus on his mission. He began his life's work—a translation of an encyclopedic scripture called the Srimad-Bhagavatam.

Finally, in 1965, at the age of sixty-nine, Prabhupada left India on a forty-day sea journey to America, carrying with him, so the story goes, only a crate of Srimad-Bhagavatams, a pair of cymbals and seven dollars. He disembarked in New York City and promptly wrote to Lord Krishna, "You are so kind upon this useless soul, but I do not know why You have brought me here." But Prabhupada had arrived at precisely the right time, at the cusp of the counterculture explosion, when a wave of disenchanted American youths were seeking alternatives to traditional American society. Word soon spread about the far-out Indian swami who meditated by chanting, over and over again.

Prabhupada began to attract a steady trickle of disciples, a shaven-headed band of homegrown missionaries, and in July 1966 he formed the International Society for Krishna Consciousness (ISKCON), which would become less formally— and quite infamously—known as the Hare Krishnas.

Within months, Prabhupada opened temples in Montreal, San Francisco, Los Angeles, Boston and Buffalo. And then, in 1968, he conceived of an ideal society based on Krishna consciousness and located in the hills of West Virginia, of all places. He named the project New Vrindavan, after the Indian city of Vrindavana, the place of Krishna's birth. Prabhupada dispatched one of his first disciples to oversee the venture, a fellow named Keith Ham who had recently undergone psychological evaluation at New York's Bellevue Hospital and now called himself Kirtanananda. The goal was to recreate Vedic culture, an ancient and agrarian Indian civilization that was said to be in perfect harmony with nature. Prabhupada claimed that anyone could live a peaceful and productive life with four acres of land and a cow.

New Vrindavan began humbly, indeed—113 acres with no electricity, no running water, the only building being a battered old pioneer shack. Within a few years, it had tripled in size, and there were some seventy-five devotees on the premises. It was then that Kirtanananda decided to build a "modest home" for his spiritual master.

Prabhupada died—or as the devotees say, "left this mortal world"—in 1977, by which time ISKCON had grown into a confederation of more than one hundred temples, schools and communities all over the world. Two years later, the ideal community he had envisioned in Appalachia had a grand opening of sorts. By then, the centerpiece of the community, the so-called modest home constructed over the course of seven long years by devotees reading do-it-yourself manuals, had taken on an unabashedly extravagant incarnation.

Surrounded by an ornate temple, a thirty-eight-room guest lodge, twelve guest cottages, a restaurant, a gift shop, footpaths lined with huge statues of deities and elephants and sacred cows, man-made lakes populated by stately swans, and a massive flower garden bordered by scores of fountains—amid what is now several thousand acres with a view of three states—is a shrine topped with turrets, minarets and a three-hundred-ton gold-leafed dome. The inside is even more lavish, featuring crystal chandeliers, hand-carved teakwood doors, gold-plated faucets, some two hundred tons of marble and two dozen stained-glass windows, four of which contain more than 1,500 pieces of glass hand-shaped into royal peacocks. For a time, Kirtanananda had envisioned a sort of spiritual theme park in New Vrindavan—Krishnaland was a name bandied about. The final product offers something short of Dollywood in its opportunity, but something beyond Graceland in its superfluity. They call it Prabhupada's Palace of Gold.

So if you ever recall flipping a couple of quarters to a bare-domed, saffron-robed devotee in an airport, this is what you paid for. They bill it as America's Taj Mahal. That it was right on my way to Calcutta—in West Virginia, not West Bengal—seemed a stroke of good fortune and an invitation to explore. So I set a course for the Palace of Gold.

It was a long drive through New England, New York, New Jersey and the gut of Pennsylvania. Along the way, I was on the lookout for a sign that a foray into Krishna consciousness was a tangent worth taking, some sort of message with spiritual implications. I found only a marquee alongside a central Pennsylvania restaurant named Clem's: ONE NATION UNDER GOD CLOSED MONDAY.

As the afternoon grew late on the fourth day of my journey toward the Krishnas, I finally reached West Virginia's thin northern panhandle, where I escaped the interstate, ironically, at the Bethlehem exit. I took a wrong turn, realizing it immediately, and a few hundred yards later I pulled into the driveway of the Bethlehem Chapel in an effort to right myself. As I turned Phileas around I noticed the message on the church sign: GOD ALLOWS U-TURNS.

About a dozen miles later, after chugging along a narrow road winding its way up a mountainside, I rounded a bend and caught a glimpse through the trees of a golden dome as conspicuous amid the emerald landscape as a fire hydrant on a putting green. Soon after came a water tower spelling out its welcome: NEW VRINDAVAN.

The palace appeared palatial, indeed, if smaller than expected. I drove past it to a nearly empty lot in front of the Palace Lodge, which was fronted by a statue of a sleepy-eyed kneeling elephant about fifteen feet high and twenty feet long. I parked right behind the pachyderm's ample rear end, feeling somehow protected by the position, yet slightly uncomfortable at the same time. There was also a young man strolling the grounds while softly playing a flute, and there appeared to be three or four peacocks strutting along the roof of the lodge. It all made for a surreal arrival in West Virginia.

I had made tentative reservations to stay at the lodge — nonrefundable, of course — but I wanted to investigate the accommodations. A woman with a stud in her nose and a sweet demeanor handed me a key, and I made my way through a maze of hallways. Over nearly every doorway and water fountain was a hand-carved plaque bearing a verse, in Sanskrit and English, from Krishna's sacred text, the Bhagavad Gita. Said one, I SHALL DELIVER YOU FROM ALL SINFUL REACTION. DO NOT WORRY. But I was worried. My tiny room consisted of two bare bunk beds with thin blankets. It was stiflingly hot. The carpets were stained. The toilet in the bathroom across the hall was clogged. I returned to the receptionist and informed her that I would be sleeping in my RV in the parking lot, if it was okay with her. Sure it was, she said, and "Hare Krishna."

There were few, if any, guests in the lodge that night. The parking lot was nearly empty. And the stars looked like eyes in the darkness. From my perch behind the elephant's posterior,

I could hear the rhythmic sound of voices coming from the temple, mumbling unfamiliar words and moving closer.

It is one of the central aspects of Krishna devotion—the chanting of the mantra: *Hare Krishna, Hare Krishna, Krishna Krishna, Hare Hare, Hare Rama, Hare Rama, Rama Rama, Hare Hare.* It is a meditation whose goal is to summon higher awareness, to revive transcendental consciousness by dismissing an illusory struggle against material nature. *Hare* is the form of addressing the energy of the Lord, and the words *krishna* and *rama* are forms of addressing the Lord himself. When devotees chant together, it is called *chirtan.* When one chants swiftly and softly to himself, it is called *japa.*

The sheer quantity of the effort is remarkable. Devotees carry around a string of *japa* beads—108 of them, plus one to show when you have chanted around all 108 beads. One journey around the string of beads is called a round. Devotees are instructed to complete at least sixteen rounds daily, which amounts to about two hours of chanting. That is, they recite the mantra 1,728 times every day. Try putting that on your to-do list.

A devotee named Tapahpunja later enlightened me as to the significance of the numbers. "The number 108 indicates the number of elevated souls in the spiritual world who have a direct association with the supreme Lord Krishna," he explained. "When our spiritual master, A. C. Bhaktivedanta Swami Prabhupada, first came to this country, he recommended sixty-four rounds. That's what great self-realized souls do."

"But that's about eight hours of chanting," I said.

He nodded. "Most Americans are just too passionate. They can't just sit for eight hours and chant Hare Krishna. So then he said, all right, do thirty-two. And no one could do that." He laughed. "So finally he said, well, at least do sixteen."

In 1987, a couple of California-based psychologists completed a study called "Personality Characteristics of Hare Krishnas" in which they evaluated devotees on a mental health scale. For the most part, their personality traits were found to be very much in the "normal" range. But one characteristic was off the scales—compulsivity, which often comes from a desire to please. Seeking love of Krishna and the approval of their spiritual leaders, devotees prefer order, ritual, routine. So they chant . . . and chant . . . and chant . . .

"It's not just the mechanical chanting of it," Tapahpunja explained. "The purpose of this prayer is to focus on a loving relationship. The actual meaning of the prayer is: My dear Lord, please allow me into your service. In other traditions— for example, within the Judeo-Christian tradition—praying for your daily bread is an important part of your spiritual activity, and it's certainly a good thing to do because at least you're recognizing the authority of God. But higher than that is to not ask God for anything."

So that is how I fell asleep that night, surrounded by men in long robes strolling the grounds, chanting, almost unintelligibly, over and over again, like a spiritual lullaby. *Hare Krishna, Hare Krishna, Krishna Krishna, Hare Hare, Hare Rama, Hare Rama, Rama Rama, Hare Hare.*

They say that in a state of deep contemplation, the mantra becomes a direct link to God. It was my thirty-fourth birthday, but at least I wasn't alone.

With the sun hanging high over the hills the next day, I had a chat with that same receptionist at the little window that served as the Palace Lodge's front desk. Glkula Taruni was her Krishna name. Teresa was what they called her when she was growing up in St. Petersburg, Florida. Glkula, whose girlish voice made her seem younger than her twenty-six years, was working at the lodge to make money during the summer. In the fall, she planned to resume pursuit of a teaching degree, although that hadn't stopped her from teaching at a Krishna boarding school in India for the past three years. When Glkula was a high school student, herself, an age when most of us are searching for a prom date, she sought the meaning of life.

"I remember walking down the hallways and thinking this world isn't real. What's this about? What are we doing here? You go to school, you grow up, you go to work, and why? What's the point? I was raised a very strict Catholic, and my grandfather was actually a Southern Baptist minister. It was an extremely Christian background," she giggled. "But I didn't just want to be a Christian because my parents believed in that, you know? I wanted to find it out on my own. So I started studying all different religions—Buddhism, Taoism, Confucianism, even different types of mythology."

It turned out, however, that her spiritual awakening came through the underground music scene—death metal, the straight edge scene, a sort of male-dominated superpunk sub-culture in which its adherents sought to be hardcore yet pure. Its adherents promoted some of the same basic behavior as the Hare Krishnas—no meat-eating, no intoxication, no gambling and no illicit sex. So it was inevitable that the two subcultures found an overlap. Some musicians became devotees and started Hare Krishna hardcore bands, which is how a sixteen-year-old girl in St. Petersburg discovered the notion of seeking Krishna consciousness.

Therein lies much of the infamy of the Hare Krishnas—the accusation that the movement preys on the vulnerable and un- formed. Indeed, what interested me most about the sect was not its existence as much as its attraction—not necessarily New Vrindavan itself, but rather what brought people there.

Glkula walked me to the community's organic gardens a few hundred feet away and introduced me to an athletic- looking man in his early fifties with a cleanly shaved head and fingernails caked with dirt. Tapahpunja was articulate and confident, and I wondered if perhaps it was no accident that I had been steered toward his garden, much in the way that filmmaker Michael Moore finds himself maneuvered toward the smiling visage of an automaker's director of public rela- tions. On the other hand, I wasn't made to feel like an in- truder in a society of dubious motivations. I noticed no furtive glances, no put-on airs, no clandestine attempt to keep me from turning over that one rock hiding all the dirty little se- crets of the Hare Krishnas. I felt welcome. Any discomfort was a product of my own biases.

"I've been here so many years that I'm kind of dedicating myself to organic farming and teaching the connection be- tween farming and spirituality—how simple living is con- ducive to higher thinking, and how that higher thinking will naturally gravitate toward higher consciousness and love for God," said Tapahpunja, as he showed me around his chemical-free collection of everything from peas to pokeweed. "So what I do here is mostly try to set a good example and talk to people in this garden."

We sat on some chairs in the center of the garden, where we were joined, off and on, by what amounted to Tapah- punja's new family—his wife of just three days (officially, at least) named Kamalavatia; his stepdaughter Krishna Prestha; his step-son-in-law Sri Thakura; and their little blonde son Var-shana, an angel-faced sixteen-month-old who spent most of his time roaming about the garden naked.

Tapahpunja had first set foot in New Vrindavan in 1974, its pre-palace days. But he grew up on a farm in northern Michigan and then in a working-class neighborhood of Detroit, back when he still called himself Terry Sheldon. Terry's parents were diehard labor organizers, so he was brought up with a yearning for social change. His adolescence began at about the same time as the conflict in Vietnam, and he spent his college-aged years organizing people against the war and what he perceived to be a corrupted American government. To the degree in which he stayed in one place, it was usually in Berkeley and Haight-Ashbury.

"I was part of that youth culture, but I was very politically active. In fact, I would chide hippies who were not politically active. I was writing at the time for an underground newspaper, and I would actually use the Hare Krishnas as an example of a group that is so apolitical that what's their social relevance? They were just going out and chanting and throwing their arms up in the air and dancing. So what? Don't they know there's a war? But at the same time, as a person living through the rigors of street life and being arrested and the whole turmoil of the time, I detected in their character something that was very peaceful. I wanted to know what it was about. I was curious, and one time I began chanting with them."

It was a common inspiration at the time. The typical devotees in the early 1970s, when Krishna consciousness was a mainstay of the flower-power movement, were white, middle class, often from a Catholic or Jewish background, usually with some college experience. Generally, they were young men and women who weren't attached to a particular culture, who found it easy—and desirable—to opt out of society.

"It was another several years before I returned to Michigan and took a step back from the whole revolution. And I couldn't help but notice that when I left Berkeley and the Bay Area, ordinary people were going: What revolution?" He laughed and searched my eyes for understanding. "I thought maybe the real revolution was inside of me, and I needed to wake up to my own problems, my own deficiencies, and work on that."

He moved to a remote piece of Michigan property with no electricity and no running water. He grew an organic garden, dabbled in astrology and played at palmistry. And then, one

TAPAHPUNJA AND FAMILY

day, a visitor arrived and began to whisper the wonders of Krishna consciousness.

"He could see the path I was following—that unless I understood the great opportunity that human life affords for self-realization, then I was just spinning my wheels. And because of his compassion at explaining that to me, without being too heavy, I woke up a little bit. So he told me about this place in West Virginia. . . ."

Terry, soon to be Tapahpunja, had been reading the works of J. R. R. Tolkien at the time, and apparently he had been captivated by the agrarian purity of the hobbits and the elevated consciousness of the elves. Two decades ago, the same book had set me on a course as well, only I had envisioned myself as the writer of the tales, not the characters within them. I had been attracted to the imagination; he had been drawn to the fantasy. I would pursue enlightenment through a writer's curiosity; he would seek it through devoted spirituality. So we both arrived at the garden in New Vrindavan along very different paths.

Then again, everybody seemed to come to the Krishna commune from unusual angles. Glkula had found it through music and metaphysical musings. Tapahpunja had fueled and had been fueled by a revolution. As for Tapahpunja's wife . . . well, that was a story all its own.

She used to be Elicia Heller, a nice Jewish girl from Rockville Center, New York. She is now Kamalavatia and covered in spiritual tattoos. On her left forearm is Lord Balaraman; on her right arm, Lord Niyananda; on her chest, Krishna and his older brother running through a field with a sacred cow.

"See, my parents were atheists. They were cultural Jews,

but they weren't religious Jews. But I always believed in God. I knew I had a relationship with God. I just didn't know who he was. And since my parents disbelieved in God, home didn't really feel like home to me."

So she ran off at the age of seventeen. She had been accepted to college early, spent about three weeks at a little school in rural Illinois and then quit abruptly, traveling the country, following the Grateful Dead, hitchhiking her way to Colorado when her money ran out.

"It was kind of funny the way it happened," she smiled. "I met a devotee when I was panhandling. He was selling *Back to Godhead* magazines, but I was totally broke. He asked for a quarter, and all I had was like seven cents in my pocket. I told him I can give everything I have. And he took it and gave me the magazine. And I was really pleased with that! So I read it."

She paused for a moment, studying an airplane that seemed to be flying in circles above the compound, while I mused over the revelation that she was pleased with this fellow for having taken her last seven cents.

"And then a few days later, I went to some kind of outdoor concert, a Woodstocky kind of thing, and I met this guy who was part of a hippie commune. He had just been out of Vietnam, and he wasn't talking. I thought he couldn't talk. So I decided I would go with him, and I wouldn't talk either. So we lived up in the Rockies for five or six weeks without talking. But he gave me a Bhagavad Gita, and all we would do is just read it. Occasionally, we would go down into Boulder, to the temple, where they gave out free food to all the hippies. For weeks, I would sit on top of the mountain—you know, naked—reading and chanting Hare Krishna. One night all the hippies from the commune dropped acid. I never had before, so I thought I'd try it. And while I was tripping, that guy I was with starting talking!"

She laughed, and it was a laugh I heard several times over the course of my visit to New Vrindavan—sort of a boy-this-sounds-rather-goofy-in-the-retelling chuckle.

"I didn't think he could talk!" she continued. "And he said, 'You have to die to be free. This whole world is an illusion.' That's all he said. And I'm going, Whoa! Then it started to click. It all started to make sense. I'm not this body. I'm really a spirit soul. I want that eternal, loving relationship with God. Everything here is an illusion because everything is temporary. It's not who we really are. And I decided I didn't want to come down from this realization. So the next morning, I moved into the temple. The first time I bowed down before Krishna—you know, you're in kind of a fetal position—I just felt safe, like it was my normal position to be in. I felt like I was home."

I toured the temple with a woman named Gopala-syapriya—call her Gopa, she said, though she was once known as Diane. She wore a light blue sari and bore a marking on her forehead called *tilak,* the sacred mud from Dwaraka which is supposed be applied on the body in twelve places, designating it as a temple of the Lord. A native of the Detroit area, she had been initiated in 1975 at New Vrindavan and had been there ever since.

"I was raised in the suburbs, and I always felt like it was so empty and so easy, and I had no spiritual life. I remember asking my father about the sky. Does it ever end? Does it stop at a certain point? And he just told me not to even try to think of stuff like that," she said, as we walked past the temple's ornate golden altars, the hand-carved chariot, the stained-glass arched ceiling and the wax figure of Prabhupada draped in a fresh garland and surrounded by sacred cows. "I was really attracted to nature. I felt like I wanted to live off the land. I didn't really want to be a part of the world, as I saw it, because it all seemed so wrong. When I went to college, I just felt like it was a joke. Everything seemed so ridiculous."

She dropped out, lived alone in a tepee in the West Virginia woods for a summer and explored various commune options until she finally found herself visiting New Vrindavan one winter. She was attracted to the austerity and the notion of a higher consciousness. Still, she wasn't ready to commit.

"But all kinds of things happened on that visit," Gopa recalled. "I had a notion that God was there."

I asked if she could give me some specific examples. She reflected for a moment.

"Someone asked me if wanted to help clean the barn, like shoveling manure and stuff. I thought, yeah, I'd love to do that. The devotees were always saying how everything they do is for Krishna, but I just wanted to do it for my body, to get back in shape. And just as I had that thought, I went to pick up a load of stuff, and my back just went . . . snap! I couldn't move. I felt like Krishna was reading my mind and showing me that this is real. This is serious. This is not to be taken lightly."

"So one of your defining moments was actually shoveling manure and having your back go out," I teased, and thankfully she laughed good-naturedly.

"Well, another thing happened on that trip. It was morning and snowing, and it was real quiet. And I was talking about what I thought of the place—how I liked it, but I felt like I didn't want to do it right now. And as soon as I said that, there was a huge clap of thunder. . . ." She looked at me with a somewhat embarrassed expression on her face. "I don't know. Maybe you're thinking it all sounds kind of silly. . . ."

"I'll be honest with you," I told her. "What I'm thinking is that a lot of people put themselves in situations where they're ready to believe, and when something happens they interpret it the way they want to."

She shrugged. "Everything just seemed so wrong everywhere I went, but everything seemed so right here."

Later, Gopa led me on a brief tour of the Palace of Gold. I once had paid $15 for a tour of Hearst Castle in San Simeon, California, and had reacted with both wonder and distaste at its extravagance. As I explored Prabhupada's palace, I experienced much the same visceral response. It was beautiful and gaudy and spiritual and goofy. The only difference was: William Randolph Hearst made no claims to purity.

The walls and floors of the temple hall feature fifty varieties of marble, which were imported from all over the world, cut into twenty thousand pieces, polished and then shaped into geometric designs. Eighteen murals, depicting Lord Krishna's pastimes, are painted on the dome, from which hangs an antique French chandelier. Prabhupada's bedroom has walls of Italian Botticino marble inlaid with Persian onyx and a ceiling decorated with nearly one thousand hand-painted flowers. The adjoining bathroom, likely never used, features a three-hundred-pound marble sink with gold-plated and rose quartz-handled faucets beneath an eighteenth-century Spanish mirror. In Prabhupada's study, surrounded by ornate gold baseboards and cornices and gold-embroidered silk brocades and antique Chinese vases, sits a wax replica of the spiritual master, himself, sitting at his desk, translating Vedic literature. And in the altar room, beneath a dome containing more than four thousand pieces of crystal, there he is again, seated on a throne, dressed not as the ascetic that he was, but as a crowned and royally garbed representative of God.

As I stared at the replica of this charismatic supermissionary, I wanted to feel a divine vibe. But I couldn't help thinking of the two or three wax museums into which I have wandered. I always find such displays spooky, probably because I can't seem to shake the memory of a particular museum in Hollywood and a young Shirley Temple, her face yellowed and flaking, her left eye loose in its socket. She looked like some sort of undead child star. I have confidence the devotees will not let Prabhupada suffer so.

All in all, the Palace of Gold was something Liberace might have visited and commented, "A little over the top, isn't it?" But Tapahpunja had suggested that the greater marvel, if that is the right word, was the journey to construction.

"It seemed that, technically, we were building a palace. But it was building us, because the cooperation it took, the inspiration, the teamwork was really wonderful. And the finished project attracted the whole world. We suddenly went from a small farm community cloistered in the hills of West Virginia to hosting fifty thousand people a year. We were the second-biggest tourist attraction in the state."

"What's the first?" I had to ask.

"The dog races," he laughed. "Wheeling Downs."

So this was America's Taj Mahal. But in coming to my own conclusions about it, I can only echo the words of my own spiritual master of sorts. Upon seeing the real Taj Mahal a century earlier, Mark Twain wrote, "I saw it in the daytime; I saw it in the moonlight; I saw it near at hand, I saw it from a distance; and I knew all the time, that of its kind it was *the* won-

der of the world, with no competitor now and no possible future competitor; and yet, it was not *my* Taj."

When Prabhupada died in 1977, the Krishnas encountered a
crisis of charisma. In his stead, the sect's Governing Body
Commission decreed that eleven gurus would carry on the tradition, to be treated with the same respect formerly paid to the
spiritual master. This zonal guru system proved to be a nearly
fatal mistake for the movement, as many of the gurus became
more concerned with empire building than furthering Krishna
consciousness. They led lives of luxury, buying castles, hob-
nobbing with royalty and rock stars, having their feet bathed
by servants. Slowly at first, and then in greater numbers, stories
emerged of activities that were anything but pure—money-
raising scams, drug-running, arms-stockpiling, beatings of dissi-
dents and worse.

ISKCON's members became increasingly divided over the
"guru issue," many of them pushing for internal reform and a
disassociation from the kind of guru worship that fueled in
some a certain power-hungry paranoia. The most vociferous
opponent of such reform was Kirtanananda, the guru at New
Vrindavan, who was said to run the most corrupt zone of them
all. In 1985, a mentally disturbed man who had been denied
initiation took matters into his own hands, beating Kirtanananda with a metal spike and sending him into a twenty-
six-day coma.

"No question he tried to kill him," Tapahpunja recalled.
"But local law enforcement cut him loose after four months.
They called it malicious wounding and let him go, which is
very typical of the way we were treated here. They kind of created a mood here about having to take the law into our own

hands. But there was a whole series of events here in the 1980s that were just draconian."

Indeed, over a period of four or five years, the extent of violence and negligence at New Vrindavan was head-spinning. A female devotee was beaten for questioning Kirtanananda's status as a guru. A two-year-old boy died from an apparent battering. Two more boys, ages four and five, suffocated in an abandoned refrigerator. A fourth boy drowned in one of the man-made lakes. Then, in 1987, the former school principal and a teacher's assistant at the now-closed Boys School of New Vrindavan were arrested after appalling accusations of child sexual abuse. The perpetrators had told the victimized children that their karma was to blame for their suffering. Indeed, this was part of an epidemic of pedophilia and physical abuse, particularly at the *gurukulas* or Krishna boarding schools. It took years for the children of the 1970s and 1980s to go public with their memories and allegations. In 2000, they filed a $400 million lawsuit against Krishna temples, which forced ISKCON to file for bankruptcy.

But there was more. A New Vrindavan resident named Tirtha (Thomas Drescher) was convicted of arson-for-insurance fraud and the murder of Stephen Bryant, a dissident devotee who had embarked on a one-man crusade against upper-level corruption in ISKCON. At the time of his conviction, Drescher was already serving a life sentence for another murder at the commune three years earlier. The day after he was apprehended, a key witness against him suffered critical injuries in a gas explosion at his New Vrindavan home. Several years later, Drescher would testify that it was all a murder-for-hire plot funded by Kirtanananda, who would eventually be sentenced to twelve years in prison for racketeering. By then, ISKCON had finally had enough, excommunicating the guru and, for a time, his entire commune.

Tapahpunja was well aware of how the gurus came to resemble the Gambinos, but he made a point of separating the Krishna transgressions from the Krishna tradition. "The phenomenon of people aspiring for spiritual life, getting to a level of purity and inspiration to others, and then making mistakes and falling down from that position . . . it's not uncommon. It goes on in every tradition in the world, and it will continue to go on," he said. "So while it is tragic, and very unfortunate, it's not something that should be looked on as a reason to question the authenticity of the movement or the credibility of the scriptures or even the lifestyle."

Are the Hare Krishnas a cult? I mustered up the courage to broach the subject with Tapahpunja, and I had the feeling he had thought out his answer well in advance.

"Well, its dictionary meaning is not pejorative. Basically, it means a following of people who are guided by particular religious principles. If you're going to use the definition that it's a group of people that blindly follow instructions and are incapable anymore of critical thinking or analysis, you can say the same thing about the U.S. Marine Corps—or for that matter, Tau Kappa Epsilon. Because of the lack of spiritual dimension in America in people's day-to-day lives, a group like we are that really tries to bring synthesis of lifestyle and philosophy becomes an easy target for using that word in a derogatory way."

The Religious Movement Resource Center in Colorado defines a destructive cult (as opposed to an alternative religion or a benign group) as "any organization that inhibits individual freedom of thought through the use of violence, deception and mind control." That certainly sounds a lot like the Hare Krishnas, at least in the 1970s and 1980s. Before things fell apart, the spiritual master, himself, supposedly used to make light of the notion that his followers were somehow brainwashed when all he saw was people seeking purity. "Brainwashing?" Prabhupada would say. "Yes, we are washing our brains." But even many of the devotees who remained on the path to purity reacted to the endless series of accusations about their leaders and the goings-on at their *gurukulas* with denial in the face of ample evidence. It smacks of an insidious sort of mind control.

Nevertheless, Tapahpunja made a valid point. Many of the movement's leaders and followers failed to maintain a standard of purity—failed miserably, in fact—but does that negate the quest itself? Do we blame all of Catholicism for pedophile priests? His suggestion that Americans tend to practice religion of convenience also resonated with me. I know many people who consider themselves sufficiently pious but who tend to categorize others as simply too religious. To avoid such apparent hypocrisy, I have chosen to distance myself from organized religion altogether, acknowledging only the cultural aspects that bring me closer to my family. Hare Krishnas have opted for the other side of the spectrum. Were they to shave their heads and dance and chant on the streets of Calcutta, India, they would largely blend into the religious landscape. But on the streets of, say, Chicago, they stick out like a saffron robe in a world of gray.

Is religion to be applauded in moderation but scorned in excess? Well, in West Virginia, it used to be grounds for being committed. About eighty miles south of New Vrindavan, there is an institution called Weston Hospital, which was once known as the West Virginia Hospital for the Insane. According to a log book I discovered during my investigative wanderings, "religious enthusiasm" was listed among the hospital's reasons for admission back in the nineteenth century. Of course, the others included grief, jealousy, disappointment, remorse, seduction, egotism, laziness, asthma, sun stroke, indigestion, dog bite, the war, imaginary female troubles, loss of lawsuit, greediness, superstition, ill treatment by husband, bad company, opium habit, snuff eating, novel reading, politics, bad whiskey, nymphomania, deranged masturbation and, finally, that Appalachian icon: parents were cousins. All of which suggests that both insanity and piety are open to interpretation.

Of the people I met at New Vrindavan, the one who interested me most was Kamalavatia's twenty-five-year-old daughter, Krishna Prestha, who had just earned her master's degree in clinical psychology. She seemed to be a sort of litmus test of the maturation of the movement and the self-empowerment of its devotees. In her early childhood, she had attended a Krishna day school in San Diego. But then her mother had decided to leave the temple for a while, having felt alienated by what she saw as a widespread abuse of power, which included an abusive marriage.

"At the time I thought, well, I'm just going to tolerate this because I'm not the body and Krishna is in control and he arranged my marriage and I'm just going to accept it," Kamalavatia explained to me. "But then, when I was pregnant with my last kid, I realized this is not safe for my children. That was the bottom line."

She moved to Amherst, Massachusetts, sent her children to public school and finally completed her college degree. She never lost her faith, even hosting her own radio show as a vehicle for preaching Krishna consciousness, but her teenaged daughter wanted nothing to do with it. "I didn't press it," said Kamalavatia. "It's better to just accept where they're at and be loving, then they'll come to what they want on their own."

Krishna Prestha nodded. "You try to find yourself in the spectrum of these little subcultures of society. I was a cheerleader. I played lacrosse. I even went through a short phase of wearing all black. Or maybe a Debbie Gibson hat," she chuckled. "It was like a quest. I just found that this is not who I am. And at the end of high school, I just rediscovered my spirituality."

"All of a sudden one day, when she was seventeen or eighteen, I came home," said her mother, "and she was chanting Hare Krishna again."

While Tapahpunja walked off to tend to his garden, his wife and stepdaughter and I discussed the past and present of the movement, and I began to receive the impression that the culture of Krishna consciousness had evolved significantly over the past dozen or so years.

"You know how sometimes things go from one extreme to another and then come to a happy medium? It's a young movement in America, started by young people. So there's a lot of maturing taking place on different levels," said Krishna Prestha. "I think, in some ways, we're going to another extreme." What she meant, I believe, is that a softening of the hierarchy had lessened the level of respect by some of the devotees for their spiritual master. In fact, she added, only half-joking, that nowadays when one bows down before a guru, one then "looks around to see if anyone saw you."

In fact, there aren't any resident gurus at New Vrindavan,

only initiating gurus who arrive periodically to initiate new devotees. The farm in the West Virginia hills seems to have become less of a commune, per se—or at least less communistic. "Before, everyone just surrendered all their material goods and just lived in the temple, very poorly and simply, and a lot of people were neglected, too. Now, people are realizing they have to get jobs and support their families. And that's the way it's done in India," said Kamalavatia.

She and Tapahpunja now earn extra money through commission on membership sales for Pre-Paid Legal Services. Even Gopa, who admitted to being less worldly than most, travels to a mall near Toledo during the holiday season and sells Christmas ornaments—never mind that she is a Krishna devotee of Jewish origins.

As for the criminal behavior that seemed so rampant at New Vrindavan, I sensed that the devotees were intent on distancing themselves from the perpetrators and the past. Kamalavatia and Krishna Prestha recalled the amazing denials and eternal regret of the mothers who had sent their children away to Krishna boarding schools. They acknowledged how women were often treated with disrespect in years past and lamented the lack of female gurus, hinting at an old boys' network. In general, they seemed to feel free to condemn and question and divulge, and I pointed out to them that this was a surprise to me. Frankly, I had expected anything but candor and criticism of the movement's flaws.

"When I joined, in the beginning, no one talked like that. We didn't even think like that," Kamalavatia admitted. "But we did a lot of things differently because Prabhupada was on the planet. I mean, just going to the morning program where everybody is up at 4 A.M. and goes to the temple . . . back then, everyone did it without question. You never even thought to not go. Now, hardly anyone goes."

Perhaps Krishna consciousness in America has become less dogmatic, less authoritarian, and somehow more sincere in its spirituality. I had arrived in the West Virginia hills thinking that I was entering the confines of a cult. I left hoping that maybe much of the corruption had been shed along with the terribly misguided believers who were its architects, that only the purest, most self-realized souls remained.

But later, when I looked further into New Vrindavan's sordid past, I discovered that the organic gardener Tapahpunja, whom I had thought earnest and straightforward, had not been just a distant observer of the "draconian" events at New Vrindavan in the 1980s. He had been a participant—guru Kirtanananda's right-hand man. He had assisted in the surveillance of now dead Stephen Bryant, had actually been with Thomas Drescher when he was arrested for the murder, and had been caught carrying written instructions about how to smuggle Drescher out of the United States. Tapahpunja fled the country soon afterward, returning at some point to be charged with racketeering and conspiracy to commit murder. Although his conviction seems to have been later vacated, I did come across a photo of him in a true-crime book—a mug shot in which he didn't look nearly so pure of spirit.

As I was leaving New Vrindavan, I caught a glimpse of a small snake slinking across the road just a few feet in front of Phileas. Gopa had mentioned seeing many snakes lately. They were coming out of hiding because it was so dry. In India, snakes are said to rank second in veneration only to the sacred cow. In fact, many homes have their own shrines to snakes, which are said to be a source of happiness and wealth when properly worshipped, loss and disease when not.

One of the earliest settlers in the vicinity of Calcutta, West Virginia, had much the same admiration for the slithering reptile. His name was Christian—Christian Schultz. He was born in New York City, well educated and wealthy, and became a judge with Supreme Court ambitions. But his hopes were thwarted by people whom he thought were his friends, and he became a bitter man. Much like Gopa at New Vrindavan, he resolved to flee what he considered a false civilization, taking refuge in the West Virginia wilderness, where he lived out the rest of his days and translated his contempt for humanity into a love for snakes. He gathered specimens of every kind, studied their habits and wrote several volumes about them. He died without many friends around him, but surrounded by serpents aplenty.

So this was a connection, albeit a tenuous one, between the world of Krishna consciousness that I was leaving and the hills and hollows of the region where I was headed. Unfortunately, I am pretty certain I flattened the snake. The meaning of this is a matter of interpretation, much like the fine line between a religion and a cult. Maybe it was a sign that I was stamping out bad karma, or perhaps courting it. Maybe some higher spirit was branding me a nonbeliever. Or—and this is my preferred construal—maybe there are just a whole bunch of snakes in West Virginia.

I climbed onto Route 2 and headed south, anticipating a lovely drive in which I would be shadowing the Ohio River for an hour or so. The first few miles were satisfying enough, as I maneuvered between the river and a sheer rock wall. There was a sign: WILDLIFE VIEWING AREA BEGINS. But for the next thirty miles, the view was marred by a succession of riverside plants—and not the leafy kind. Moundsville Calcining Plant. Columbian Chemicals Company. Chlor-Alkali & Derivatives. Mile after mile of concrete and steel, a depressing corridor of bins and boilers and chutes and conveyors and smokestacks and transformers. It was a Riverkeeper's industrial nightmare.

Just south of Bens Run, I entered the sparsely populated (7,513 residents) province of Pleasants County. A few minutes later I arrived in St. Marys, the county seat, where I turned inland onto Route 16 and headed into the hills. A right turn on King Ridge Road took me along, appropriately, a majestic tree-lined ridge meandering past mobile homes. Soon, the road dropped down beneath a leafy canopy and into a series of switchbacks, until finally I found myself in a sunlit hollow, hardly the black hole of Calcutta.

But Calcutta is, indeed, the name of this classic Appalachian holler, although nobody is quite sure how that came about. P. J. O'Rourke once described India's Calcutta, home to crowded millions, as "a dundering flux of a place that seemed in total disarray." West Virginia's Calcutta, home to a few dozen, is largely unpolluted and blessedly uncomplicated. I later found a photograph of the place, taken from atop the ridge in about 1908. Besides a post office and a general store, which were no longer in service, the settlement between the hills looked very much the same. It consists primarily of the eighty-one-year-old Calcutta United Methodist Church and a handful of homes belonging to one extended family. There is a family reunion every third Sunday in July, held at the church picnic shelter alongside French Creek, but it must be a rather redundant affair. Everybody in Calcutta's holler—except for one household, I was told—is a Bills.

For nearly its entire existence, the hollow has been populated by the descendants of Revolutionary War veteran John
Williams. When his son, William Williams, fought in the War
of 1812, there were several others named Williams in the
same company. So he changed the surname to Bills. Eventually, he made his way to Pleasants County, arriving in 1841
and purchasing land that included a tract along the upper waters of French Creek. Williams' son, Joseph, inherited the
land, which was cleared and farmed as the years went by.
Upon Joseph's death, his property was divided among his thirteen children. Aaron, the youngest, was given the home farm.

I parked Phileas near the church and walked across the
road toward the few houses that constitute Calcutta. There
was a young blonde woman standing there, watching her
three-year-old son burn off energy. We slipped into a conversation, which was inevitable. Anonymity is impossible in Calcutta, West Virginia.

Twenty-seven-year-old Amy Northrop is the great-
granddaughter of Aaron Bills, which I suppose makes her the
great-great-great-great-granddaughter of the Virginia farmer
who fought in America's revolution. Her parents live in the
house next door. Her great-aunt owns the one on the other
side. A Noah's Ark of animals wandered around the property—
a couple of dogs, two stray cats, a pair of horses. Some cows
grazed in a backyard field. There was a goat tied to a post.

"That's my dad's goat—the Calcutta Kid," she explained.

Apparently, there were wasps around, too, because at that
moment her three-year-old, who had been poking into various
places, began wailing—"I got stung! I got stung!" His unruf-
fled mother settled him down with a bandage, and he continued his explorations.

The assorted animals weren't quite the peacocks and elephants that had surrounded me that morning, but as Amy began to describe life in Calcutta, it sounded to me like the kind of commune—secluded, simple, tied to the land and a place of worship—that New Vrindavan might have aspired to, had its builders not opted to include a palace on the premises.

"I loved growing up here. My grandma and grandpa lived here. All my cousins lived here. We were all in 4-H club together. We'd ride our bikes and swim in the crick," she said, nodding toward French Creek. "We had a club out in the woods, and we even paid dues. And we had a lemonade stand in the summer. We made a fortune off that lemonade stand."

"Here?"

"Yeah, we did!"

"Who comes through here?"

"Well, at the time they were drilling an oil rig down the road here, and those guys would come up three or four times a day and buy lemonade off us. We made a lot of money!" she chuckled. "Then we took it all and bought something stupid—rafts for the crick, I think. Anyway, I wanted my kids to grow up here."

As if on cue, a school bus winded its way along the switchbacks and into the hollow and let out Amy's five-year-old son, home from his first day in kindergarten. His younger brother, apparently recovered from his wasp encounter, ran right up to him and welcomed him with a tight hug.

"Mom! Look what I did!" said the five-year-old, running to his mother. He opened his lunchbox to reveal that it was completely empty.

"You ate it all? You little piggy!" she smiled. "Now, go change your clothes."

Watching the display, I missed my boys more than ever. And I missed their mother, who happens to be named Amy. Besides her three children, Calcutta's Amy also has five step-children. She said her ex-husband, the father of her three sons, lives "somewhere in Williamstown," which is just down the river a bit. "He hasn't seen the kids in over a year," she added.

I asked Amy if she ever considered living anywhere else but Calcutta.

"Yes. I moved to Parkersburg," she said. Parkersburg is the relative metropolis twenty miles away. "Actually, I made it as far as Florida. But I was back two weeks later. I was nineteen, and for some reason I decided I didn't want to live in this small town anymore. A friend of mine had decided to live in Florida. So we packed up and moved to . . . oh, man, what's that big one down there?"

"Miami?"

"Uh-uh."

"Orlando?"

"Yeah, Orlando. I hated it. I was so homesick. I was bawlin' and squawlin'. I had been workin' at Shoney's before I left, and they mailed my last check to me in Florida. I took the twenty-six dollars, filled up my car and came home. Drove straight through."

Amy's great-grandfather, Aaron Bills, and his wife Fanny had eight children. Charlie was the name of the youngest. Charlie's wife, Gin, lives in a little white house at the bottom of the winding road into Calcutta. Her full name is Mary Virginia Bills—that's Mary Virginia near St. Marys, West Virginia. She was born in 1914, she said, in another holler three-and-a-half miles down the creek.

"I'm eighty-seven now. I'll be eighty-eight on my birthday," she explained.

Gin also claimed to be five-foot-two, or at least she was once. "I'm a-shrinkin'," she chuckled, as she sat on the arm of a porch bench. Indeed, she was a lovable little lady who laughed often, but life hasn't always been laughter and leisure for Gin Bills. I asked her about her husband, whom she had wed in 1930. They were married for fifty-eight years.

"He was killed. . . . Right up in the corner of that field," she said, peering and pointing into the distance. It happened nearly a decade and a half earlier, but she remembered the moment like it was yesterday.

"He went out to cut down a wild cherry tree. He said, 'When I get back, we'll go to Parkersburg.' Then he didn't come. He didn't come. He didn't come. I went outside, and I could hear the saw runnin'. And I thought, well, he's a-cuttin' up that tree. So I went back in, and later I went back out again. And the saw was still runnin' yet. So I got to pullin' weeds. I had to do somethin'. The phone rang, and I went and got it. Then I went back out, and the saw had quit. Still, he didn't come. And he didn't come. I stood there and watched. I couldn't see him, but the tree was down. And I thought, well, I'm goin' to see what's wrong. So I went up there, and that's when I found him. The tree fell on top of him. It'll be fourteen years on the twenty-eighth of October."

Gin and Charlie had met at Calcutta's church. She still attends every Sunday, and she always has, no matter what it took to get there. In her youth, she and her family would walk the three-and-a-half miles to church every Sunday morning, then walk home, then return for second services Sunday night. That's fourteen miles to salvation every Sunday.

Gin was the third oldest of nine children, and the oldest girl. Her father worked at local oil wells and kept a small farm. When Gin was just nine years old, she was forced to quit school for a period of time when her mother was confined to a hospital. "She was gone for nine weeks with a gall bladder and appendicitis. I done the work, the cookin', the churnin', the bakin' bread, stuff like that. I kept the kids. I was the housemother."

She returned to school, attending through the eighth grade, and then she was sent off to high school in St. Mary's. "Me and a cousin, we had to walk nine miles to school—that's a-goin' and a-comin'. I said if I ever got outta there alive, I'd never go back. And I didn't. One year! When you walk through snow drifts clear 'bove your knees, you don't go back! And they wouldn't let us wear slacks or nothin'!"

GIN BILLS

"So what did you wear?"

"Just dresses or skirts."

"You walked nine miles there and back through the snow while wearing a skirt?"

"Well, we'd wear our four-buckle Arctics, but the snow went down the boots. . . ."

And they used to have some rough winters in Pleasants County. Not so much over the past decade or so, but once upon a time it used to snow something fierce.

"My husband used to walk through the snow clear up to his waist and feed the cattle night and mornin'. We had a cat and a dog, and he'd say, 'C'mon, babies. Let's go feed the cows.'" She peered again out toward the fallen cherry tree. "I can hear him sayin' that yet. . . ."

Nowadays, her sons take care of her cows. Gin used to like to mow the lawn, but they won't let her do that either, ever since she had her three heart attacks. And she loved to make piece quilts, crafting hundreds over the years, but severe arthritis in her hands put an end to that. She had cataracts in her eyes and a bandage on her nose and a bend to her back. It isn't easy getting old. Then again, as the Hare Krishnas would say, "Every day is another day closer to getting out of prison."

Gin had only escaped the confines of Pleasants County on a handful of occasions, and I wondered if she had encountered a great deal of diversity in her life.

"Do any black folks live in the area?"

"No. Maybe in St. Marys. I don't know."

"Have you ever met any?"

She thought for a moment. "No. Can't say as I have. But I think they're the same as we are. That's the way I look at it.

God wouldn't have made all colors of races if he hadn't had a purpose for 'em."

"What about different religions? I mean, I happen to be Jewish. Am I the first Jew you've ever met?"

"Hmmm . . . Yep, you just may be." She smiled, and then she added with a chuckle, "Now don't you go tryin' to convert me!" Then, suddenly serious, she said, "I tell you what I think. Maybe I'm wrong. I don't know. But I think we all serve the same God. You serve the same one I do."

"But when your husband died, did you question your faith?"

"No," she shook her head slowly. "I just asked why did it have to happen to him. But what is to be will be. I've always said that, and I always will. What is to be will be."

The philosophy brought me back to New Vrindavan for a moment, to a comment Kamalavatia had made. "The law of karma says you have a certain destiny of pleasure and a certain destiny of suffering," she said, "and no matter how much money you have or how many possessions you have, if you're meant to suffer, you'll suffer."

Gin sighed and shrugged her shoulders slightly. A butterfly fluttered across the porch, and a wind chime announced a breeze. "Since my husband's been gone, it gets pretty darn lonesome. But then you get over that spell, and I like it here. I don't even like to go to town—to St. Marys. I go in, get what I need and get out. I'm just not used to the city. I'm a country girl. I'm a hillbilly."

She laughed, as pure a laugh as I have ever heard, conveying both self-deprecation and a certain self-satisfaction. "Yep, I'm just a plain ol' hillbilly. That's all there is to it."

Sounds to me like a self-realized soul.

THE LEGACY OF
BLACK DIAMONDS

CONGO, OHIO

There it is before you—smiling, frowning, inviting, grand,
mean, insipid, or savage, and always mute with an air of
whispering, "come find out."
—JOSEPH CONRAD, FROM "HEART OF DARKNESS"

One doesn't immediately think of Ohio when envisioning Appalachia, but as much as one-third of the state can be labeled as such—twenty-nine counties spread out south of Columbus and east of Cincinnati. Some of these have been able to cling to niche industries or attractions—wineries in Adams County, a couple of universities in Athens County, the lure of the Amish in Holmes County—but many parts of Appalachian Ohio are impoverished and isolated, having predicated much of their survival on an industry of inherently dwindling capacity.

The region's struggles began thousands of years ago with the mammoth glaciers of the Ice Age, which flattened land to the north, removing hills and rocks and leaving soil well-suited for farmland. But the ice stopped here, leaving sandstone rocks and hills and valleys, all of it too rugged for major highways but just right for the occasional flash flood. The topsoil was poor, but the natural resources beneath the hills were abundant with possibility.

One hundred years ago, there were more than one thousand coal mines in Ohio, employing fifty thousand miners. Company towns sprang up around these holes in the ground, drawing thousands of people to remote areas, a rich ethnic mix of immigrants and pioneers willing to dig deep. One such coal-mining center—in the rugged hills of Perry County, southeast of Columbus—consisted of several small towns and rural townships built largely around mines owned by the Sunday Creek Coal Company. These became known as the Little Cities of Black Diamonds.

Black diamonds are a paradox of time. It took thousands of years for plants to live and die in swamps, to accumulate, to fossilize, to be buried under mud and silt and transformed over the geologic ages into coal. Every twelve inches of coal thickness is estimated to represent about ten thousand years. So given the eons necessary for its creation, it is ironic how fast civilization sprang up around the efforts at extraction—and how fleeting the lives of such communities could be. In Perry County, where the coal seams were fourteen feet thick in some places, many coal company towns barely lasted a generation.

While it is still a multibillion-dollar industry today, coal production in Ohio is half of what it was just three decades earlier. There are slightly more than 3,000 miners in the state, working about 130 mines—less than 10 percent of the total from a century ago. Appalachian Ohio is pockmarked with ghost towns, once-had-beens with whimsical, ephemeral names like Mudsock and Bogus and Knockemstiff; Moonville and Rain Rock and Rogue's Hollow; Hamburger and Hobo and Utopia. Ghost towns in these parts tend not to be the tumbleweeds-and-flapping-shutters variety. Many have been replaced by highways and housing developments, or the forests have swallowed them, or the elements have worn them into anonymity.

If there is an analogy, it is perhaps the white diamonds of Africa. By any name, the Democratic Republic of Congo, formerly known as Zaire and, before that, Belgian Congo, has long received little in return for its natural resources. Belgium extracted ivory, rubber, uranium and diamonds and left no infrastructure that wasn't directly aimed at feeding colonial greed. Today, rebel groups and the government fight for control of Congo's diamond mines amid a civil war that has killed millions and created refugees of millions more, a crisis nearly unprecedented in its scope and its shameful lack of global attention.

Diamonds finance armies, and the men with the guns maintain order through terror. They smuggle the diamonds into neighboring dictatorships, receiving more guns and cash in exchange, and the jewels eventually make their way to the world's great cities and the necks and fingers of the well-to-do, who don't have a care in the world about how it arrived in the Tiffany's box. The rich (the powerful cartels and armies and launderers and bejeweled) get richer, while the poor (the West African diamond miners) are virtual slaves. And when a diamond mine is depleted, it and the surrounding community are often left to die, abandoned and engulfed by the desert's shift-ing sands.

Such are the similarities with Ohio's Little Cities of Black Diamonds. Consider San Toy, for instance, which used to be just a few miles up the road from Congo. In the first quarter of the twentieth century, it was a prosperous town created by the Sunday Creek Coal Company around two of its mines. Leg-end has it that it received its name in a backhanded manner. The company had invested in an unsuccessful Broadway mu-sical called *San Toy*. When a handful of executives surveyed the town, one told another, "Let's hope this isn't another *San Toy*." (Of course, the most troubling part of that story is that if the company had invested in a different show, there might have been a mean little coal town in Ohio named Frocks and Frills or My Lady Molly.)

San Toy thrived for a while. At its peak, in 1917, it had its own streetcar line, a theater and the only hospital in the county. But violence proved to be its downfall. Murders were somewhat commonplace there, the town being full of men who liked to drink, fight and carry guns and knives. As one local later recalled, "It was a tough place. If you took a walk up the railroad tracks with a lantern, somebody'd shoot it out." In 1924, a group of overworked, underpaid and angry miners rolled a coal car full of burning railroad ties into Mine #1. The resulting fire destroyed not only the mine, but also the theater and the hospital. Three years later, faced with a need to mod-ernize Mine #2, the company decided to abandon it instead. San Toy cleared out, and the few who stayed turned to brew-ing moonshine in an attempt to survive. By 1931, there were only nineteen registered voters remaining. They voted seven-teen to two to desert San Toy.

If there was a subtext to my journey from Calcutta to
Congo, it was this very notion—that it could all change in an
instant. I crossed the Ohio River, which looked pristine and
handsome until I steered south on Route 7, flirting with the
riverbank, and caught sight of an industrial plant silhouetted
in the fading light, looking like some sort of massive pipe
organ coughing smoke into the West Virginia sky. Through
Marietta, then west on Highway 550, driving into the sunset
and past an old CHEW MAIL POUCH TOBACCO advertisement
painted on the side of a dying barn. North on Highway 13,
shadowed by Sunday Creek, now the color of sewage as the result of acid mine drainage. Through the hamlet of Chauncey,
where expressionless Ohioans sat on front porches, holding fly
swatters and staring at passing cars.

I searched for a soundtrack. National Public Radio was
playing jazz, which I don't normally prefer, but there was
something fitting in the improvisation, the unexpected
melodic variations. A mile beyond Chauncey, traffic slowed to
a crawl, blocked by the spectacle of two fire trucks, two police
cars, an ambulance, a tow truck and two cars in a ditch on the
side of the road. One was perpendicular to the roadway; the
other lay on its side with its roof sheered off.

Just north of that was more evidence of life's precarious-
ness, a road leading to, as the sign said, MINE DISASTER SITE.
Coal miners live and die with the dangers of their profession—
slag falls and cave-ins, crippling broken bones and black lung
disease, poisonous gases and fires. On November 5, 1930, the
killer was an explosion that ripped through the Millfield site,
which was the hub of hundreds of shafts run by the Sunday
Creek Coal Company. The cause of the blast was said to be
gases ignited by a simple spark between a trolley car and its

railing. Eighty-two men died, including the company's top executives, who were touring the mine, ironically, to inspect new safety equipment. In an instant, sixty women were widowed. More than 150 children lost fathers. One mother buried five sons. It was the worst mining disaster in Ohio history.

Coal mining is safer these days, but not safe. While it was an all-time low, twenty-seven people did lose their lives in coal mines in 2002, a number palatable only relative to the past. Just three decades earlier, there were more than a hundred coal mining deaths. A century ago, the number exceeded two thousand annually.

I made a brief stop for provisions in the once bustling town of Glouster, where much of Main Street was boarded up, but a Kroger's supermarket was open for business. Maybe my expectations colored my perceptions, or maybe the lighting was bad, but everyone inside looked sickly to me—either grossly overweight or frighteningly thin, with heavy-lidded eyes and stringy hair and skin so pale it was colorless. Coal, the product of heat and pressure, is known in many places as "buried sunshine," in much the same way that garlic is the "stinking rose." I used to think of it as an optimistic phrase. But I sensed a melancholy cloud hanging over these hills.

As the sun was setting, I pulled into a campsite at Burr Oak State Park, on the southern edge of Perry County, just a few miles from Congo. Phileas and I were all alone, perched on a knoll in the heart of darkness, surrounded only by night as black as coal.

Corning, Ohio, just north of Burr Oak, was little more than a tiny business district clinging to a crossroads, but it was once the railroad hub of the Sunday Creek Valley. When the

Zanesville and Western Railroad reached the village in 1890, it spurred creation of another mining community a few miles to the east of town. To open up the coal field, a tunnel was dug from Corning to this new settlement, which came to be called Congo. It was estimated that there were more than four hundred million tons of coal in the Congo mine, enough for some four decades of labor.

Histories diverge on the source of its name. One version claims it came from a man nicknamed "Congo" Mooney, an African-American who migrated from Alabama in the late 1880s and became a strong and popular voice in the region's rail camps. Another suggests the name derived from the coal company's tendency to segregate workers. A large number of Appalachian miners at the turn of the twentieth century were southern black laborers drawn to the coal mines by offers of free transportation north, steady work at high wages and inexpensive company housing. Many found their way to Congo, although the record shows that by 1900 only 51 of Congo's 1,129 residents were black. On one hill, which came to be called White Hill, were mostly workers of Hungarian descent. I was told that the other hill, largely populated by black miners, was known as Colored Hill. But the history books call it Nigger Hill, christened at about the same time the U.S. Supreme Court was affirming the notion of separate but equal.

It was a feudal system of sorts, the coal companies being the barons of the manor, the miners being the serfs. The company houses, some 250 of them arranged in rows down both hills, were identical in every aspect except workers could choose between one- and two-bedroom residences—at a rental rate of $2 per room per month. There was a company school, a company-run hotel and a company store. To keep peddlers out, and to keep miners in, the company actually constructed a fence around Congo. Miners were paid with company money and had to shop on credit at the company's establishment, where prices were often higher and debts often outstripped funds. So after laboring on his knees in a puddle for an entire shift or stooping for hours in a narrow seam of coal, a miner might go to retrieve his paycheck and find an empty envelope.

Nevertheless, hope ran high on Congo's hills. I came across a description of Perry County, written about a century earlier in the heyday of Ohio coal mining, which described the community as "a wide-awake burg whose adjacent coal mines are its chief source of wealth." It also gushed about how the region offered "all the charms of yore, with the advantages of the present, and the alluring possibilities of a glorious future."

The mine closed in the 1950s. The coal company skipped town. And Congo began its slow spiral toward irrelevance. The Congo I discovered, past a series of trailers and double-wides along a wooded ridge, was not a ghost town in the traditional missing-community sense, but rather in the ailing-community sense. It is still there, still breathing on life support, a phantom of its former self.

The curvy lanes on Congo's two hills sloped down into increasingly desperate circumstances. So-called Colored Hill was like a living landfill. Trash was strewn everywhere—between decrepit trailers, beside toppled children's toys, around cars rusted through like metallic Swiss cheese. On this Tuesday afternoon, mulleted-and-tattooed types in stained shirts milled around unsalvageable cars set on blocks. Obese men rested cans of Budweiser on their bellies and stared steely-eyed from lawn chairs. An old wild-haired woman in a muumuu shook the filth out of a rug on her front porch.

White Hill, just a few hundred feet north, was a bit quieter and slightly more appealing. The Congo Community Church still stood, a gray yawn of a building with a couple of faded stained-glass windows, but it stood for nothing anymore, the preacher having left less than a year earlier in search of a more receptive flock. Among the twenty or thirty low-slung houses crowding the road on each side were a handful of pleasant enough homes. But the rest seemed to be either deserted or in a wretched state of disrepair with roofs buckling, gutters falling loose, frayed banners waving in death convulsions and paint peeling like sunburned skin. There was no longer a fence around Congo, but it felt uninviting all the same.

At the top of White Hill was the former Stenson's Bar, which had served the hard-drinking miners for nearly a century, from the town's inception through the 1980s. I have seen a photograph from decades earlier depicting the bar in better days, showing a trio of men leaning over the porch railing and chatting with a fellow driving a couple of horses. There was no longer a porch railing. The entire left side of the porch itself had collapsed. Much of the roof was in the process of doing the same. A light bulb, probably decades old, hung from a wire suspended from the ceiling, swinging lifeless. Vines crept up through porch slats and along the side of the building, which was completely boarded up, with the exception of two second-floor windows, which stared vacantly like a skull's eye sockets. The leaning brick chimney appeared ready to crumble at the first strong breeze.

Next to the deserted tavern was a house in marginally better shape. Its white exterior had been scraped and stained by the elements into a sickly gray. The roof was charred in one corner. The chimney had fallen into itself. A torn and limp American flag hung from a rusty post like a sad metaphor. The concrete steps leading up to the porch were cracked and split down the middle. All three doors leading inside from the porch were boarded up. Still, it seemed only half-abandoned, which is actually a more spine-chilling sort of neglect. Shards of glass had been swept into a corner of the porch. The porch light was on. And in one window, infested with cobwebs like curtains, there was a basket of flowers. It was eminently creepy, as if some shadowy figure was peering from behind a cracked upstairs window every time I turned my back.

Feeling either daring or foolhardy, I knocked on the door. No answer. More knocks. No answer. One more knock and—

FORMERLY CONGO'S BAR

thank goodness—no answer. I slinked around the back of the house, through the weeds, where a pile of garbage lay like a patio dumping ground. In the midst of it all were a couple of discarded items symbolizing something—I wasn't quite sure what—about Congo, Ohio. One was a tattered Old Glory, suffocating amid the refuse. The other was a Diehard battery.

Across from the abandoned buildings were a couple of signs. One announced SLOW CHILDREN AT PLAY, which I always misread, forgetting to pause between the first two words. The other was supposed to say WELCOME TO CONGO, but vandals had been at it, smashing it to pieces, turning the salutation into a collection of plastic shards in the weeds. The sign had essentially become a window framing the dry leaves of the forest behind it. All that remained, hanging precariously to the frame, were the last two letters: GO. The temptation was to obey.

Alongside the Congo Community Church was a modest house, better maintained than most on the hill, complemented by a modest garden. Alongside the modest house, paying due attention to the modest garden, I spied a modest man in a white tank top, bluejeans and sneakers. He wore a neat, white beard and an Ohio State Buckeyes cap. Jack Jones was his name, and he proved to be an affable antidote to uninviting Congo.

Jack had been born in that house seventy-two years earlier, had shared it with his parents and five siblings, sleeping three to a bed. His widowed older sister, Maxine, lives there now, surviving on about $1,000 a month from Social Security and a small pension. A tiny woman, too small for her skin, she padded out to her front stoop in slippers.

"She can't see very good," Jack said.

"I can't see anymore," echoed Maxine, her voice unexpectedly loud in relation to her size. Nevertheless, she padded back into the house and returned a couple of minutes later holding a fistful of old photographs. The septuagenarian siblings and I sat on plastic lawn chairs beneath a cacophony of wind chimes and a pageant of hummingbirds, as they shared with me their illustrated history of Congo.

Maxine squinted at a photograph and then offered a toothless grin. "That's our older brother," she said, "with our pet coon."

She handed me another photo, this one of the fourth through sixth grades at Congo School, which was now just a collection of rotting wood and furnaces in the woods just up the hill. The photo was from 1935. Some three dozen dusty-faced children posed stiffly with one adult, a male teacher wearing a tie, glasses and a self-consciously serious expression. Maxine, seventy years younger, was in the middle of the second row.

"Brings to mind *The Grapes of Wrath*, doesn't it?" Jack commented.

Maxine howled with delight. "I'll tell ya, to me there was no place like it. We all got along good. We all played together. We fought together. If someone beat up on him," she said, pointing to her little brother, "I'd go down the road and beat up on them."

Jack shrugged. "Nobody had a lot of money, but—"

"But we had a garden every year," interrupted Maxine, "and we canned everything. That's how you got to eat."

"We're in the process of cannin' peaches today," Jack nodded.

"Yeah, we're gonna can peaches." His sister smiled. "We used to live on relief. They call it food stamps now. We used to walk clear to Corning. . . ."

"Three miles up and three miles back," Jack expounded.

"To get our food supplies—grapefruit and flour and sugar and cabbage and stuff."

Somebody made a fortune off the Little Cities of Black Diamonds. The coal barons. The railroad companies. But certainly not the miners themselves. John Jones, their father, worked all his life in the coal mine, getting up early, journeying toward the center of the earth, then returning home in the late afternoon and soaking his blackened body before sitting down for a well-earned but barely afforded supper. He dug for buried sunshine day after day, right up to the day he dropped dead from a heart attack at age fifty-five. Jack was just fifteen at the time. A couple of years later, he graduated high school and went right to work in the mine.

"But not for very long. I had all I wanted out of it," he admitted. "Really, all I wanted to do was get away from here and get a job. But I made eighteen dollars and twenty-five cents a day at the mine back in fifty-one, which was real good money. Real good. Then I was in the army for two years, in Korea for thirteen months. After that, I worked in a chemical factory, at a brickyard, a tile plant, a machine shop, a liquor store. I worked on the railroad. I sold Amway products. . . ."

Maxine pulled out another photo, a posed shot of the Congo Buckeyes, the local baseball nine, including a young Jack Jones in the back row. Baseball was a significant part of Congo's culture. In fact, probably the town's most famous native is a fellow named John Churry, who spent parts of four seasons as a third-string catcher for the Chicago Cubs in the 1920s, appearing in a grand total of twelve big league games.

There was once a ball field in Congo, although the terrain in the land of Black Diamonds made it tough to find an area large enough and flat enough for a baseball diamond. The only suitable space included a dramatic slope in the outfield. It was said that a ball hit to deep right field would take the fielder down the hill and practically out of sight. "You could just barely see his head," recalled Jack, whose baseball career was much like the course of his working career. He was a utility player, used wherever he was needed. "Mostly I was a catcher," he said, "because everybody was afraid to catch."

I shouldn't have been surprised at Congo's affinity for the national pastime. The Stars and Stripes were flying everywhere on White Hill, rising from weedy lawns, hanging off leaning porches, an affecting blend of patriotism and poverty. The memory of September 11th was still fresh in the minds of people for whom the Pentagon and Wall Street were distant monoliths of no direct influence on their hardscrabble lives.

"I was in the house, in my bed, watchin' the seven o'clock news, and I saw it," Maxine recalled. "I almost passed out. I said, 'Oh, my God no!'" She shook her head in disbelief. "And all them people in there it fell upon . . ."

"I was at home, and my son called me," said Jack. "He said they're tearin' the hell out of New York City, runnin' planes into buildings and all. So I turned it on. It made me sick. It just made me sick."

"I got cold chills all over me," added Maxine, still shaking her head. "I said, 'Oh, my God! Them poor people!' And it's gonna happen again. If we don't go over there, they're comin' over here again."

JACK AND MAXINE

All the same, I couldn't help but wonder whether they felt let down by the America they had experienced. Jack grew up in an impoverished and largely overlooked part of the country, watched his overworked father die before his time, hopped from job to job in a region where carving out a living was about as easy as carving out a mountain, and shipped off to Korea for an experience so dreadful that it was the one thing he didn't want to talk about, except to say, "It was a whole different world. It wasn't nice." So I wondered: Had his country given him the equivalent of an empty pay envelope?

Jack wouldn't take the bait. "No. It's what you make of it, you know. It's not my fault I was born here. It's not anybody's fault. I mean, this is where my parents were. My mom always said she didn't know she was poor until the government told her she was."

The Jones family remained in Congo, even after John Jones died and after the mine closed and most of the old families moved away. I was curious as to why they stayed.

"I really don't know." Jack scratched his bearded chin. "I think the people who stay in Appalachia are pretty hard workin'. The people who move in, most of them are on welfare."

"They won't work!" Maxine shouted, nearly jumping out of her slippers. "Welfare takes care of 'em. They just have one baby after another, so the welfare'll keep 'em. And their kids run 'round half naked all the time. It's a shame."

"You see some of the houses down the street here, and you just want to cry." Jack sighed, nodding toward the bottom of the hill. "When you look at the homes and the people livin' in 'em, and you think of what used to be . . ."

Congo used to be something, yes—not necessarily something grand, but something more than a broken-down repository of stunted dreams. However, it isn't dead yet. It hasn't yet gone the way of San Toy and Knockemstiff and Rogue's Hollow. Towns dwindle for many reasons—industrial abandonment, an alteration of transportation routes, natural disaster, the various winds of change. But towns die, completely and irrecoverably, due to a prevailing sense of resignation. It is hard work to save a town that has no business enduring. Rare is the resident who is determined to defy a doomed destiny. In San Toy, when nineteen people remained, all but two voted to forsake the settlement.

But Jack Jones and a few others were doing their part to save Congo. So it was that, at the top of White Hill, not far from the vandalized welcome sign that shouted only GO, was a large banner hung between two trees and offering an opposite message: CONGO HOMECOMING.

Jack was part of an organization that called itself Citizens for Congo: People for the Future. He had come to a leadership position in the group in much the same way he found himself playing catcher for the Congo Buckeyes. "Nobody wanted to be president," he said, "so they elected me."

Every summer, beginning with the town's centennial in 1991, the town has hosted the Congo Homecoming at a tiny community park alongside the fading church, a sort of oasis among the deserted with a small pavilion overlooking a clearing in the woods. In the clearing is a basketball court featuring one net attached to a rim with duct tape. In the center of the concrete court is the word "Congo" painted in red cursive, as if the town were aspiring to a higher station through polished penmanship. Jack and his cohorts raise money for the Congo Homecoming through donations, bake sales, even a $350 grant from Ohio's Hill Country Heritage Area Program. Everyone brings a covered dish to the potluck meal. A band plays country music. The children play games. The adults—former residents and their extended families—pay homage to the Congo they knew and loved.

"Everybody that used to live here comes back," Maxine insisted. The most recent barbecue had occurred a month before my arrival. The theme was a luau, a "Bongo in the Congo," and some 150 people showed up, more than the current population of the community.

"Even people from out of town," said Jack, "they've come to me and said, 'Don't ever stop having this.' That's one of the reasons I accepted the challenge—to try to keep this town from dying, to get people back here. It's a way to preserve the memory of this place."

And this brings the African Congo analogy full circle. As the diamonds find their way around the world and evolve from rough stones into polished jewels, they tend to shed their history. Usually, they leave no clue as to their origins, the struggles that brought them from the darkness of the mines to bright light allowing reflection. It would be a shame if this Black Diamond town suffered the same fate.

LET MY PEOPLE GO

CAIRO, ILLINOIS

*"We's safe, Huck, we's safe! Jump up and crack yo' heels!
Dat's de good ole Cairo at las', I jis knows it!"*
—MARK TWAIN, ADVENTURES OF HUCKLEBERRY FINN

Southern Illinois has long been known as Little Egypt for its geography and its topography. It is situated between two of the nation's great arteries, the Mississippi River to the west and the Ohio River to the east, which flow gradually southward and toward each other, shaping the southern half of the state into a rounded point. Complementing its Nile-like location are scattered burial mounds in the Mississippi Valley, mysterious constructions by a native people who had long ceased to exist by the time the Europeans arrived. Pyramid-like, they suggest an advanced and ancient culture along the great river.

The Little Egypt designation received spiritual support

from the disastrous winters of 1830 and 1831 in Illinois, the so-called Winter of Deep Snow. Snowfall is said to have covered the ground from September to April. The start of the next growing season was delayed until June, then cut short by a killer frost in September, followed by another harsh winter. Settlers in northern Illinois apparently had to rely on corn grown in the state's sixteen southernmost counties, summoning comparisons to the Book of Genesis: "The famine was all over the face of the earth. . . . And all countries came into Egypt for to buy grain. . . ."

My own journey into Little Egypt felt like forty years in the desert. For the past few days, I had been rejuvenated and comforted by another visit with my family outside of Chicago, but nothing saps a renewed spirit like a drive down I-57, a singularly uninspiring road through the heart of the Heartland. Compared to what I had recently experienced—the harmony of the Hudson River Valley, the perfectly pitched New England countryside, the crescendos of Pennsylvania, the adagio of the Bluegrass, the legato roll of western Appalachia—this humdrum highway was one long, flat note.

Since I could find no appropriate soundtrack, I turned to AM radio to talk me through it. As I passed by Kankakee, a folksy preacher counseled: "You get God's love right, and you can get everything else right." Toward Buckley, a smug moralist flapped her gums: "I am very much against young adults dating until after high school. . . ." On the outskirts of Champaign, a halting rookie news reader: "Blood reserves in the Community Blood Services of Urbana are seriously low right now. . . ." By Arcola, a monotone update: "British Prime Minister Tony Blair voiced support for the U.S. policy on Iraq. . . ." Near Mattoon, a giddy football analyst: "Alabama's going to have trouble moving the ball against Oklahoma. . . ." In Effingham, a soothing voice: "People are committed to let the love of God show in their lives. . . ." In Salem, a carefully inflected bit of bad news: "The Dow dropped three hundred thirty-five points today. . . ."

I spent the night in Mount Vernon, one of those Interstate crossroads suffering a neon franchise invasion, and the following morning I pushed deep into Little Egypt, where the names of hamlets further evoked the Middle East here in the Midwest—Dongola, Karnak, Thebes. The southernmost city in the southernmost county, at the tip of Illinois where the muddy brown waters of the Mississippi and the deep blue currents of the Ohio join in one magnificent fluvial encounter, is Cairo, the self-proclaimed capital of Little Egypt. The locals pronounce it to rhyme with "pharaoh."

As in the nation along the Nile, the residue of slavery resonates here, where there is a remarkably mixed legacy. Indeed, the history of Cairo is nearly a microcosm of the ebb and flow of race relations in America over the past two centuries. It is a dichotomous place. Cairo is an Illinois burg, but it is closer to Mississippi than it is to Chicago. It was a Union stronghold during the Civil War, but it is farther south than Richmond, Virginia, the Confederate capital. It was a stop along the Underground Railroad, but also the site of a horrifying lynching. Along the "blues highway" route from the Mississippi Delta to Chicago, this was where the North began. It has been reported that a curtain separating the whites in the front of a northbound bus from the blacks in the back was taken down once the bus reached Cairo. Yet Cairo later became a symbol of entrenched Jim Crowism, experiencing one of the latest and longest-sustained civil rights conflicts in the nation. It still hasn't recovered.

If you remember *Huckleberry Finn,* runaways Huck and Jim planned to head from slaveholding northern Missouri down the Mississippi River to Cairo, where they hoped to take a steamboat up the Ohio River to freedom. But they were forced to continue their arduous journey after they missed the town in the darkness. In Mark Twain's prescient tale, Cairo was lost in the fog.

The first thing one notices upon arriving is the CAIRO sign painted above a gate in a levee at the northern edge of town. This is a city behind walls—a triangular tract of land with levees on three sides, a place so low in elevation and so squeezed between the waterways that all attempts to establish a settlement in the eighteenth century were unsuccessful due to frequent flooding. Permanent settlement finally arrived in 1818, the same year Illinois achieved statehood. A couple of the city's founders were originally from Alexandria, Virginia, and they may have enjoyed the notion of continuing the Egyptian theme when naming the town between the rivers. Two years later, twenty slaves helped to erect Cairo's first buildings.

There were dreams of a river metropolis, an urban center expected to surpass St. Louis and Cincinnati, but the city struggled as a port until the railroad arrived. When the Illinois Central was completed through Cairo in 1856, connecting the city to both Chicago (by train) and New Orleans (by way of a steamboat line), expectations grew even higher. In *Life on the Mississippi,* Twain wrote, "Cairo has a heavy railroad and a river trade, and her situation at the junction of the two great rivers is so advantageous that she cannot well help prospering." And for a time, she did. In 1859, Cairo became the seat of Alexander County.

Then came the Civil War, and Cairo became one of the most important pieces of real estate in the country. By June 1861, there were twelve thousand Union soldiers in and around Cairo, which had been quickly identified as an ideal location from which to wage a war. General Ulysses Grant was headquartered here. Soldiers and equipment arrived by railroad and then headed downriver to split the Confederacy. Cairo became an enormous military encampment with a huge parade grounds surrounded by barracks and protected by Fort Defiance. *The New York Times* referred to the city as "the Gibraltar of the West."

The war transformed Cairo. When it began, the city counted 2,200 residents, just 55 of them black. But over the next few years, the Union relocated large numbers of freed slaves to Cairo, skirting the technicalities of the Fugitive Slave Act by calling them contraband of war. These former captives formed the basis for a significant element of the city's population into the twentieth century, as the growing black segment was fed by a steady migration from the South.

The 1920 U.S. Census recorded more than fifteen thousand residents of Cairo, but its population may have peaked between censuses—at around twenty-one thousand in 1927, just before the onset of the Depression reduced the numbers considerably. This seems to have been when Cairo reached its tipping point, when its future hung in the balance. Either it was going to continue to grow into a shining success story along the river or it was going to lose momentum and begin a gradual fade into semiobscurity.

A city's fate is at the mercy of both chance and a Darwinian formula of economic trends and societal shifts. It seems like Cairo should have ranked among the survivors. Its location

was a challenge, but also a unique opportunity. It was a transportation hub. It wasn't within a hundred miles of a bona fide
metropolis. It offered historical cachet, strategic possibilities,
even an evocative name. But, generally speaking, Cairo harbored too little foresight and too much prejudice.

Many residents of Little Egypt had gone south to fight for
the Confederacy. Williamson County, north of Cairo, had
even attempted to secede from the Union. Here, in the lower
Land of Lincoln, southern sentiment lingered for decades like
driftwood in a Mississippi eddy. In Cairo, the city's expanding
black population brought increased racial polarization. When
it became evident that the river-based economy was fading, indicating a need to develop an industrial base beyond the river-
front, a proposal was made to expand the city's boundaries by
incorporating a mostly black settlement called Future City,
just to the north of Cairo. The proposal failed, largely because
city officials were wary of significantly increasing the number
of black voters. Surrounded on all sides by floodwalls, Cairo
developed a fortress mentality, and it rotted from within.

Cairo's first day of infamy occurred on November 11, 1909,
when William James, a middle-aged black man, was lynched
for allegedly slaying a white woman. A mob traveled some
thirty miles north to the town of Belknap, apprehended James
and returned him to Cairo for a grisly public execution. Still
not satisfied, the mob then broke into the county jail and
dragged a white alleged murderer, Henry Salzner, out of his
cell. They strung him up from a telephone poll. The behavior
was explained away by a Reverend George Babcock of the
Church of the Redeemer in Cairo as "necessary for the inflic-
tion of justice."

Justice, of course, is what Cairo's African-American residents were seeking, and over the years the black community took baby steps toward that goal. Many of the earliest protests were led by a relentless local schoolteacher named Hattie Kendrick. In the 1940s, she sued over pay inequities between black and white teachers in the city's segregated schools. None other than Thurgood Marshall, then chief counsel of the NAACP, successfully argued the case. Years later, when Marshall was sitting on the U.S. Supreme Court and another case involving the city's racial practices appeared before him, he reportedly said, "This is from Cairo, Illinois. I know all about that place. . . ." In the 1950s, Kendrick was a plaintiff in several other local civil rights cases, including a push for school integration. And in the early 1960s, student-led demonstrations led to the integration of several restaurants and theaters.

But Cairo's African-American community still found themselves without representation in city government and without recourse in response to discrimination. A seminal event—indeed, a symbol of Cairo's self-destruction—occurred in 1963, when the city chose to prevent the integration of a swimming pool in the heart of town by filling it with concrete.

The city's black citizens seethed with resentment, which finally boiled over on July 15, 1967, when Robert L. Hunt, Jr., a 19-year-old black soldier visiting relatives, died while in police custody. After being detained for reportedly driving without an operational headlight, which evolved into charges of resisting arrest, he was reportedly found hanged by his T-shirt in his jail cell. The death was labeled a suicide, but when a black mortician took one look at the body, he placed a 2:30 A.M. phone call to a fellow named Preston Ewing, Jr., a twenty-two-year-old, fresh out of the University of Illinois, who had only recently taken over for Kendrick as president of the local chapter of the NAACP. Thirty-five years later, I called on him again.

Walt Whitman once wrote, "A great city is that which has the greatest men and women. If it be a few ragged huts it is still the greatest city in the whole world." I located Preston Ewing in a one-story brown brick edifice that houses both Cairo's police department and the city's municipal offices. I found him chatting with his friend the mayor, who is white. Three decades ago, he represented an unwelcome disruption of the status quo in Cairo, an agent of "outside agitators" fanning the flames of racial discontent, despite having been born and raised there. He was jailed for marching in protest without a permit, thrown in the same cell where Robert Hunt drew his last breath. Today, Preston Ewing is the city treasurer.

More than that, he seemed to be something of a city patriarch, an everybody-knows-his-name sort of fixture, not so much helping to govern the city as helping to guide it. "I'm treasurer of the city, but the town is small. It doesn't take long to count the money," he chuckled. "So I do all these other things." This was evident in the waves and greetings thrown his way, by mostly white patrons, as we sat for lunch in a diner along Washington Avenue, the main thoroughfare. It was the kind of place in which we might have been met by cold stares four decades earlier. I sensed that this affable, straight-backed black man was a 57-year-old symbol of how a 185-year-old community had embraced a new public face.

Preston's father was from Cotton Plant, Arkansas. His mother was born in Moscow, Tennessee. Hearing there were jobs in Cairo, they arrived there during the Depression, just as the city began its precipitous decline. Preston Ewing, Sr.

wound up driving a mail truck, but he wasn't allowed to use the post office's restroom. Later, he became a Pullman porter, traveling from coast to coast. But Cairo remained his home.

Preston Ewing, Jr. grew up before segregated public housing was even introduced in the city. He still lives on the same block, although he now owns two houses adjacent to one another. It was an integrated block in a town with segregated institutions. The kids might play sandlot baseball together. But the whites went to this school, and the blacks went to that school, and their teams would never meet on the field for official competition. If the white kids had a swimming pool, the black kids had the Ohio River. The whites stayed on one side of St. Mary's Park; the blacks kept to the other. Preston doesn't particularly recall chafing from the shackles of segregation. That was just the way it was in Cairo.

"Living in a small town, there's really nothing new once you've grown accustomed to it," he said between sips of iced tea. "I can remember going to the all-black movie theater, the Opera House, the first movie theater I ever went to. Then later, when I got a girlfriend, we went to the Lincoln Theater, which was also a black theater. Then when they closed the Lincoln down, we went to the Gem Theater. The blacks had to sit up in the balcony. And I always wondered then: Why do they give us the best seats?"

It was a memory indicative of what emerged as a glass-half-full personality, a man more focused on a city's possibilities than its decline. Perhaps that is why, just a few months out of college, he accepted the position with the NAACP, having been specifically chosen by Hattie Kendrick to replace her. The challenge was obvious. In fact, in 1966, when Kendrick testified before the Illinois State Advisory Committee to the

U.S. Commission on Civil Rights, she was asked if she had heard of the Civil Rights Act of 1964. She replied, "I've heard of it, but it hasn't gotten here yet."

Like his father once did on the Pullman cars, Preston often traveled the country, only his mission was to assure that blacks were receiving equal opportunities in recently desegregated schools. But the real conflict exploded in his own backyard with the death of Robert Hunt in the county jail, followed by Preston's middle-of-the-night trip to the morgue. Sitting across from me at the diner, he stared down at his plate and recalled the agony of the moment: "When I saw all those marks on his body, I realized that even if he did hang himself, he sure took a hell of a beating before he did it."

Of course, the hanging itself was in doubt. When Preston was placed in that same jail cell a couple of years later, he found that its wire mesh ceiling was too malleable to support the weight of a man. And Hunt's T-shirt, the one he supposedly used to hang himself, showed no signs of having been stretched at all. Cairo had found a martyr. Four days of riots, leading to a call for the Illinois National Guard to restore order, were only the beginning. Said Preston, "It jump-started what we call the last civil rights movement in America."

We climbed into Preston's red Chevrolet Caprice Classic and embarked on a tour of Cairo, then and now. "The whites here, they watched TV. They knew there were civil rights movements in the South, and they thought it had bypassed them," he explained. "So their initial reaction was: Wait a minute. This can't be happening here."

They responded by organizing a White Citizens Council, dedicated to preserving the status quo. As a counter to that, the

United Front, a coalition of black organizations and white supporters, was formed and headquartered at St. Columba Church on Fourteenth Street. The United Front Church, as it was called, was a place of numinous resistance. In July 1969, a United Front delegation traveled north to Springfield to petition the governor for help. They were refused admittance to his office, and dozens were arrested, some of them spending weeks in jail. Later, the United Front Choir even put out an album of civil rights songs called *On the Battlefield in Cairo, Illinois*. The cover of the album featured a gun and a Bible. "The gun was for your sure-enough protection," said one member. "The Bible was for your direction."

There are some thirty churches in Cairo, and while the United Front Church no longer exists, the Cairo Baptist Church does. As Preston drove me past it, we discussed its pastor, Reverend Larry Potts. In January 1968, he clubbed to death a seventy-three-year-old black man whom he accused of attempting to rape his wife. He was cleared by a coroner's jury, and no trial was ever held. Later that year, in response to a federal mandate forcing Cairo's schools to desegregate, Potts led the formation of an all-white private school that he called Camelot. Potts and his colleagues claimed the school didn't discriminate against African-American students, just that none had ever applied.

Potts, now in his seventies, still preaches. "He invites black folks to his church now," said my tour guide. "He does what he believes to be politically correct."

"Has he had a change of heart?"

Preston pondered the possibility for half a second. "No. I don't think so. I think it's an adaptive thing. Nobody wants to be known as a racist now."

It was like that everywhere Preston took me. He showed me present-day Cairo; I saw stories from its past. We passed a baseball field toward the northern end of town, and I reflected on the city's decision to avoid integration of the ballpark by discontinuing its Little League program. We toured Riverlore, an eleven-room, magnolia-fringed mansion built by a riverboat captain in 1865—and purchased by the city for only $240,000 in 1999 with an eye toward turning it into a B&B—and all I could think of was how it was an historic monument to anticipation, an unfulfilled expectation of prosperity just around the corner.

Preston pointed out the McBride Projects, formerly all-black public housing known as the Pyramid Courts, and I heard the echoes of gunshots. More than 150 nights of shooting incidents were reported between 1967 and 1973, mostly between the obdurate whites and the black residents of the projects. There are stories of children sleeping on floors or in bathtubs to stay out of the line of fire. Nobody was killed—it was essentially psychological warfare—but it continued for years. Indeed, *The New York Times* observed in 1973, "Probably no other American locality in recent years has lived through such persistent, systematic, stubborn racial violence as this tiny city at the southern tip of Illinois. . . . While the major battlefields of the sixties—Watts, Detroit, Newark—have regained a measure of equilibrium, Cairo's shooting spree goes on and on."

Still, the protests in Cairo had an admirable insolence about them. Maybe it was the lateness of the civil rights hour. When men in sheets burned a cross at the Pyramid Courts, protesters responded by marching through town carrying signs: THE HELL WITH A BURNING CROSS. They carried the scorched

cross through town, too. In August 1970, the American Nazi
Party marched in Cairo in support of local white residents. A
few months later, every black police officer in the city resigned.

The centerpiece of protest was a boycott of downtown
white businesses that refused to hire black workers. The me-
dian annual income in Alexander County at the time was
less than $3,000 for black families, but the African-American
community had grown to nearly 40 percent of Cairo's population, and spending power can have a cumulative impact.
So the blacks stopped shopping locally, organizing a "Freedom Ride" cab to take people back and forth to the stores
outside of town. The boycott began in April 1969. It lasted
for several years.

ABANDONED CAIRO

Cairo's white business owners essentially opted to let the town die rather than acquiesce to the march of enlightenment. By late 1971, there was hardly anything left for the black community to picket. Seventeen establishments went out of business. As one protester later reflected, "It accomplished a goal—but a victory, no. Because everybody loses in a situation like that."

Preston turned his Caprice onto Commercial Street, once the heart of the business district, and it seemed like we had ventured into a ghost town. For several blocks, almost every building, some of them four stories high, stood in a state of depressing decay. Doors were boarded up, mailboxes were rusted shut, display windows were cracked and revealed only fallen plaster and cobwebs. Faded lettering on walls and marquees hinted at former glory. In a desperate attempt to resuscitate the area, the city has been leasing storefronts for $1 a year. But still there had been few takers. Commercial Street was dead.

Despite the oppressive heat, the intersection of Commercial and Eighth Street sent a cold shiver down my spine. There was once an impressive piece of architecture called Hustler's Arch here, a prominent Cairo landmark from which banners were hung during holidays and fairs. This was the site of that lynching so many years earlier. In those days, such atrocities were often captured in photographs, which were turned into macabre postcards that locals would mail to friends and family as if bragging about the town's new fire truck. There is such a series depicting the ghastly demise of Will James. The rope broke before he died, at which point his body was riddled with bullets, dragged for a mile to the alleged scene of the crime and then burned in the presence of thousands of spectators. The last postcard shows James's charred head on a stake. But nearly a century later, Hustler's Arch was gone, along with most signs of life, save a handful of pigeons cooing on a rusted rooftop. It seemed to be some sort of cosmic comeuppance.

Commercial Street was only a more salient example of a feature throughout twenty-first-century Cairo—evidence of a city in atrophy. Every other house on every other block seemed to be abandoned. Windows were boarded tight or missing completely, like eyes gouged out. Large brick buildings—churches, schools, warehouses—withered from nonuse. What was once a hospital was now a collection of broken windows, scattered graffiti and vines growing up the walls and into the open wounds.

Cairo was like the Tom Hanks character in *Big*, who suddenly becomes twelve years old again while still wearing a grown man's suit. But it wasn't a result of neglect as much as numbers—the city's infrastructure remained while its inhabitants did not. By 1970, Cairo's population had plummeted to 9,348, with 39 percent of the residents African-American. Over the next few censuses, the city's population dropped to 8,277 in 1970, then 5,931 in 1980, then 4,846 in 1990. The last census, in 2000, counted just 3,632 folks in Cairo. Nearly two-thirds of the population is black. It had been a mass white exodus from the capital of Little Egypt.

There are nearly the same number of buildings standing, the same amount of grass to mow, the same mileage of sewer lines, but fewer than one-fifth the population of eight decades ago. It has become a governmental challenge to simply maintain the community. "I tell people, Don't think of restoring this town to what it used to be. Think of stabilizing it, preserving what you've got. Hold on to the population," said Preston. "You can't stop decline until you stabilize."

There is potential, as yet woefully unfulfilled, for Cairo to regain its footing, to fashion a future by trumpeting its history. We headed a few hundred feet west on Sixth Street, and Preston pointed out what looked like brick caves tunneled into the base of Ohio Street, along the river levee. Only a few years earlier, when the city was putting in new sidewalks, the workers noticed that the broken concrete would go into free fall. They had happened upon storage chambers, built by the Illinois Central but used by the Underground Railroad to hide slaves before secreting them aboard northbound trains. Preston hopes to locate enough money to turn the site into a park someday, but for now the crumbling vaults just sit there like a half-excavated pharaoh's tomb.

Preston's dream park would encompass yet another place of obvious historical significance, the site where Ulysses Grant set up his wartime headquarters. But the building was torn down in 1967. "This was a southern town," Preston shrugged. "Even though he had his headquarters here and was one of the lead generals of the Civil War and became president, you find me something here with Grant's name on it. Grant was a Republican, and these were southern Democrats." Today, the site of U. S. Grant's war room is now a bar and grill overlooking the Ohio River.

Between the Underground Railroad vaults and the river lies the floodwall, and on it a faded sign, obviously decades old: WELCOME TO HISTORICAL CAIRO: GATEWAY TO THE SOUTH. Below the sign, I spotted a plaque boasting how at one time the flags of every nation of the world flew atop Cairo's levee wall. Nearly two hundred flagpoles protruded from the top of the wall like metal beard stubble, but not a single flag. "When I became treasurer, the city was going through money problems," said Preston. "So I had that discontinued. It was an expensive project."

One Cairo icon still standing, at the northern part of Commercial Street, is a nondescript low-slung building known as the Cavalier Club. Started in 1935 and still operational, it has long been a popular stop along the blues highway. The blues are essentially struggles put to song, and a number of blues legends were either born, raised or seasoned in Cairo—Pinetop Perkins, Robert Nighthawk, George "Harmonica" Smith. In fact, a recently released collection of recordings by Henry Townsend, made between 1969–74, is called *Cairo Blues*. It isn't the only notable example of Cairo's battles expressed lyrically. One of the era's more notable civil rights songs, "If You Miss Me from the Back of the Bus," added a verse on the heels of Cairo's confrontations: *If you miss me in the Mississippi River . . . and you can't find me nowhere . . . come on down to the city pool. . . . I'll be swimming in there. . . .*

Preston drove me to the corner of Twenty-fourth and Sycamore, where the municipal pool used to be. Cairo, short on funds, hasn't built a new one. The nearest place to swim is about eight miles away, and the city runs buses two or three days a week from the public housing to Charleston, Missouri. The site, once such a profound symbol of Cairo's racial divide, was now a concrete slab beneath a do-it-yourself car wash, owned by a fellow who used to march with Preston as a young kid. We parked the car, and I snapped a photo of Preston, standing in what once might have been the deep end.

"Well," he said, a slight grin creasing his face, "I finally made it into the swimming pool."

The street protests in Cairo largely came to an end in 1973, but the battles continued to be waged in the courts of law. One of the most significant moments came in 1980, when the federal courts ordered a change in Cairo's government from at-large representation to a ward system, ensuring the election of black representatives. Two black aldermen were elected later that year, the first in nearly seven decades. There are now African-Americans on juries, on the housing authority, in the police commissioner's office and running the school system. There has never been a black mayor in Cairo, but Preston suggested the next election just might result in the first.

"Of course, there are still people with racist attitudes," Preston mused, "but they don't express them openly. I'm sure white people get together and use certain words and talk about how things have changed. But you don't hear it coming from the government anymore."

The last serious potential race conflict occurred in 1991,

PRESTON EWING, JR.

when an unarmed black man was shot more than a dozen times by a white Cairo police officer. It evoked flashbacks of 1967, to the nineteen-year-old soldier whose death sparked a transformational uprising. This time, however, the police officer was quickly convicted of murder.

Before the end of our tour, Preston made a stop at his house—or actually, his houses. This is a place where homes cost little more than a moderately fancy car. Preston lives in one house and works in another next door, a commute I can appreciate. As he spent a few minutes looking for an old edition of the *Yale Law Journal*, which referenced how his father had been banned from using the post office restroom, I examined the items he had chosen to hang on his wall—a photograph of his three daughters in Chicago (an accountant, an attorney and a doctor), a 1968 Civil Liberties Award, a 1998 Citizen of the Year award from the National Association of Social Workers. In a bookcase were dozens of thick binders. They had titles like "Failed Lynch Attempts—1910" and "Sit-ins of 1962." These were the collected research of a man convinced that what comes next depends on an understanding of what came before.

During the peak of the civil rights struggles, he had been as much a recorder of events as a participant. An avid photographer, he published a page in the newspaper every Friday consisting mostly of photos and informational captions about the various incidents and confrontations in Cairo. Ironically, the newspaper was based in East St. Louis, more than one hundred miles away. It was his only option. "If you went and looked at microfilm of the Cairo paper, you'd think no civil rights movement took place there. You can't find it. So we had to get the word out," he said. Even then some 1,200 copies of the *East St. Louis Monitor* were stolen and burned on at least one occasion.

Years later, Preston combined many of those photos with eyewitness interviews and created a book about Cairo's civil rights movement between 1967 and 1973. The title of the book: *Let My People Go*. "I didn't just mean black folks," he insisted. "I meant white folks, too, because they were not free. They were under the burden of maintaining the same practices that had existed before the Civil War. Here we were, in 1967, and they were still under those pressures to maintain the status quo."

But I think that argument, however balanced and generous, lets the racists off the hook too easily. It's the same reason I get an uncomfortable feeling when someone dismisses a grandparent's racism by shrugging, "It's just that generation." Enlightened thought should trump social pressure. Prejudice by default is still prejudice. There were abolitionists in colonial days. There were gentiles who hid Jews in Nazi Germany. And there were plenty of white folks in Cairo who marched on behalf of the black community.

Preston's photographs are simple black-and-whites about blacks and whites and their complicated relationship in an uncertain time—a maid walking her employer's child to school, unsmiling Cairo cops in dark sunglasses, a young black man and his infant son sitting in front of a poster of Malcolm X, a row of white kids on bicycles watching a parade of black picketers, a local fireman flipping the bird to those same picketers. Preston's favorite photograph is of a tired, young black woman holding a stark white sign, and on it in bold lettering is one word: DIGNITY.

"Because that's what it was all about," he said.

His collected histories, clippings and photographs from the city's nearly two-hundred-year civil rights struggle have a future of public display—in the Ewing/Kendrick Museum, a black history museum named after Preston's father and the mother of civil rights in Cairo. The delicious irony is this: The museum bearing his father's name is slated for the second floor of the post office building.

"I played a joke on the people at the post office," said Preston. "I told them there was no statute of limitations, and I was going to sue them for their mistreatment of my father. But I made a deal with them that if they let me use the restroom, I would consider myself made whole again." He allowed a deep, mellow laugh, the kind of chuckle that accompanies overdue justice.

We finally returned to the municipal offices, but before I bid farewell to the Cairo city treasurer he took me aside, somewhat surreptitiously, and handed me a small cardboard box. "Here, take it. I couldn't believe Cairo never had a flag! So I designed one."

I thanked him profusely, returned to Phileas and opened the box, curious as to what image Preston Ewing chose as a symbol of Cairo, Illinois. It was a steamboat puffing its way downstream—a symbol of progress, however slow—and beneath it was an olive branch.

At the southern end of Cairo, past the houses and the billboards and the levees, is a precarious and oft-flooded stretch of land. The sign says: FORT DEFIANCE PARK: CONFLUENCE OF AMERICA. Here, where once there were cannons, there stands now a two-story tower, the Boatmen's Memorial, dedicated to those who lost their lives on the water. The top floor offers a terrific view of the confluence of the rivers, but I wanted a closer look. I walked past a handful of picnic benches, down a dirt-and-grass path, to a beach of soft mud littered with driftwood and river refuse. Stepping carefully, I made my way to the southernmost square foot of land, the very tip of Illinois, a truly remarkable yet somehow unspectacular spot. It was, after all, just an unmarked patch of mud.

To my left was a bridge spanning the Ohio River and leading into Kentucky. To my right was a bridge over the Mississippi River and into Missouri. The late afternoon sun reflected off the windshields of silhouetted semitrailers as they rumbled across state lines. The merger of the two great rivers suggested two massive freight trains arriving at a crossroads at the same time. By this point, the blue Ohio, having emphatically separated the Midwest from the South, had traveled nearly one thousand miles from Pittsburgh. The muddy brown Mississippi, in the process of cleaving the nation in two, had journeyed nearly the same distance from Minnesota's Lake Itasca.

For about a half-mile or so, the two rivers struggled to merge, commingling in ebbs and flows as if they were a pair of strong hands intertwined. But when two rivers join, no matter how much time and glory both carry in their currents, only one survives. Here, the Mississippi was the stronger, so the brown water won the encounter and continued—different yet the same—along its journey to the sea.

But there was still a long way to go.

SEARCHING FOR KING DAVID

JERUSALEM, ARKANSAS

A good name is rather to be chosen than riches.
— KING SOLOMON

Ever since I moved from the Midwest to the West Coast several years ago, I have been warned consistently by friends and family about the massive earthquake bound to strike my place of residence. They may, indeed, be right. But I rationalize my fate this way: No place in America is safe from natural disaster.

The nation's entire middle section, from Texas to the Dakotas, is tornado territory. The Gulf Coast and Eastern Seaboard are hurricane magnets. Florida is a global thunderstorm capital. Hawaii is a Krakatoa waiting to happen. The valleys of the Ohio and Mississippi Rivers are flood plains. The high desert is an annual tinderbox. The West Coast is wrinkled with fault lines. Below-zero temperatures chill the upper Midwest for weeks at a time. Triple-digit heat stifles the Southwest. Overlay all of the impending doom, and it leaves about four square miles of safety in the fifty states. Unless you live in Nutbush, Tennessee, you may be living on borrowed time.

Such a fatalistic perspective is further emboldened by incongruous calamities—the heat wave that kills dozens in Chicago, the deep freeze in Florida, the tornado that rips through Salt Lake City and, perhaps most famous of all, the earthquake that made the Mississippi River change its course.

I drove forty miles south of Cairo, to New Madrid, Missouri, a quaint town with a population of several thousand on the west bank of the Mississippi. It is a crowded piece of American geography. Missouri, Illinois, Kentucky, Tennessee and Arkansas converge in the vicinity. Founded in 1789 and named after Madrid, Spain, the town was first envisioned as the capital of a Spanish colony. But this attempt to check American expansion never materialized, and New Madrid now calls itself "the Oldest American City West of the Mississippi." It is not, however, the Oldest American City West of the Mississippi in Continuous Existence. Barely two decades after its inception, New Madrid was essentially destroyed.

On December 16, 1811, a massive earthquake rattled the region, followed by another on January 23 and yet another, the biggest yet, on February 6. The three tremors, collectively known as the New Madrid earthquakes, are widely believed to constitute three of the ten most powerful quakes ever in the contiguous United States. Scientists believe that each would have measured more than 8.0 on the Richter scale, had there been a Richter scale in the winter of 1811–12. Nearly a century later, the infamous San Francisco earthquake of 1906 would affect an area of sixty thousand square miles. But the seismic event around New Madrid disturbed more than one million square miles. It was reported that chimneys toppled in Cincinnati. Log cabins collapsed in St. Louis. Chandeliers rattled in Washington, D.C. Store shelves shook on Long Island. Church bells sounded in Boston. The waters danced on the Great Lakes. Clocks stopped in Charleston, South Carolina.

Closer to the epicenter, which was just southwest of New Madrid along the St. Francis River in Arkansas, the destruction was remarkable. Because the quake was concentrated in a sparsely populated region, the loss of life was minimal. But five towns in three states basically disappeared. Stories emerged of forests falling like pixie sticks over an area of 150,000 acres and fish flopping in the mud of streams suddenly run dry. The whole midsection of the Mississippi River writhed and heaved, submerging many boats and washing others ashore. Bridges collapsed. Bluffs tumbled into the water. Whole islands vanished. Apparently, the Mississippi riverbed rose high enough to cause the river to temporarily flow backward for hundreds of miles. Near the Kentucky-Tennessee border, a few miles from the river, an enormous tract of land sank like a giant footprint and was filled with gushing waters. Ninety-square-mile Reelfoot Lake was created in a matter of minutes.

Consider, too, that this came at a time when there was a tremendous void in the understanding of earthquakes. To a great many skittish Americans, the event simply reinforced evangelical religious notions of Judgment Day. In a letter to a friend, one barely literate fellow from Kentucky wrote, "A lot of people thinks that the devil has come here. Some thinks that this is the beginning of the world coming to an end." Ethnologist and explorer Henry Schoolcraft opted for a more poetic analysis: "The rivers they boiled like a pot over coals, and mortals fell prostrate, and prayed for their souls."

In the past two decades, scientists have learned that earthquakes in the central Mississippi Valley are not so unusual. Strong quakes have struck often in the geologic past, and minor tremors occur frequently in the area—some two hundred each year. Scientists estimate a 90 percent probability that another substantial earthquake will strike the region by the middle of the twenty-first century, and this time it would be far more deadly now that the region is home to millions of people. The doomsayers warn that if a quake of such magnitude were to arrive again, it could be the worst natural disaster in U.S. history. If the river were already near flood stage, perhaps a quarter of Arkansas might be inundated. Sixty percent of Memphis would be destroyed. Thousands would die amid some $50 billion in damage.

All of which may explain the Great Non-Event of 1990.

It began when a moderate earthquake (4.5 on the Richter scale) shook southeast Missouri in early autumn. Afterward, somebody discovered that a pseudo-scientist named Iben Browning, who claimed to have predicted the previous year's Loma Prieta ("World Series") earthquake, had forecast an even bigger one for the central Mississippi Valley on December 3. His prediction was vague, his methodology suspect. Nevertheless, fear moved through the region like a seismic wave. The Arkansas State Health Department was put on disaster alert. Residents began stockpiling food and supplies. Sales of earthquake insurance soared. People stayed home from work and slept in tents. Schools closed for as long as a week around the fated date. The media pounced on the possibility, taking over every motel room near New Madrid.

Then December 3 arrived. And nothing happened.

There was, however, one similarity between the earthquake of 1811 and the non-earthquake of 1990: People found religion. Churches posted signs suggesting "the end is near," and attendance reportedly doubled in the weeks leading up to the projected disaster. Of course, this isn't the first time that apocalyptic notions influenced behavior in the vicinity of the Ozarks. Sometimes, it breeds fear; occasionally it feeds hatred.

I steered toward the boot heel of Missouri, the projection in the state's southeast corner that exists because of one man's stubbornness. Every state border and peculiar panhandle tells a tale. The original Mason-Dixon line, dividing Maryland and Pennsylvania, was first drawn to settle a charter dispute between two families, the Calverts and the Penns. The desire to create a buffer zone between squabbling Washington farmers and Montana miners resulted in Idaho's narrow bottleneck. The northern border of Tennessee isn't a straight line, rising slightly at the Tennessee River, because a surveyor miscalculated. And Missouri's boot heel was cobbled together by intransigence. Back when Arkansas was being created in 1836, a plantation owner near the river port of Caruthersville refused to become part of the new state, believing it would damage his commercial ties with St. Louis. So he rallied neighboring towns to his cause, and the Missouri border was extended south some thirty miles to include his backyard.

So it was that I crossed the state line while heading west on Highway 62, even though Arkansas is due south of Missouri. According to a manufactured billboard, I had arrived in THE NATURAL STATE, and indeed everything seemed to be hued in earth tones—the leaves on the trees aging toward autumn, the russet meadows, the sallow fields, the salmon-colored mud, the dirt roads, the mucky creeks, the creeping kudzu, the tall grass, the hay rolls, the stacked lumber, the weather-stained roofs, the rusted roadside mailboxes, the brown herds of cattle and swaybacked chestnut horses. Earthy, too—conveying a down-home informality—were the names of the establishments along my Arkansas journey. J.D.'s Catfish Market. Jill's Hardy Café Fishin' Hole. Scooter Bob's Ozark Country Dining. Cousin Bubba's Creekside Buffet. The state is allergic to pretension.

It happened to be the eve of Rosh Hashanah, the celebration of the Jewish New Year. The fact that I was heading toward Jerusalem via the Ozarks was a piece of irony I could not leave unexplored.

In the mid-twentieth century, northern Arkansas was home to a cockroach named Gerald Smith, described as "the most prominent anti-Semite in America." Smith built a gleaming seven-story statue of Jesus in Eureka Springs, from where he spewed his evangelical, rabble-rousing hate-mongering. He has been called the father of Ozarks tourism, but he was also a key figure in the Christian Identity movement, which views Jews not as the children of God but the seed of Satan.

With its homogeneity and pockets of extreme isolation, the Ozarks provide perfect cover for right-wing hate groups. Mix in fundamentalist churches with apocalyptic teachings. Throw in a dash of resentment kindled by privation, and you have a cultural stew ripe for radical zealots. In fact, the Southern Poverty Law Center estimates that more than thirty anti-Semitic, racist, separatist groups exist in the Ozark Mountains today.

One such group was the Covenant, the Sword and the Arm of the Lord, led by James Ellison, who believed that Jews are financing the training of blacks to take over major American cities. God apparently told Ellison to stay away from metropolises, where there weren't enough righteous people left to spare them. He eventually started a community on a peninsula jutting into Bull Shoals Lake, near the Arkansas-Missouri border. There, they began stashing guns and grenades and poison gas, as well as food and survival gear, believing that society was on the verge of economic and social collapse and that the members of the CSA were destined to rebuild it. Ellison offered a course called "Endtime Overcomer Survival Training School," providing lessons in everything from urban warfare to wilderness survival. A mock village was erected for target practice, featuring pop-up cut-outs of blacks, Jews and law enforcers.

The CSA was responsible for bombing a Jewish Community Center in Indiana and for a church arson in Missouri, but in 1983 the group began to plot a more ambitious scheme—a violent act with a large body count, sure to get the government's attention. Ellison cased the possible target himself, but the CSA was raided by law enforcement before it could carry out its plans. The raid occurred on April 19, 1985. Ten years to the day later, Timothy McVeigh destroyed what the CSA had originally targeted—the federal building in Oklahoma City.

Hate groups with religious pretensions are often populated by people who believe traditional churches have become too secular. But as I rolled toward Jerusalem, I noticed sign after sign indicating that piety and pop culture had merged into a sort of comic sales pitch of salvation. Forget the parables. Bring on the one-liners. A sign at the Cornerstone Church in Bertrand, Missouri, announced, BEAT THE CHRISTMAS RUSH. COME TO CHURCH THIS SUNDAY! In Arkansas, the Christian Church in Levisy Flat declared, WE SET THE SAIL, GOD MAKES

THE WIND. The Antioch Baptist Church in the hamlet of Rushing advised, IT'S HARD TO STUMBLE WHEN ON YOUR KNEES. On the outskirts of Clinton, Arkansas, the First General Baptist Church cautioned, FORBIDDEN FRUITS CREATE MANY JAMS.

Religion is big business, and business is market driven, so it was only a matter of time before local church leaders took to advertising a product that doesn't always sell itself. And anyway, I'll take the folks who market moralizing with a wink and a rim shot over the ones who do it with a sneer and a shotgun.

The last half of my drive through northern Arkansas took me over Strawberry River, the White River and the Little Red River into the thick emerald woodlands of the Ozarks. It was a roller coaster of a ride, the signs shouting things like CROOKED AND STEEP NEXT 20 MILES. The roads, empty of traffic, snaked along forested ridges, higher and higher until the occasional clearing provided a magnificent view of the mountains rising one behind another in thick green waves. Finally, as I descended into the foothills, I spied a roadside barn, not far from the turnoff to Jerusalem. On its roof was painted, graffiti-like, a large yellow cross and a message in blood red and Ozark green: JESUS IS COMING SOON.

Nope. Just me.

I spent the night at a KOA in Morrilton and awoke to a crisp September day washed clean by an overnight downpour. I headed back into the hills, north on Route 95 until I reached a fork in the road that elicited a grin. According to the sign, Jerusalem was to the left. To the right was Cleveland. Veering left, I soon crossed a fog-shrouded bridge over Point Remove Creek. Thereafter a fine layer of mist seemed to trail me into Jerusalem, which arrived eight miles later.

It is difficult to categorize Jerusalem. Its residents are not quite the hill people of the Ozarks, not quite the planter class of the Delta and not quite the lumberjacks stalking the timberland of much of east-central Arkansas. Folks in Jerusalem tend to raise chickens and hogs—and an occasional beauty queen or two. Indeed, probably the hamlet's most famous natives are a couple of identical twins who were crowned Miss Arkansas in succeeding years. Their names, and I couldn't make this up: Leanne and Lynnanne Derryberry.

The few lines about the town in local history books suggest the people submitted at least two possible names for their new settlement—Jerusalem and Wilson. The U.S. Postmaster General went for the more exotic offering, but Jerusalem is basically just a curve in a rarely traveled highway. It used to be far more isolated than it is now. Electricity didn't arrive until after World War II. There weren't paved roads or modern telephone lines in the area until 1960. But it is still a far holler from the beaten path.

A sturdy brick U.S. post office serves the couple hundred residents. JERUSALEM, ARKANSAS 72080, it announced, with the K leaning at a 45-degree angle. Across from it was a locally owned service station, the Circle H. Around the bend, there were a trio of churches of assorted denominations. They surrounded the Jerusalem Volunteer Fire Department with its bright red truck idling in the driveway, well positioned to handle the fire and brimstone nearby. Behind it stood a community center that used to be the Jerusalem school. Several dirt and gravel roads vectored out from the highway, tangents with names like Granny Hollow Road and Razorback Lane, disappearing over hills into the Arkansas outback. Other than that, Jerusalem was just humble homes and humidity.

I stepped into the Circle H, which was a service station in the most useful sense of the word. It was a gas station, where it wasn't uncommon for young men to pull up in thirsty four-wheeled ATVs. It was a small general store, selling everything from bullets to Spam. And it was a restaurant with a handful of tables and a lunch menu offering the four food groups of Arkansas—egg rolls, corndogs, pizza sticks and cheeseburgers.

I must have appeared out of my element as I entered because the woman working the cash register examined me suspiciously.

"Are you lost?"

"No."

"Are you a salesman?"

"No."

"Are you an insurance man?"

"Uh-uh."

"Well, what are you?"

"I'm a writer."

"Haven't heard that one before."

She rang up a customer and explained, "I get a lot of people that come in here and kind of look around. They're either wantin' to wait 'til people clear out because they're lost and they don't want anyone knowing or they're looking for the owners and tryin' to sell somethin' we don't need. I've watched the owners' back for four years. And they've watched mine for four years. It's just a habit. I get to see how people can take a razz. You took it real easy. Some people I scare. The UPS man will run if he sees me here. Especially workin' in a small place like this, you know who comes and goes. You know ever'body in the community. Ever'body knows ever'body's business. You can't sneeze around here—"

She was interrupted by an older man wearing the local uniform of overalls and a camouflage cap. He paid for some snack food and told the woman he was in the midst of mowing his lawn.

"When you're done, don't be a stranger. Come and do my lawn!" she grinned

"I don't know where you live," he replied.

"Sure you do. Follow the grass trail. It's so tall I lost a kid in it the other day."

Her name was Sherri. She had been born in California but grew up in, as she put it, "a real small town just two mountains over from here." She was thirty-two and had four kids between the ages of nine and nineteen, two each between her and her husband from previous marriages. We chatted about nothing of significance until I noticed a computer printout that she had been reading between customers. It was an essay a friend had sent her about the September 11th attacks. Contrary to most of the Americans I queried, her most vivid memory of that day was not of the devastation but rather a woman's fear of reprisal.

"I didn't get to work until noon that day. When we got here, everyone was speechless. There were a lot of 'em gathered here, tryin' to sort it out. Is it true? Did it really happen? And there was a very nice little lady that lives down the road. I believe she's from India. I felt so sorry for her because she just stood in here and cried. It shook her up bad. She said, 'What if they're all going to start coming for me?' I said, 'For what? We know you. You're here with us.' "

I asked her if the people around Jerusalem were generally supportive of the U.S. government's gathering war efforts.

She shrugged. "Yes and no. As for me . . ." There was a long pause, as if she was making a philosophical commitment about the war for the first time. "No. What good is it going to do? A lot of people are going to be hurt that didn't have anything to do with it. Somebody's family member is going and not coming back. I don't believe in politicians and Congress and a lot of the horseshit they say. They can say one thing and do another, and that's wrong. It's a holy war. It's not anything to do with a lot of things they're talkin' about. Why can't everyone just get their heads together, get 'em out of their butts. I mean, they know right from wrong. Do it."

This seemed to be a central tenet of Sherri's philosophy. "There are some people who don't know right from wrong," she continued. "They don't know how to treat people, how to treat their family. People don't respect one another. They don't respect their property. But if you teach them when they're young, then you've got the foundation to build on. I'm about simplicity. I want my children to be raised knowin' right from wrong. I don't ever want to hear them lie or steal from anybody. And I want them to understand the value of life. Appreciate what you have. You don't have to have all these material things to make you happy."

And with her Jerusalem sermon concluded, she rang up a bag of ice and some beef jerky. But before I could make it out the door, Sherri offered a parting shot, so to speak. "I'll warn you," she said with a mischievous look in her eyes. "People 'round here aren't afraid to shoot first and ask questions later."

I had given myself a mission in this town. Before embarking on my road trip, I had logged on to the Internet in what I anticipated would be a fruitless attempt to find information about Jerusalem, Arkansas. I scrolled through dozens of irrelevant offerings, paying scant attention to the screen until I came across a couple of lines that stopped me in midsurf. It was a genealogical reference to an Arkansas farmer who died in Jerusalem around the turn of the twentieth century. His name was King David Byers.

As the reader may have noticed, I revel in such coincidences, so I continued my research, locating a message board posting by a woman in Idaho who claimed to be the great-great-granddaughter of the man. She offered me a few factoids and a tale or two about her ancestor, as well as a best-she-could-figure-it family tree. She thought maybe there were still a few of her distant relatives in Conway County, Arkansas, and gave me a few names to try. So several months later, some eight thousand miles into my journey, here I was, in Jerusalem, quite literally searching for a sign of King David.

I started with the post office and a friendly sort there named Harrol Barnes. He knew of a few Byerses in the region, he said, but mostly over in Cleveland, and all of them were African-American. Although I couldn't discount a distant relation, I knew that the man in which I was interested had tried to enlist with the Confederacy during the Civil War. Besides, "King David from Cleveland" just didn't have quite the same ring to it. So there were no more Byerses left in Jerusalem, but I ran my finger down the branches of the family tree, looking for another name that might ring a bell.

"How about Reid?"

"Reid?"

I squinted at my notes. "Darrell Reid."

He smiled. Harrol knew Darrell. He lived a few hundred feet away, across from the Circle H, on Reid Lane, first house on the left. It was that easy.

The Reid house on Reid Lane was a slice of *Sanford & Son*

in the Ozark foothills. The yard around the modest home was littered with toothpaste containers and smashed plastic bottles, carpet sections and stained cartons, long-abandoned work gloves and discarded sandals. A roofed section adjacent to the house had been turned into a junkyard full of old couches, laundry baskets, boxes, tires, cords, filthy cloth rags, even a dated and rusted Marine Corps recruiting sign.

There was a tiny mobile home across the street, not an uncommon sight in Arkansas, where one in seven homes is "manufactured housing." In 2000, Governor Mike Huckabee even made stereotypical headlines by moving into a triple-wide while the governor's mansion was being renovated.

Darrell's wife, Betty, a sixty-six-year-old woman with bleached frizzy blonde hair and red-painted toes, met me at the door and warmly invited me inside, where it was only slightly more orderly. "I collect ever'thin'," she explained, and she wasn't kidding. There were quilts on the walls, on the floor, over much of the furniture. There was a collection of little terrapin shells against one wall, looking like a pile of helmets for an army of monkeys. And there was a gun rack in a corner, filled with enough rifles and shotguns and crossbows to equip such an army.

"This right here is mine," said Betty, showing me a .410 double-barrel shotgun. "I love this little gun, and every one of my grandkids wants it. They want me to will it to 'em when I die. I tell 'em I'm never gonna die. I'm just gonna live forever."

She pointed to a deer head mounted on a wood-paneled wall behind me. Her grandson Jeremy had killed it with one shot from atop a bluff. "It's an eight-point buck," she marveled. "He drove all around showin' ever'body because it was the biggest deer that had been killed in this area in quite some time. He kept saying, 'I'm a-gittin' it mounted. I'm a-gittin' it mounted.' And here it is."

Yes, there it was, staring at the clutter in the Reid family den, looking somewhat appalled.

Betty and Darrell settled in a couple of Edith-and-Archie chairs in the middle of the den. Darrell, who had just turned seventy, wore a neat beard and a rather impassive expression. He was a bit hard of hearing, as it turns out. "I hear for both of us," Betty explained. She talked for both of them, too.

The long and short of the Reid love story is that it was a long trip to go a short distance. Darrell had spent his early childhood a few miles west in Cleveland. When he was ten, his family moved to the West Coast. When he was thirteen, he moved in with his grandparents in Oklahoma. At sixteen, he returned to

DARRELL AND BETTY REID

California. At nineteen, during the Korean War, he joined the navy, serving on an aircraft carrier that took him throughout the Pacific and a tanker that toured the Mediterranean Sea.

One day, he returned to Conway County to visit an uncle, who happened to be an old friend of Betty Church's family. Yes, Church. In Jerusalem. It gets better. They were introduced and dated for a couple of weeks before Darrell went back aboard ship. He was gone eighteen months, came back through town for a week, then returned to California. He worked three months on a ranch there, then set off again for Arkansas, where he and Betty were married after spending a grand total of three weeks together.

"They said it wouldn't last," Betty declared, "and it may not. But we've been married forty-eight years."

It was only after the wedding that Betty was informed that her great-grandmother had been a Reid, that she and her husband were distant cousins. "I couldn't believe it! I confronted my mother. I said, 'How come you didn't tell me so I wouldn't marry my cousin?' We have never really figured out how much related we are, but it's a long way off."

For more than a decade, Betty and Darrell lived in California, but she couldn't wait to return home. When they moved to Jerusalem, Darrell found a job at a cotton mill, but he didn't like the hours. Then he worked at a Firestone plant, but he was allergic to one of the materials they used. Finally, he snagged a job delivering propane, and he stuck to it for twenty-one years. Now retired, the Reids still go out five or six days a month reading meters for the local electric company.

"It gives us a chance to get out of the house, and I love seeing the country 'round here — in the fall, especially," Betty explained. "We go out together. We don't get a whole lot of time, just the two of us. You wouldn't believe how our house is. There's always somebody here."

It seems Betty collects grandchildren, too. Her four children, each of whom lives no more than a dozen miles away, have given them eight grandchildren and another fourteen step-grandchildren. Three of them were currently living, per their choice, at the four-bedroom Reid house on Reid Lane.

"It's 'cuz she spoils 'em," quipped Darrell, and then he returned to his silence.

I have a stock question I tend to ask many of the folks I encounter, regarding the most exciting thing they can recall happening in their town. It gives them an opportunity to reflect on the years, on their values, on their definition of what thrills. Usually, the question vexes them a bit. There is an awkward pause, often followed by a less-than-thrilling memory. Betty didn't hesitate for a moment.

"We built a new church, the Freewill Baptist Church. We had about thirty thousand dollars in the building fund. The foundation alone cost about seventeen thousand dollars. We thought . . . hmmm . . . we'll never build this church. But we started up with it, and the money started coming in. We started having fund-raisers. We raised a little bit here, a little bit there. People would send us donations. And you know what? We've got about one hundred thousand dollars in that church, and it's all paid for. We had our dedication last December. God blessed us richly."

Which brings us to King David, of course.

I related what I had discovered about him to Darrell and Betty, who knew nothing except that Darrell's grandmother was born a Byers. "There's been a lot of research and background done on the Reid family, but not very much on

KING DAVID'S GRAVE—MAYBE . . .

Grandma Reid's side of the family . . . and I don't know why," Betty mused.

There actually seem to have been three King Davids in the Byers clan. The first was born in 1809 in Ohio and had nine children over a twenty-eight-year-span. His seventh child, who was born in Georgia, was also called King David. Although this fellow didn't slay any Goliaths, he and his biblical namesake had a couple of things in common. For instance, both participated in a bloody civil war and were part of a fighting band of malcontents. King David Byers was fifteen in 1864 when he tried to join the Confederate army, but he was rejected because he was too young. So he signed up with the Union instead. So much for loyalty. Most of his mates in the

Third Tennessee Mounted Infantry Union Volunteers were deserters from the Confederate army.

"Maybe he was just looking for a fight," I told Darrell. "Does that sound like your family?"

Betty answered for him. "Yes. Yes." She chuckled. "There's some rednecks and rebels on his side of the family."

By 1890, the Byers family seems to have settled in the Jerusalem area. King David had a daughter, Emma—Darrell's grandmother—and a son, Noah, who named one of his sons King David, as well. But everyone called him Dave.

"Where did they live in Jerusalem?" I wondered.

Betty thought for a moment. "Over on Mount Zion road, I believe."

This was too much. "So let me get this straight. Your maiden name is Church, and you moved to Jerusalem and married the great-grandson of King David, who appears to have lived on a road called Mount Zion."

"That's about it," said Betty.

I would later search for King David's grave in the Appleton Cemetery, about five miles up the road. Half-hidden among the marked gravestones of various members of the Byers family was a particularly ancient-looking stone etched with an illegible hand-drawn scrawl. Perhaps this was the final resting place of the patriarch himself. I couldn't be sure. I had to settle, instead, for taking a snapshot of his descendants. Darrell and Betty stood shoulder to shoulder, one cradling a rifle, the other holding a shotgun, like some sort of NRA reimagination of *American Gothic*.

After all, who needs a slingshot when you can use a .410 double barrel?

FOREVER MINE

BAGDAD, ARIZONA

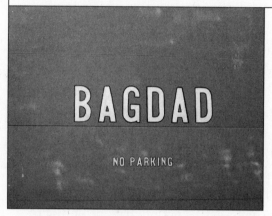

Since the desert does not act, it seems to be waiting—
but waiting for what?
— EDWARD ABBEY

It is a long way from Jerusalem to Bagdad, more than 1,300 miles, most of it along a mind-numbing stretch of pavement known as Interstate 40. I have often joined the chorus of travelers who malign the interstates for their near absolute lack of appeal. Indeed, I would suggest that a ten-mile drive through Vermont is more memorable than a thousand-mile trek across I-40. But I feel it is my duty, as a chronicler of American marvels, to offer the other side of the coin, before tossing it into a tollbooth.

The U.S. interstate system is admittedly a wonder of the modern age. I often imagine the awe with which an early twentieth-century driver would view twenty-first-century interstate traffic, how the first mile-a-minute man, a daredevil in his day, would today be honked at by a little old lady in an Airstreamer for going too slow in the passing lane. One hundred years ago, there were less than two hundred miles of paved roads in America. Today, there are roughly forty-three thousand miles of interstates. This represents just one percent of the nation's highway miles, but superhighways carry nearly one-fourth of America's traffic. In fact, for every route mile on the interstates, there are some sixty thousand daily person miles. Since its inception nearly a half-century ago, more than twenty trillion person miles have been traveled over the interstate system—enough to send one quarter of the U.S. population to the moon, which, come to think of it, isn't a bad idea.

As early as 1939, Franklin Roosevelt had proposed a system of "direct interregional highways," a notion that one of his critics derided as "another ascent into the stratosphere of New Deal jitterbug economics." I don't quite know what that means, but it sounds rather obstinate and ornery. FDR's bigger problem was that reality was no match for imagination. Some observers thought his plan paled in comparison to the popular "Futurama" exhibit at the 1939 New York World's Fair, which fantasized about fourteen-lane superhighways from coast to coast, with vehicles moving at more than a hundred miles per hour and the space between the cars regulated by radio beams. It wasn't until 1956 that Congress green-lighted construction of the interstate system, which was perhaps the largest public works program in history.

Few people remember that the interstates were created almost as much for defense as for transportation, designed to accommodate the speedy movement of military equipment and personnel during the Cold War's nadir. The official name is actually the Dwight D. Eisenhower System of Interstate and Defense Highways. It was said to be Ike's favorite domestic program because, according to his biographer Stephen Ambrose, "More than any single action by the government since the end of the war, this one would change the face of America."

Of course, one might argue that, by expanding mobility and thus employment freedom for rural Americans, the interstates transformed America by killing off certain small towns with character and history, to be replaced by cookie-cutter suburbs and glorified truck stops.

But still, let's give the interstates their due. A 1996 report by public policy consultants to the American Highway Users Alliance contended that the interstates have saved nearly two hundred thousand lives over the years by being by far the safest component of the nation's highway system and have profoundly benefited the economy by reducing freight costs, broadening shoppers' options and increasing retail competition, thus lowering consumer prices. Superhighways, said the report, have "positioned the United States to remain the world's preeminent power into the twenty-first century."

On the other hand, the ride from the middle of Arkansas to the middle of Arizona was excruciating. The interstates offer only vague impressions of one's surroundings. Towns? You barely get a sense of the states. As I struggled across America— listening to a book on tape about the Bataan Death March—I began to think of the states as a simple succession of colors. Oklahoma was red. The Texas panhandle was a dull green. New Mexico was purplish brown. Arizona was pink and beige. Of course, maybe these were just the dominant colors on the relentlessly repeated billboards touting travel stops and trading posts that always prove far less impressive than the effort at advertising.

Exactly where the interstates have taken us was made most clear to me at my first I-40 campsite, just past El Reno, Oklahoma. It was a KOA Kampground behind a Cherokee Trading Post, whose billboards had shouted "Live Buffalo!" over the course of some fifty miles. Such is the dominant cultural opportunity along Interstate 40—a series of ethnic exaggerations posing as souvenir shops with names like Chief Yellow Horse Trading Post, Ortega's Indian Ruins and Fort Courage. This was once Indian Territory; now it is intermittent Injun Kitsch.

I walked into the gloaming, up a steep hill to a small enclosure behind a chain link fence, which served as a pathetic paddock. There, alongside the smooth hum of interstate travel and the occasional rumble of cross-country transport, surrounded by the neon blaze of a Texaco and a Love's Travel Stop, next to a trading post selling moccasins and arrowheads and a restaurant offering buffalo burgers, was a broad-shouldered bison chewing on a big pile of hay. A roadside mascot in the form of an enormous wooden Indian stared down with a sad and frightened expression. The animal turned to me, and I could read resignation and ridicule in his eyes: "Well done, white man."

At least in Arizona I was able to glimpse one of my favorite things about the wide-open West—the opportunity to witness a freight train in its entirety, beginning to end, all in one eyeful. Sometimes it brings into focus the size of the train, sometimes the enormity of the surroundings. Either way, one feels slight in comparison.

By the time I arrived in forested Flagstaff and turned south on Route 89A through a gauntlet of pines, the sky was a swirl of low stratus clouds, not quite the sun-drenched Arizona morning I expected. I descended, along a series of switchbacks, more than two thousand feet into a steep canyon, past pines clinging to sheer sandstone walls. It was like driving along a groove in the Earth. Finally, I arrived in a valley surrounded by curious pinnacles and promontories, where the tourists swarmed and there wasn't a single parking space to be had.

I have good friends who named their daughter Sedona. Now I know why.

About twenty-five miles later, I began the trek back up, along a sweeping serpentine trail and into the town of Jerome, a hamlet resting on the shoulders and crown of a mountain. In its heyday, Jerome was a hard-living copper-mining town of 15,000 residents, 21 bars and 8 houses of prostitution. Today, many of its 450 inhabitants are artists. No wonder. It calls itself, quite appropriately, "the mile high town with the fifty mile views."

Beyond Jerome, I continued to climb, past 5,500 feet, 6,000 feet, 6,500 feet. I half-anticipated a sign: NEXT EXIT: PEARLY GATES. Instead, there was this: DO NOT STOP FOR HITCHHIKERS. Finally, at 7,023 feet, my descent began into a wide valley and the city of Prescott. After lunch at a delicatessen, I returned to hugging the hips of mountains, from where it became clear that I was also riding the fringe of a rainstorm.

At a poorly marked road, I veered west toward the Arizona wilderness, beneath a gray shroud of a sky. The sign said: BAGDAD 42 MILES. The mile markers counted down. . . . 41 . . . 40 . . . 39 . . . Trees dwindled into scrub brush, and scrub brush into dry grass. This was wide-open ranching country of cattle guards and occasional turnoffs to distant homesteads. Except for a stray cow or two, I was alone. . . . 32 . . . 31 . . . 30 . . . The grass morphed into boulders of all sizes, as if a mountain had exploded into ten thousand pieces, interrupted sporadically by sickly stunted cacti. The ominous sky became a drizzle, and the drizzle became a rain, causing water to gather in slick puddles on the road. . . . 21 . . . 20 . . . 19 . . . The rain became a deluge, punctuated by sharp bolts of lightning. Phileas kicked up thick sprays, his windshield wipers working furiously. . . . 14 . . . 13 . . . 12 . . . As I crossed a swath of mud known as the Santa Maria River, a turkey vulture swooped in front of me and then soared away. I had visions of skidding off the road into a ditch, my body to be picked clean by coyotes in an area thereafter known as Dead Writer's Gulch. . . . 9 . . . 8 . . . 7 . . . I passed the gated entrance to Pike's, an old miners' bar surrounded by ghostly trailers. The gate was down and locked. The wooden sign said, PIKE'S: RUNNING A STRAIGHT BUSINESS ON A CROOKED ROAD. . . . 3 . . . 2 . . . 1 . . . Finally. WELCOME TO BAGDAD, ARIZONA . . . THE BEST COPPER TOWN ANYWHERE.

Before immersing myself in Bagdad, I pursued a brief tangent into absurdity. Bagdad is twenty-two miles from Nothing. Literally. There is a hint of further civilization a half hour away, reached by veering west at a junction four miles before the entrance to town, rising and dipping for eleven miles through desolate hills, then speeding seven miles north on Highway 97 to a settlement that is nothing more than a turnoff featuring a ramshackle service station surrounded by several rotting vehicles.

This is Nothing, population 4.

NOTHING TOWING said the sign. Nearby, there was a scrawled proclamation of sorts, something along the lines of a nihilistic pledge of allegiance: TOWN OF NOTHING, AZ . . . FOUNDED 1977 . . . THE STAUNCH CITIZENS OF NOTHING ARE FULL OF HOPE, FAITH AND BELIEVE IN THE WORK ETHIC. THRU THE YEARS THESE DEDICATED PEOPLE HAD FAITH IN NOTHING, HOPED FOR NOTHING, WORKED AT NOTHING, FOR NOTHING . . .

The self-proclaimed sheriff of Nothing—and he showed me the badge to prove it—was a thin fifty-one-year-old man who looked like a soldier in an army of tramps. He wore a helmetlike cloth hat festooned with vulture feathers and rabbit tails. A red bandanna hung around his neck, as well as a thin stretch of rope fastened to a digital clock, which hung at his waist like an amulet. His beard was scruffy and brown, probably a dark red when it was clean. He called himself Jim Outback.

"It's 'cuz I live out back here," he said, pointing into the wilds beyond the service station. The four inhabitants of Nothing reside on the premises. Buddy and Betty Kenworthy, who live with their stepdaughter in an adjacent trailer, are the owners of the establishment, which basically preys on unfortunate travelers and occasional whimsical tourists. On the other side of Nothing, a couple hundred feet away, an abandoned and graying school bus is home to an ancient fellow named Johnny.

"Here he comes now," said Jim. "He's our town drunk."

Johnny shuffled through the door, toothless and grinning, and mumbled something that sounded like, "Objuster hagger umph."

Jim had been working the Nothing service station for fifteen years and had lived "out back" for slightly longer. "When you

want something done, you call Jim Outback. See, the beginning letters of each name are JOB, so you get the job done."

"What kind of job are we talking about?"

"Anything you gotta do here. All the hard work. Buddy's
had a triple-bypass and three hernia operations. He can't do
nothing. And the girls can't do anything. So Buddy drives, and
I help with the wrecks. We offer a gas station, tire change,
soda, beer, candy, chips, coffee, conversation, jokes. This is
the only place where I can come and do Nothing all day and
get paid for it."

Johnny, hovering over our conversation, interjected, "Og-
gerbitter wobber out baggumha peccup," and began to giggle
uncontrollably.

I motioned to the assortment of dented and rusted hulks littered throughout Nothing, making it look a bit like a post-
apocalyptic drive-in theater. "Where do you find these?"

"They leave 'em on the side of the road," Jim explained.
"Most of 'em are Mexicans. They pack eight or nine or ten
people in a car and then, when it breaks down, they abandon
it. Then another car that's not quite full will come by, and
they'll all cram into that and keep going."

"Yunno what ya kin do," Johnny broke in, suddenly almost
coherent—or maybe I had just learned the language. "If ya
ever wanna live er, git broke down and have 'im tow ya in.
Then refoos to leave."

"Is that what happened to you?"

"Yep. Happeduh me."

"He's been here longer than I have—'bout eighteen years,"
Jim nodded.

"And I bin workin' for Nothing ever since!" Johnny declared.

It was the pun that wouldn't die. The walls were papered with pithy notes from passersby, most enjoying the obvious play on words. There was even one written by Nothing's most famous unexpected visitor, Frank Zappa, whose bus broke down for a couple of hours. "Free," he wrote, "is when you have to pay for Nothing." There were T-shirts for sale with similar turns of phrase: HAPPINESS IS KNOWING NOTHING . . . THANK GOD FOR NOTHING . . . WHEN YOU'VE SEEN NOTHING, YOU'VE SEEN EVERYTHING. Also available were assorted hats, mugs, shot glasses, key chains, postcards and refrigerator magnets. Nothing was its own miniature cottage industry.

The service station's front lot contained a handful of crates bearing half-hearted warnings. BEWARE OF COPPERHEADS, said one. There were pennies inside. BEWARE WHITE BAT, said another, which contained, of course, part of a baseball bat painted white. Behind the crates was a large cage containing about a dozen chirping cockateels and parakeets. I noticed one of them floating facedown in a water dish and pointed it out to Jim.

"Whoops," he winced. "I'll have to tell the boss's wife. . . ."

But Jim is more than just an employee of Nothing. He is old-school Arizona, a throwback, something of an anachronism.

"I'm a prospector, see. It's a gold claim where I'm at. I'm digging tunnels under the ground."

"Have you found much?"

"Oh, yeah," he said, letting his voice trail off cryptically.

A native of Tucson and a former bounty hunter for a bail bondsman, Jim lives in a box canyon two miles back of Nothing, in a little hut constructed out of tarps strung on poles over a Dodge van. He rolls up the sides of his makeshift hut in the heat of summer and warms himself by a fire in a twenty-gallon drum in the dead of winter.

"I came out here to get away from people because of all the stuff that's comin' down. Something's gonna happen, and I'll be out here. And all the city folks won't know how to live out here."

"What are you surrounded by out there?" I wondered.

"Rocks. Cactus. Prickly pears. Everything."

"What about animals?"

"I got javelinas, deer, quail, jackrabbits, squirrels, chipmunks, cats. I got lots of cats. I raise six-toed cats—six toes on each foot."

"Heguttum cats serstuh geridderum rodents," Johnny explained.

JIM OUTBACK IN NOTHING

"I got about thirty-two cats at my place and one dog," Jim continued. "I call 'im Pooperdog. When he was a little baby, he pooped about eight or nine times a day. It never stopped."

It was one of the few occasions along my journey in which I regretted receiving too much information. "So these animals, are they friends or food?"

"Around my camp, they're all friends. If I do need something fast, it's all there, but I don't want to scare off my population. You never hunt your own country. 'Course you never know when you're gonna run into a pack of coyotes or a rattlesnake," he cautioned, patting a .22-caliber rifle that he had rested against a T-shirt display. "But if you run off a rattlesnake, you're passing up a good meal. You skin 'em. You sell their skin and rattler to a tourist. Then you cook the meat in beer batter, from the old beer you didn't drink the night before. Whip it up with a little jalapeño. Then you use the McDonald's sweet-and-sour sauce. . . ."

"You actually make it sound pretty good."

"It is really good. You gotta try it. People say it tastes like chicken. But I say it tastes like rattlesnake."

I noticed that Jim had been watching television when I walked in, one of those asinine made-for-TV courtroom charades in which an arrogant judge makes a snap judgment regarding a trifling matter involving two moronic adversaries. I pointed out that, for all his reclusive tendencies and rattlesnake recipes, Jim certainly wasn't cutting himself off from the rest of the world.

"No, I'm not. I have a TV back there, too," he said, nodding toward his wilderness retreat. "I have a solar panel as big as this countertop, and I run a bank of batteries. I got a little black-and-white and a radio and lights that run on 12 volts. I don't want to be cut off from the world. I gotta be informed."

Jim scratched his cloth-helmeted head. "Last September 11th, I was sittin' there watchin' TV, and I didn't believe what the hell was goin' on. I was pissed. I'm still pissed. And something's gonna come down. There's a movie called *The Day After*. Remember that? Remember what caused it? There were ships in Asian ports, in Asian seas, attacking a man in purple robes. And where are we now? Where are our ships? In his seas. Saddam Hussein's got nuclear capability. And he always likes purple." He shrugged and tried to lasso his thoughts. "But that's the madness in my motive, and the motive in my madness."

"You live pretty darn close to a town named Bagdad, though."

"Right. Well, you gotta have a place to get supplies when things happen," he replied, letting the irony slip by. "I have several friends there who are gonna come out here when something big happens. Don't matter if it's in the dead of summer. They'll bring all their winter gear, petroleum, canned goods, everything they can get, and we're all gonna meet out at my place. We're gonna take the tow truck loaded with diesel tanks, generators and anything else we want. We'll go deep in there, create a little fortress and hide out until it's all done."

He pointed skyward. "See, we've got a military flight pattern that goes right through here. I saw eight big black stealth bombers fly through here one day. That was awesome. At first I thought they were big turkey vultures. But that day, September the 11th, all of a sudden, there was nothing. Days and days and days of nothing. There was no highway work, no nothing. Everybody just shut down. It's the beginning of it, see? That's what happens at the beginning of the movie."

"But that's just fiction. . . ."

"And now it's becoming reality," he insisted, and he puffed out his chest. "I got my bio suit out and my gas mask all ready. I got bandolier ammo belts and thirty-round clips and stuff. See, I'm an ex-Green Beret, too. I did recon into North Vietnam when we pulled out all those POWs. We brought back forty-eight Americans POWs, and we brought back French, German and Italian POWs that had been there over fifteen years. So I'm ready to dance. All I need is for the band to play."

Environmental philosopher Paul Shepard once wrote, "To the desert go prophets and hermits; through deserts go pilgrims and exiles." Jim Outback is one of these, but I'm not sure which one. I hopped onto the highway and headed back into the hills, leaving Nothing behind.

Unlike Nothing, travelers don't just happen upon Bagdad. The residents joke that other towns have *through* traffic, but Bagdad has *to* traffic. The highway into Bagdad continues as Main Street for another mile, past a welded copper sculpture depicting a male and female miner, past a strip mall called Copper Plaza, an American Legion post, a high school and athletic fields, until it dead-ends abruptly at a chain link fence—DO NOT ENTER—at the copper mine.

The town's other principal road, Lindahl Road, runs perpendicular to Main Street, past a fire station, a tiny museum, a nine-hole golf course, a Baptist church and a few miles of brush-covered hills. But eventually, it, too, ends at the copper mine, an immense open pit, measuring one mile across by half a mile wide, carved into giant narrowing concentric circles, each just wide enough to carry a truckload of treasure. Despite its size, the mine is only visible from the upper reaches of Bagdad's hills. It doesn't hover over the town in the manner of, say, a South Dakota grain elevator. But make no mistake, the copper mine is the be all and end all in Bagdad.

There is a copper star on the state flag of Arizona, which has been the nation's leading producer of the mineral since the 1880s. Bagdad's existence dates back to 1882, when a couple of men located the first claims on the banks of Copper Creek. The following year, a fellow named John Lawler bought the claims and named the town, so say the legends, because his brother loved to read tales of the *Arabian Nights*. A less plausible story suggests that a father and son were mining in the area, and the son, chipping high-grade ore, said, "Pass me another bag, Dad." Of course, that would explain the spelling.

There are still Arabian pretensions in Bagdad. Businesses have names like Aladdin Glass. The high school athletic teams call themselves the Sultans and the Lady Sultans. At the junior high school, they are the Sheiks. But the Middle Eastern ties only go so far. "When all that was happening during the Gulf War," one resident admitted, "we always made sure everybody knew our Bagdad was spelled without an *h*."

The Bagdad mine was unique in that it developed from a prospect into a bona fide copper mine without the support of a major company. It was a company town—not entirely unlike the coal-mining hamlet of Congo, Ohio—but nonunion Bagdad prided itself on its family atmosphere. The mine maintained its independence for nearly ninety years before merging with the Cyprus Mines Corporation in 1973. A few years later, Cyprus built houses as permanent residences to replace old frame buildings, all in a Spanish style with red tile roofs and cream stucco walls. There isn't much ornamentation to differentiate one from another—maybe a basketball hoop or a cow skull fastened to a wall. In fact, teenaged girls in Bagdad have been known to flirt with boys from out of town, only to tease, "I live in the white house with the red roof." It is Bagdad's version of giving a fake phone number.

Bagdad's centennial came and went without a hitch. One hundred years is a long life for a company town. In 1984, however, the community almost went the way of the hundreds of other mining settlements that died young or dwindled considerably. Imports were hurting the American copper industry, and copper had fallen to barely sixty cents a pound, far below what U.S. producers claimed was the break-even point. Cyprus-Bagdad laid off 550 workers, nearly the entire force, and shut down mining operations.

One hundred and two years after its inception, there began a mass exodus from Bagdad, reaching such proportions that the Yavapai County Humane Society posted notices begging people not to leave their pets behind. Threatened with the loss of two-thirds of its student body, the school system hinted that it might be forced to shut down at the end of the year. Someone even posted a hand-painted sign on the edge of town: "Last family out please turn off the lights."

But Bagdad survived. Eight months later, the mine reopened for business. The price of copper rebounded. Hundreds of employees were rehired. By 1988, Cyprus-Bagdad was said to be the most profitable of the company's thirty holdings. A few years later, the mine was acquired by the Phelps Dodge Mining Company, the second-largest copper company in the world. The locals grumble about the new rules and regulations and corporate hierarchy, but the trucks still come and go from Bagdad all day, loaded with mineral wealth, and as long as they do, the town endures.

Nevertheless, as I sat in a tiny public library and worked my way through random news clippings, I came to the realization that death hovers over Bagdad like a summer storm cloud. Over the previous decade or so, this isolated hamlet had been associated with more than its share of tragedy. In 1993, a twenty-seven-year-old resident was charged with the shooting death of her husband. That same year, a Bagdad couple was fatally shot by their son while visiting Oregon. Three years later, a local man was charged with second-degree murder after he hit another man with a gun and it discharged, killing a five-year-old girl. At about the same time, a four-year-old daughter of Bagdad natives died when their trailer exploded in Nevada. A few months after that, four people died in a small plane crash on the outskirts of town. In October 2001, a truck driver was fatally injured when his brakes failed as he descended the haul road into the copper mine. And only six months before my arrival, two Bagdad teens lost their lives when their car overturned on the highway. That is a lot of violent death for a town of fewer than two thousand souls.

Supposedly, Bagdad even has a resident weeping ghost, the White Witch, who roams the region in a blood-stained gown, mourning her husband killed in the Spanish-American War. But saddest of all, I think, is the prospect of loss without closure, sacrifice without certainty, like the unfinished narrative of Bagdad's own Dennis Pike.

On March 23, 1972, Lieutenant Commander Pike was flying an A7E Corsair, a state-of-the-art light attack jet, in a mission targeting a section of the Ho Chi Minh Trail in Southern Laos. Just a couple of weeks earlier, the A7E had temporarily been grounded after engine problems forced a pilot to eject and then be fished out of the ocean. But the pilots had agreed to fly them again. After all, they were the World Famous Golden Dragons—some of the best bombers in the navy fleet. Only a couple of years earlier, the squadron had been cited for its safety record during extensive combat, going accident free over the course of fifty-five months. During Dennis Pike's first cruise, from November 1970 to July 1971, the Golden Dragons' "Laotion Highway Patrol" had set another precedent by dropping fifteen million pounds of ordnance without losing a single aircraft.

After successfully completing his mission, Dennis was returning to the USS *Kitty Hawk* when he reported engine vibrations and what he thought was a compressor stall. His wingman, observing smoke swirling from his flight leader's exhaust, instructed him to turn east. "Negative, too many vibrations," was the reply. "I'm going to have to leave it. I'm going to do a shallow drop and head for the water." That was the last anyone heard or saw of him. Moments later, the wingman closed to within half a mile and made several observations that became clues of paramount significance. He reported seeing a cloud of white smoke, tiny particles resembling glittering pieces of canopy and an object tumbling through the air that appeared to be the ejection seat. No parachute was sighted.

Lieutenant Commander Pike had apparently ejected over rugged jungle-covered mountains in an area heavily populated by communist forces. Search and rescue efforts found nothing—no emergency beeper signals, no voice contact, no aircraft wreckage, no sign of the pilot. After three days, the formal search was terminated. Dennis Pike was listed as missing in action. Thirty years later, he can be found only on Panel 2W, Row 119 of the Vietnam Veterans Memorial.

There are no Pikes left in Bagdad. Indeed, the Pike name had only been left behind on Pike's Bar on the outskirts of town, which had been built by Dennis's grandparents during the Depression. Still, I wondered if the memory of Dennis Pike lingered in Bagdad. At a time when soldiers were once again preparing to risk their lives in a controversial war, did the memory of one lost pilot still haunt his hometown?

I made a few phone calls and was directed first to Bagdad High School, to a yard behind the main office, steps away from the football field and its tiny press box bearing the smiling caricature of a Sultan. There stood two trees, both planted in 1973. One was dedicated to a Lieutenant Colonel William Thompson, whose family had resided in Bagdad, although he never had. The plaque by the other tree read: THE FREEDOM TREE: WITH THE VISION OF UNIVERSAL FREEDOM FOR ALL MANKIND, THIS TREE IS DEDICATED TO LT. DENNIS PIKE AND ALL PRISONERS OF WAR AND MISSING IN ACTION.

As I stared at the branches, lost in thought, I was startled by a bell ringing, followed by a student stampede. They chatted and flirted and whooped with adolescent energy, and I wondered if they had ever stopped to consider the profundity of the trees they passed every day. By the time most of them were born, Dennis Pike already had been missing for more than a decade-and-a-half. But he had been about their age, a wide-eyed high school dreamer, when the urge to be a jet pilot took hold.

The school had misplaced its 1958 yearbook. There were two 1957s and two 1959s, but Dennis Pike's senior year was missing. Bagdad is the kind of town, however, where someone always knows someone who knew somebody. So it wasn't difficult to locate one. I found it in the possession of eighty-seven-year-old Jeannette Walters and her daughter, Kathryn, at the Sycamore Mobile Home Park in the hills above Bagdad.

"I feel like there'll be a time when they find out about Dennis," said Jeannette. She had lived in Bagdad since 1936, when it was just a mining camp with tent houses.

Dennis had signed Kathryn's yearbook. "Good Ole Dennis," he wrote, next to his photograph. On page 19, amid the class prophecy predicting where everyone was going to be twenty years later, was this line: "Hey, look at that jet! That could be Dennis. He's a pilot now."

But as I leafed through the small world of Bagdad, circa 1958, I quickly realized that this wasn't only a story about Dennis Pike. It was about Dennis Pike and Lou Ann Roe. There they were, Dennis and Lou Ann, coeditors of the senior class yearbook. And Dennis and Lou Ann posing with the school band—she with her trumpet, he with his trombone. And Dennis and Lou Ann, king and queen of the Halloween Carnival. One yearbook page offered what it called the "Last Will and Testament" of the members of the graduating class. Among the personal trivia—nicknames, pet sayings, ambitions—was a category revealing where each student could usually be found. Dennis's said, "At Lou Ann's." Lou Ann's said, "With Dennis."

"I can remember when he and Lou Ann got married. It was one of the biggest weddings around," a woman named Sharon Gibson told me a while later, as we stood on the porch of Bagdad's community center, along with Sharon's eighty-four-year-old mother, Mabel Clarkson. They share a house in Bagdad, but they come from a family of impatient generations. In just a few months, fifty-eight-year-old Sharon was expecting to become a great-grandmother. Mabel would be a great-great-grandmother.

Mabel—whose maiden name, if you can believe it, is Hussen—has lived in Bagdad since 1945, moving in just two months after Dennis's parents, Stanley and Gladys Pike. Her daughter Sharon was three years younger than Dennis. They knew the Pikes well, and their memories of the family were tinged with both woe and whimsy.

They told me how the two Pike boys always wanted to pilot jets. Jim, the older one, became a navigator in the air force. Dennis wanted to join the air force, too, after serving as ROTC cadet colonel at Arizona State University, but they wouldn't let him fly because he had a form of color blindness. So he accepted an interservice transfer to the navy, which accepted him gladly. Dennis and Lou Ann and their three children eventually found themselves in Lemoore, California, but Dennis made unscheduled appearances in the skies over Bagdad as often as he could.

"When his folks still lived here, he would come real low, and everybody in Bagdad would stand and watch him. He'd zoom right in over the mine," Mabel recalled.

"Yeah, he would buzz us," Sharon sighed, trying to smile. "We knew it was Dennis. He didn't just do it once."

It was apparently well within character for the man everyone affectionately called Dennis the Menace. Saddest of all is the loss of the life of the party.

"Just not long ago, we heard a plane real low over Bagdad," said Mabel, "and I said, 'Oh, my gosh! Is Dennis home?'" She laughed when she said it, but there were tears in her eyes.

Johnnie Wood wept openly when discussing Dennis Pike. She was eighty-seven, and shuffled around with the help of a walker. She had known Lou Ann's family since the days when they lived in Paris, Texas, before they all moved to Bagdad in the 1950s. Nearly a half-century later, home for Johnnie was a tiny single-wide on a modest dusty lot at the mobile home park. We sat on the only two chairs in the cramped quarters, beneath framed pictures of her late husband in his navy uniform and her grandson in air force attire.

"Dennis was a great kid, just the best person," she said, removing her glasses to wipe her eyes. "I remember one time he almost wrecked his motor-sickle in front of Lou Ann's house. . . ." She began to laugh, which turned into a sob, and she couldn't finish the thought. We sat there in silence for a while. Then she handed me a sheet of paper, apparently given to anyone who wears Dennis Pike's MIA bracelet. While I read about his military career—how he flew 163 combat missions on his first cruise, received 16 air strike medals, earned the Distinguished Flying Cross and the Naval Commendation Medal and a Bronze Star—Johnnie fished around in a kitchen drawer for something. She returned and offered me a small POW/MIA sticker bearing Dennis Pike's name and a message in the form of a mission: BRING THEM HOME.

I had discovered quite a bit about Dennis Pike in Bagdad, slowly attaching a human face to the name on the Vietnam memorial. But it wasn't enough. The emotions were enduring and very real, but they were still relatively removed from the tragedy. Communal grief, no matter how small the community, is not personal devastation. It is not nearly the kind of anguish felt by the families so directly touched by the tragedy.

I am not saying Bagdad's citizens didn't grieve. They did, and some still do. But their lives weren't dramatically changed by the events of March 23, 1972. Thirty years later, theirs isn't a sorrow that lingers daily. I had learned much about the kind of man Dennis Pike was. I wanted to know what he still is. So

Johnnie Wood handed me one more piece of paper before I left Bagdad. It was Lou Ann Pike's phone number.

A few days later, on my way home through California, I stopped about thirty miles south of Fresno and a few miles east of Lemoore Naval Air Station, at a house with a POW/MIA flag flying from a pole in the front yard, right alongside Old Glory.

"We never should have been in there to begin with," Lou Ann began, as she served me a supper of ham sandwiches and baked beans on plastic patriotic plates left over from the Fourth of July.

I could still see the young queen of the Halloween Carnival in the face of the woman who sat across the table. She was sixty-one now, had never remarried, but had gone back to college to get her teaching credentials after Dennis went missing. She now taught U.S. history to eighth graders, schooling them in the Constitution and devoting an entire wall of her classroom to the POW/MIA issue.

"You get a different kind of history lesson in my class," she said. "I've had kids tell me I must be crazy if I believe my husband is still alive, and I tell them they're crazy if they think he can't be. If you believe in something, you've got to fight for it."

Sometimes, apparently, if you don't believe in something, you still have to fight. I asked Lou Ann—and her eldest daughter, Denise, who had joined us—how Dennis felt about the war in Vietnam.

"He wasn't too keen on it," said Lou Ann. "I don't think he really felt we needed to be there."

"I was only about ten or eleven, but my interpretation is that he didn't feel it was worth fighting. I think he felt: I love my job, but this is the bad part," Denise added in a high, sweet voice that didn't seem to match her appearance, but only made it easier for me to imagine the little girl who lost her father thirty years earlier. Denise had her father's dark hair, and she had inherited his love of flying, too, recently building her own experimental aircraft—an RV6A low-wing two-seater.

"I wanted a faster airplane," she smiled. "Speed is in my blood."

That flying was in Dennis Pike's blood was never in doubt. "It was all he ever wanted to do," said Lou Ann. Well, aside from dating her. "We went out a couple of times, and I wasn't that interested until somebody else got him," she laughed. "Then I had to have him back."

"Typical female," Denise winked.

"His father, Stanley, really liked me," Lou Ann continued. "I played piano at a band concert once, and he turned to Dennis and said, 'You'd better set your eye for that one.' And Dennis said, 'I've already been dating her, Dad.' "

Perhaps that was part of the reason the story of Dennis Pike touched me so deeply. I had met my wife under similar circumstances, amid the maelstrom of high school, and we were somewhat taken aback by the realization that we had lucked into a soulmate before we had mastered the intricacies of parallel parking. We had grown into adulthood together, as two parts of a whole, and we were now about the same age that Dennis and Lou Ann were in March 1972. The possibility of one of us, one part of the whole, being classified as missing was a thought so painful that it was nearly inconceivable. Or maybe, too, it was the fact that my father is just eleven days younger than Dennis Pike, thus I could imagine being in his children's shoes as well.

LOU ANN AND DENISE WITH DENNIS IN THE BACKGROUND

So I saw Dennis Pike through the eyes of the people who knew him best, and he became more than just a name on a memorial, more than just a few photographs in an old high school yearbook. He played guitar in a jazz band. He listened to Waylon Jennings and Johnny Cash. He loved motorcycles and was rather addicted to sunflower seeds. He was the kind of an officer who preferred to socialize with enlisted men. And he may have thought himself somewhat invincible.

"Dennis was personnel officer in the squadron," said Lou Ann. "He made sure that everybody had their life insurance policies up to date, their wills, this and that. But he didn't do that for his own family." She served me a slice of angel food cake. "I don't think he thought he needed it."

Lou Ann hadn't harbored many fears about her husband's safety during his first cruise, but when he returned for his second deployment, she had an uneasy feeling about his fate. They said their good-byes in San Diego. This time, Dennis didn't tell his nine-year-old son, Vince, that he was to take care of the family as the temporary man of the house. Last time around, Vince had taken him literally, telling everyone else what to do. Dennis had been forced to send a tape recording a few weeks later, reminding him that mom was still boss. But this time, the father's last words to his eldest daughter were: "Now, don't you get married before I get home." Denise still hasn't.

One month after he left, on a bright spring morning, a car pulled up to the house, and Lou Ann saw the somber faces of the base commander, the base chaplain and the commanding officer's wife. Your husband is missing in action, they said. At first it seemed preferable to the alternative.

"Your first reaction," I asked, choosing my words carefully. "Was it hope?"

She nodded. "You're thinking they'll find him any time. . . ."

Lou Ann also thought back to a conversation with her husband just after he returned from survival training, having lost about thirteen pounds in one week, his feet covered with blisters and open sores. She told him, "I think I'd rather you be dead than be tortured by the enemy." He replied, "Don't ever say that. My family will keep me going. I'll come back to you guys. You don't have to worry about that."

That first year, Lou Ann answered more than five hundred letters from people who wore an MIA bracelet with Dennis Pike's name on it. Then the weeks became months, and the months became years, and the inquiries grew less frequent as time eroded optimism and "bringing them home" became less of a cause celebre. In 1978, the navy began proceedings to re-examine Dennis Pike's status, but not in a hopeful direction. There was a trial of sorts—family members at one table, a navy representative at another. The family tried to prove he was alive; the navy tried to establish that he wasn't. In the end, his status was changed from missing in action to presumed killed in action, which effectively cut off the salary Lou Ann had been receiving, giving her a widow's compensation instead.

Not long after, there was a knock on the door of the house in which Lou Ann and Dennis had planned to grow old. The family had never really been offered any counseling in the early weeks and months, but here was a counselor from the base, standing on the front stoop, offering to help. "You're six years too late," Lou Ann replied.

Over the years, Lou Ann has substituted action for mourn-ing, enlisting with groups like the National League of POW/MIA families, agreeing to television interviews, joining marches and campouts and various other campaigns for atten-tion. Once a year, she travels to Washington, D.C., for a de-briefing, to find out if there is new information, reports, rumors, anything. For nearly two decades, she was given few hints as to what might have happened on that night over Laos.

Then, in 1990, a retired CIA agent contacted Lou Ann with some startling intelligence. He had been sitting on a mountaintop in Laos in 1972, intercepting radio transmis-sions, tracking the movements of enemy troops. He claimed that a transmission indicated that a Lieutenant Pike had been captured near the Ho Chi Minh Trail. The agent knew when Dennis had been shot down. He knew where they had taken him to fix his broken leg. He had written down the name of the prison camp, the date he had been brought there and the date he had been transported, the agent believed, to Moscow. The man had given the CIA the information years earlier—a report that would have constituted the single most significant piece of knowledge in the lives of a grieving family. The CIA never told them.

A decade later, the navy informed Lou Ann that some Vietnamese military reports had been discovered in Hanoi. The information stated that three planes had been shot down over Laos in 1972—one of them, indeed, in March. A parachute and documents had been recovered. There was no mention of the pilot.

As of this writing, there are some two thousand Americans missing and unaccounted for from the war in Vietnam. Nearly six hundred disappeared in Laos. The Laotians admitted holding "tens of tens" of American prisoners, but negotiations for their release never took place. Meanwhile, as the world moves on, the Pike family continues a search for something, even if it is only personal closure.

"Some years you feel he's alive. Some years you feel he's dead," Denise explained. But about ten years ago, a dream convinced her that the loss of her father was fated and final. "You know when you're not quite asleep, but not quite awake? All of a sudden, I was in the desert at night. It was very beautiful. And he was there in fatigues, my dad was, and he said, 'You know what, I'm fine. Go on with your life. Don't worry about me.'" She fell silent for a moment. "In my heart, I think he's dead."

Lou Ann, however, has had occasional dreams, too, and in hers Dennis comes to the door looking much the same, but with gray hair. She has never held a memorial service for her husband and has never considered remarrying. She still buys him a present for his birthday every July 2, although it is usually something she needs. And every day, she opens the mailbox hopeful that maybe someone might have discovered something regarding the whereabouts of the missing part of her whole.

"I married for better or for worse. But I live in limbo," she said, fingering the MIA bracelet around her wrist. "I'm not a wife, and I'm not a widow."

Of the two trees planted at Bagdad High School, one has sprouted an explosion of maroon leaves. The other, Dennis Pike's tree, stands bare, its branches empty, its trunk leaning precariously. It is dead. But rumor has it that a mysterious man wearing an MIA bracelet has vowed to pay for a new tree, which would be replanted on the site of the old one in the hope that it might bloom once more.

DESERT PILGRIMS

MECCA, CALIFORNIA

Riches are not from abundance of worldly goods,
but from a contented mind.
— MOHAMMED

The Joshua tree grows naturally only in the Mojave Desert, surviving with panache amid the arid wasteland and contorting itself into such goofy shapes that it appears to be almost a caricature of vegetation. Driving through a grove of Joshua trees, as I did along U.S. 93 in west-central Arizona, one feels as if the pages of Dr. Seuss are coming to life. One can imagine a Ruffle-Necked Sala-ma-goox gorging itself on the tree's fleshy fruit, or a Harp-Twanging Snarp peering from behind a cluster of yellow green sepals, or a Biffer-Baum Bird flitting from branch to branch. Mormon pioneers are said to have named this species, otherwise known as *yucca brevifolia*, because its appearance suggested the Old

Testament prophet Joshua with upraised arms, waving them toward the Promised Land. Instead, the trees waved me west on U.S. 60 through a series of desert towns full of brown faces and open spaces and conditions so desperate that milk trucks have been converted into homes. The trees seemed better suited for desert survival.

I crossed the Colorado River along Interstate 10, and I was home again, in a manner of speaking. California greets the weary traveler not with a hearty hello, but with an agricultural inspection station. This always strikes me as either misleading or misguided. Either they are really looking for something else—say, illegal immigrants instead of illicit avocados—or they are wasting everyone's time on forbidden fruit. I could have a trunk full of heroin, biological weapons and the dismembered limbs of the Partridge Family, but God forbid I bring in an unauthorized grapefruit.

It was already late afternoon when the inspector waved me through, so I spent the night just over the border, in Blythe, at a campground on the west bank of the river and only a few hundred feet from the interstate. The following morning, as I continued west, the desert resumed with a vengeance. It was a seventy-mile stretch of parched earth, an enormous weedy sandbox rimmed by various mountain ranges. The exits were few and far between, and there were exactly two settlements along the way, both surrounded by sad palm trees standing in circles, most of them decapitated. It was sixty miles before I saw my first billboard—for the General Patton Museum in Chiriaco Summit, a building surrounded by American flags and an air of testosterone. I didn't at all feel like stopping there. Not today.

Finally, I came to my exit. North would take me into Joshua Tree National Park, but I headed south into the foothills of the Orocopia Mountains. Over the course of twenty miles, Box Canyon Road descended gradually from sixteen hundred feet above sea level to well below it. On the interstate, I had felt like I was skimming over the desert; here it seemed that I was plowing through it. On either side of me were jagged rock walls, formed by geological cataclysm over the years and ending abruptly only at the point, almost exactly at sea level, where the road crossed the San Andreas Fault. It was as desolate a place as any I had visited. There were no other cars in sight, not even a suggestion of civilization. It was just dust and rock and a blazing sun and me.

My first mistake was one of curiosity. Midway through Box Canyon, there came a gravel turnoff with a little sign that I thought might have been a map of the area. I made an impulsive decision to pull over and inspect. When I noticed that the ground was softer than I had anticipated, I tried to veer back onto the road—through a particularly lumpy section of gravel. That was mistake number two. I maneuvered a bit too slowly. Mistake number three. And when Phileas began to sink into the soft earth, I panicked and hit the accelerator hard, spinning my wheels deeper and deeper. Mistake number four.

The hottest September temperature ever recorded in the United States happened in these parts, the thermometer peaking at 126 degrees on September 2, 1950. It wasn't quite that sweltering when I arrived, but the effort was there. And here I was, deep in the desert, surrounded only by walls of rock baking in the sun, carrying a cell phone with no signal, sitting ten miles from the highway and another ten miles from the nearest town, along a road so infrequently traveled that it might be hours before another soul wandered through. And I was stuck, like a camel in quicksand.

Granted, I had the benefit of Phileas as my companion—
enough food, water and shelter in my little self-enclosed uni-
verse to last days, even weeks, alone in the desert. But I had
visions of night falling and beasts converging on my citadel on
wheels—spotted bats and prairie falcons and desert tortoises
and the like, the kinds of animals that have evolved toward enduring this barren wilderness. I have not. So I stood by the
side of the road and waited for a desert miracle.

It arrived only about a half hour later, in the form of Stefan
and Claudia, a couple from Germany, who had chosen to take
a whimsical ride through Box Canyon as part of their three-
week vacation through the American West. They spoke pass-
able English and certainly displayed more patience and
selflessness than your typical ugly American would have
shown upon encountering a broken-down Volvo in the Bavar-
ian Alps. We tried pushing Phileas and rocking Phileas, and
nothing moved, except for a few discs in my back that weren't
supposed to. So they offered me a ride into the next town, over
the fault line, out of the canyon, past an unexpected section of
citrus groves and trellised grapes and farm workers bent at
their task beneath the midday sun. Stefan and Claudia
dropped me at a service station, where I phoned for a tow
truck and was informed that it would be a while.

The service station was alongside a small convenience
store called Leon's Other Place. I approached a man who appeared to be an authority figure.

"Are you Leon?"

"One of them. My father is, too."

"Where's the place that makes this the Other Place?"

He smiled. "Right across the street." And, indeed, there was
Leon's Market a few hundred feet away.

I waited for several hours in Leon's Other Place, watching the comings and goings of a town that seemed to be populated entirely by Hispanic men and women. Nearly every conversation was in Spanish. Most of the signs were bilingual. LOITERING OR ALCOHOLIC BEVERAGES ARE PROHIBITED. NO SE PERMITE BEBIDAS ALCOHOLICAS O BEBAR. I watched three young men walk out with 24-ounce cans of beer in brown paper bags.

I strolled outside briefly, trying to avoid the worst of the sun, which felt like a flame. Leon's Other Place was part of a cement slab that served as a strip mall containing three other establishments—a billiard parlor (Dos Amigos Billiards), a clothing store (Los 4 Hermanos) and a hair salon (Mina's). It was the middle of the day in the middle of the week, and all three were closed. A man in a short beard sat with his back against the cement wall, his knees pulled up to his chest, hiding in the shade of the building and ignoring the passing scream, every half hour or so, of a Southern Pacific freight train across the street.

Back inside, I paid for some prepackaged deli food and read the local newspaper, choosing the one in English, not the one with the bold headline: ALERTA NACIONAL POR EL 9/11. A man sitting in the booth next to me was eating Fritos and a submarine sandwich and reading the paper, too.

"Fuckin' al-Qaeda," he muttered.

It was September 11th, and this was Mecca.

The tow truck driver finally appeared a couple of hours later. He was Latino, born and raised in nearby Indio. He had a Chihuahua in his lap and a sticker on his windshield that said, "And the flag was still there." I offered a handshake to my desert savior, here on the first anniversary of the terrorist attacks, near a town named after the holy place toward which the hijackers had prayed before murdering some three thousand Americans (in part because America supports the existence of the only democracy in the Middle East).

"Hello, I'm Brad."

"Hi," he replied, "I'm Israel."

Perhaps it is the stuff of sermons.

The term "mecca" has become a vastly overused linguistic reference point in America, particularly in California. The state's travel and tourism literature is littered with self-reverential self-references. California has been described as a "mecca for outdoor activities". . . . a "multicultural mecca". . . . an "electoral mecca". . . . a "mecca of opportunity." It says much about American perspective that we have usurped this term, putting aside its gravity so that it can be included in a brochure. Small wonder, then, that America's Mecca—in California—attracts pilgrims of a different sort. While some two million Muslims make the pilgrimage to the birthplace of Mohammed each year as one of the pillars of Islam, the trip is supposed to be taken only by those who can afford it. Saudi Arabia's Mecca is not meant as a destination for the poor. But California's Mecca makes no such distinctions.

It wasn't always a destination of last resort, and it wasn't always called Mecca. It is said to be the oldest settlement in the Coachella Valley, which stretches from Palm Springs to the Salton Sea. In the mid-nineteenth century, the Southern Pacific Railroad drilled several artesian wells here, and the area became a great water station, a stop for gold-seekers, stagecoaches and steam trains. Back then, it was known as Walters, named after a railroad official. But in 1904 a lawyer and realtor named R. Holtby Myers began land speculation, and apparently left it to his wife to come up with a new name for his venture. She noticed the topography and aridity and was reminded of the Middle East. Other nearby town sites, destined to flicker and fail, were given exotic names like Biskra, Arabia and Oasis. This one she called Mecca. The Arabic motif continued for several years. The general store was called The Bazaar, and it was across the street from the Caravansary Hotel. One of the valley newspapers, *The Desert Barnacle*, thought itself clever by printing the phrase: "Allah roads lead to Mecca."

Adding to the Arabian experience is the fact that the Coachella Valley is home to some 250,000 date palms producing nearly 35 million pounds of dates each year. Over 90 percent of the commercial date acreage in the United States is in California, and of that 95 percent is in the valley around Mecca. In fact, the annual National Date Festival is held just up the road in Indio, a celebration that includes an Arabian Nights Pageant and camel races. I assume that somewhere some brochure refers to it as a "date mecca."

An interesting fact about date trees is that they are propagated by offshoots, rather than planted from seeds. Young trees, growing from the base of the parent tree, are carefully cut away and replanted elsewhere. This might serve as a metaphor for what Mecca has become—a starting point for transplanted Latinos, who remove themselves from their mother country in the hopes that a new start in a land of opportunity would blossom into something resembling the American Dream. For the most part, the Mecca of today is a home base for Mexican migrant farm workers. They are the foundation of the nation's nearly $30 billion fruit-and-vegetable industry, yet they remain perhaps the most marginalized class of people in the country.

Two hundred years ago, nine out of every ten American workers were involved in farming. A century ago, some 40 percent of the American workforce labored on farms. Today, the number is closer to two percent. As family farms have been replaced by corporate farms, production has been increasingly concentrated in the hands of a small number of large growers. The largest one percent of America's farms produce more than one-quarter of the agricultural output. Technology and education have become vital components of the industry. Growers study at universities and examine consumer-preference studies. They utilize genetically engineered seeds and computer-controlled soil analysis. But when it comes to planting and harvesting, particularly in the orchards and vegetable fields, these high-tech, big-time farmer-businessmen still rely on the skilled hands and strong backs of seasonal laborers.

California's first seasonal farm workers, in the mid-1800s, were generally Native Americans or poor white pioneers. By 1880, the fruit-and-vegetable industry had come of age, and there was a need for a more vulnerable population that could be overworked and underpaid. As a result, over 75 percent of the state's farm laborers were Chinese. Congress responded to this development with typical xenophobia by passing the Chinese Exclusion Act, suspending immigration of Chinese workers. So the Japanese took their place, representing the majority of farm workers by 1910. When laws were passed limiting Japanese immigration, Mexicans filled the void.

When the Depression began, half of California's farm workers were from south of the border. But the arrival of hundreds of thousands of dust-bowl refugees created a labor surplus, which meant high unemployment, which translated to the usual anti-immigrant rants, which led to mass deportations. Between 1930 and 1933, more than three hundred thousand Mexicans were forcibly repatriated. At the same time, FDR's New Deal spurred a series of basic federal labor protections, from the minimum wage to unemployment compensation to child labor laws, all of which were specifically denied to farm workers. It was as if the government rubberstamped their second-class status. As Tom Joad put it in *The Grapes of Wrath*, "They're workin' away our spirits, tryin' to make us cringe and crawl, takin' away our decency." So, naturally, as the economy improved and poor white workers found better options, Mexican laborers became all the rage once more. Out of every ten California farm workers today, nine of them are Latino.

In part because of the general informality of agricultural labor, anywhere from 50 to 90 percent of California's farm workers are undocumented immigrants. "Illegal aliens" is what the folks call them who fear the negative impact of new arrivals and see the border as a battleground. Hundreds of millions of dollars are already spent on patrolling the United States-Mexico border, where more than one-third of INS employees are posted. With the help of motion detectors and infrared sensors and helicopters with searchlights, they apprehend more than 1.5 million people each year. Almost all are Mexicans who agree to return voluntarily and who generally make another attempt at crossing as soon as possible, often the same day. It is all one big game, really. INS pads its numbers, sometimes catching the same group of people eight or ten days in a row. And the migrants get a chance to try again.

But this game can also be deadly serious. The border crossing can be a terrifying ordeal. INS agents have seen infants floated across the Rio Grande in inner tubes, bands of immigrants lost in the desert, men cut in half while trying to jump onto moving trains. Still, they keep coming. It is estimated that some two million people cross the border illegally each year, most of whom do it to find work for a few months before returning home with relative riches. But about three hundred thousand of them settle in the United States annually, and when they reach the other side, where do they go? To a place like Mecca, an unincorporated community with one foot in Mexico and the other on the lowest rung of America's socio-economic ladder.

There are approximately two thousand people in the Mecca vicinity, but it is difficult to say. A lot of them don't wish to be officially counted. Many live in several low-income apartment complexes, which are interspersed among stucco houses with Spanish-style roofing. These appear to be a step up from the kind of housing that had been the cause of much concern a couple of decades earlier, when one of the big landlords in town was actually a devout Muslim, an Iranian by birth. His tenants, all farm laborers and their families, lived in shacks and sheds under such deplorable conditions that they referred to it as Ciudad Perdido—the Lost City. Eventually, the Lost City was condemned, and apparently the Iranian landlord, a retired Beverly Hills psychologist, was run out of town. Of course, American anger over a little hostage situation in his native country at the time may have played a role in his departure.

But that was a generation ago. We have come a long way. Now the enemy was Iraq.

So the Arabian theme has faded in Mecca, and life there currently revolves around places like the Azteca restaurant, serving Mexican-American cuisine, and the Sanctuary of Our

Lady of Guadalupe. Stroll through town, and you see groups of men, perhaps out of work for the day or the season, sitting on overturned plastic crates in the shade of stunted palm trees, bantering in Spanish with their hats low over their eyes. You notice stray dogs, too, everywhere, staggering in the heat, nosing through the garbage or wandering across the desert as if in search of coyote cousins. In the barren stretches between Mecca's streets, mounds of trash lie like corner landfills. Beer cases, car batteries, shredded tires, rubber shoes, shopping carts, crushed school desks. The open areas claimed by nobody seem to be cared for by nobody. Then again, trying to keep this town clean must be a bit like trying to dust the desert.

At 189 feet below sea level, Mecca is, indeed, about as low

COACHELLA VALLEY HIGH SCHOOL

as it gets, a destination for the disenfranchised, discarded and degraded. It is the kind of unforgiving place about which Mark Twain once wrote, "Here the people live who begin the revolutions"—a dusty hamlet with no business existing, let alone surviving, amid the shifting sands. But that seems to be Mecca's recurring theme—turning a whole lot of nothing into a little something.

There are manifestations of it in the industry that has found a home in the township and, in a manner of speaking, turns water into wine. Nearly three hundred truckloads of wood and agricultural residue are hauled to Mecca each week, where the Colman Energy power plant turns it into electricity. Nearby, at First Nation Recovery, six thousand pounds of tires are processed every hour and turned into crumb rubber, which is used to create everything from dock bumpers to floor mats. Both operations are located in an eco-industrial park on a reservation belonging to the Cabazon Band of Mission Indians, a tribe that only a few years ago had dwindled to a few dozen members caught in a cycle of poverty. But the Cabazons have been catapulted into the economic mainstream, thanks to the Fantasy Springs Casino, located on a parcel of the reservation along I-10.

Waste becomes power. Scraps are recycled into value. A ragged band of Indians finds riches. Something out of nothing. Of course, the theme wouldn't be complete without a visit to the Salton Sea.

I had first spotted it upon exiting Box Canyon. It looked like a desert mirage of massive proportions, a land-locked ocean, and that's essentially what it is. It is a man-made phenomenon—that is, it was formed by human error. At about the time Mecca was coming into existence, a real estate developer and an engineer dug a small channel from the Colorado River in an attempt to divert water (read: steal from Mexico) to irrigate rich farmland in what would be called the Imperial Valley. But in 1905, spring flooding caused the water to breach the banks of their rudimentary canal and pour into the valley at an alarming rate. Farms and settlements were inundated. Nearly four hundred square miles of desert were drowned. The water gushed into an ancient seabed known as the Salton Sink for more than a year until President Teddy Roosevelt ordered the Southern Pacific Railroad to close the break at all costs. For weeks, the railroad dumped a carload of rocks into the river every five minutes, until finally the flow was stopped. What was left was the Salton Sea, the largest inland body of water in the state.

The irrigated farms in the Coachella and Imperial valleys use one trillion gallons of Colorado River water each year. The farmers flush the salts from their soils with this water, and it drains downhill into the sea, which is already 25 percent saltier than the Pacific Ocean. With no outlet, water escapes only by evaporation, leaving behind contaminants from the agricultural runoff. Hundreds of thousands of birds have died from disease there, even though it has become a critical migratory stop in the Pacific. The fish in it are said to be unfit for consumption by pregnant women. It is California's version of the Dead Sea.

But I have to admit, I loved what I saw of the Salton Sea. They say you can smell it long before you see it, a putrid stink that wafts over Mecca when the wind blows north. But I have a poor sense of smell, something my wife and diaper-wearing sons would corroborate. So later that evening, I decided to drive down the sea's eastern shore, past scenery alternating between weedy desert waste and lush groves of citrus and date palms. I parked Phileas at a nearly empty campground, which proved to be one of those King-of-the-Road experiences.

All it took to charm me was a sunset. I watched the great red orb settle behind the Santa Rosa Mountains, lighting the peaks like candles—bright orange fringed by red, then lavender, then blue, until it melted into the deepening sky. When the sky went dark, the stars came out in hordes, and a crescent moon hung like a little white grin in the heavens. The inland ocean seemed to drink it all in, and I began to appreciate a loveliness in the Salton Sea. Which brought my thoughts back to Mecca again because it, too, seemed to exist where it wasn't supposed to be. And it, too, offered a lesson in potential.

Behind the Catholic church in Mecca, a road simply ceases at a garbage-strewn stretch of nothingness extending into the desert for miles. There is a sign there. It says simply, END. But really Mecca is a new beginning.

Earlier that day, on the morning of September 11th, drum and bagpipe processions from New York City's five boroughs had begun a slow march toward the site of the former World Trade Center, where thousands converged to hear the names, read aloud over the course of two hours, of 2,801 people missing and dead. Thousands more marched to the newly renovated walls of the Pentagon or mourned on a wind-rippled field in Pennsylvania. But at the same time, extremists at a London mosque were celebrating what they billed as "A Towering Day in History." And U.S. military bases were on their highest state of alert. And there were protests in Paris and Manila and Singapore against a possible U.S. strike in Iraq. And more than half of the respondents to a radio poll in

Moscow said the United States "deserved" the previous year's attacks.

That night, just as the numbers 9-1-1 were being drawn for the New York lottery, President Bush would address the nation from Ellis Island, with the Statue of Liberty as a backdrop. "We value every life," he said. "Our enemies value none—not even the innocent, not even their own. And we seek the freedom and opportunity that give meaning and value to life."

Meanwhile, in Mecca, California, a sort of land-locked Ellis Island where opportunity often avoids the innocents, several hundred students gathered for an assembly at Mecca School, a collection of dust-colored buildings set beside a grove of tall palm trees. They saluted the flag. A couple of youngsters sang "The Star-Spangled Banner." Some eighth graders recited poems and essays they had written about September 11th, and there was a presentation explaining the tragic chronology of that day. The highlight of the morning was an appearance by officers from the sheriff's department, who tried to explain the intentions behind the attacks.

"A lot of students know what happened that day, but they don't know why it happened," school principal Manuela Silvestre later explained.

Soft-spoken, serious and barely taller than many of her students, Manuela was in her first weeks as principal, having arrived in the community fourteen years ago as a kindergarten teacher. Born in Mexico, she had been brought to the United States at the age of three. You'll find better medical care there, the doctors told her parents. Manuela had been diagnosed with polio. Two of her cousins had contracted the disease, as well. They stayed in Mexico, and they didn't survive. Manuela is forty-one. She walks with some difficulty, but with head held high.

"To me, it's natural. I've never known anything different because I was three months old. That's who I am. I don't see it as a handicap."

Her parents were farm workers—migrants for several years until they settled in the Coachella Valley when their daughter started school. Manuela grew up as a witness to the injustices and hardships heaped upon America's most disadvantaged class of laborers—threats and false promises from contractors, workers cheated out of their wages, fluctuating periods of unemployment, substandard housing, routine exposure to potentially deadly pesticides, lower life expectancy and higher infant mortality rate, the three hundred children who die each year as a result of farm-work-related accidents, the two-thirds of migrant households that live below the poverty line. But like the birds at the Salton Sea, Mexicans continue to migrate to California and place their fate in the hands of a system poisoned by greed. This may be why Manuela dreamed of becoming a lawyer.

"Those were my intentions," she said, sitting at her desk in a lightly decorated workspace. It was my first visit in a long while to the principal's office. "I had a four-year college scholarship, but my parents wouldn't allow me to go four years out of state anywhere. I was the oldest. I was female. And nobody had done it in my family. So that was something new for them. We compromised. My dad said go two years to College of the Desert in Palm Desert, and then we'll decide if you can transfer out or not. At COD I started working in a library to put myself through school. I was making minimum wage. Somebody came in and said, 'You know, you're real good. Why don't you just work in daycare? I have a friend who owns one. You can make a little more money.' I've been in education ever since."

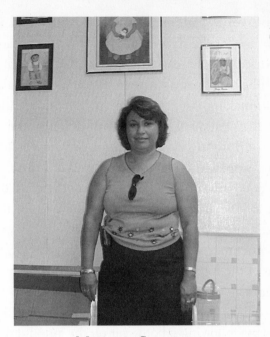

Manuela Silvestre

The migrant worker is a shadowy figure to most Americans, just a fleeting glimpse from a passing car of figures stooped among parallel rows of crops. But while their labor does not define their lives, the two are inseparable. Many migrant parents find it difficult to justify sending their kids to school instead of into the fields and orchards, where they can provide for the family. In fact, more than one-third of all migrant children over the age of seven toil alongside their parents. They move from one temporary home to another, fitting in schooling when the agricultural seasons allow it.

About half of the nine-hundred-plus students in the fourth through eighth grades at Mecca School are children of what Manuela refers to as traditional migrants. They follow the

grape harvest into California's Central Valley and return to
Mecca in time for the start of the school year. Another 35 percent, however, are the children of mobility migrant workers.
These families follow, for instance, the apple crop all the way
to Oregon, making their way back to Mecca by October. Or
they work the potato fields as far north as Idaho and return in
December. Obviously, this presents a unique challenge—on
top of the language obstacles—to those trying to maintain
some sort of continuity in the education of these children.

"Some of the students do go to school when they're up
north, and it's very hard to even track their educational record
because sometimes we don't receive it from the other school.
And some of the kids don't go to school at all. They come in,
and we have to play the catch-up game, trying to get them
back on course," said Manuela. "The government bases our
money for the following school year on the amount of students
we have in October. So every year we have this number of students, and then in December we get one or two hundred
more. But we don't get the money for them."

In 1966, the federal government tried to address these
problems by creating the migrant education program, catering
to the special needs of migrant children in various ways—from
hiring tutors and counselors to streamlining the transfer of
records. Still, as early as the first grade, half of all migrant children fall below national scholastic averages. The typical migrant student is two years below their grade level in reading
and math skills. Nearly half of them drop out of high school.

"We do have a migrant program," said Manuela. "We have
what's called a resource teacher. She goes out to the class-
rooms where the migrant students are and works on an individual basis with them or in little groups, making sure they

know what the homework is and that they understand the concept being taught."

"How many resource teachers are there?" I asked, thinking of the hundreds of students requiring the assistance.

"For migrants on our campus? One."

Making matters more difficult is the fact that migrant children tend to be saddled with adult responsibilities in the home. Four out of five migrant parents do not speak English, so it often falls to the bilingual children to serve as a conduit between the margins and the mainstream. They serve as translators, negotiators, bill payers. And meanwhile, they watch as their family's fortunes are determined by forces out of their control—the droughts, freezes, crop diseases and market prices that constitute agriculture's inherent unpredictability. They see their parents toil under backbreaking conditions at scandalous wages with no sign of being able to climb aboard an economic track toward prosperity. It must make for a sad sort of fatalism. Welcome to America, indeed.

All of this is why the principal of Mecca School thought it was so important to try to explain September 11th to her students. "We have to teach them that we can't judge people and that we have freedom. And if they attack us, it's because they want to take that freedom away from us," Manuela explained. "I think it's also our job to make sure that they understand what the U.S. offers for them—that if their parents brought them over, they had a reason. They wanted something better for them."

Mecca is perhaps a half hour from Palm Springs and its satellite upscale destinations like Palm Desert and Rancho Mirage, where celebrities and politicians and captains of industry barricade themselves from the riffraff, either in one of the dozens of gated resorts or at the Betty Ford Center. The parents of many of Manuela's students, the ones who don't work the land, work maintenance on the golf courses and in the hotels, tending the fairways and fluffing the pillows of the well-to-do. They leave dusty Mecca every day for the lush playground of the stars, where streets like Gene Autry Trail and Bob Hope Drive are lined with upscale boutiques.

"It is a different world, especially for our students," said Manuela. "When you take them on a field trip, especially the ones that never left Mecca, you can see their faces. You're driving on this big yellow bus, and you can see their eyes opening."

Amazing, isn't it, how desperation and disenfranchisement can live so close to consumption and entitlement—two socioeconomic extremes sharing a section of desert, one immersed in its harsh realities, the other escaping into a perpetual mirage. But Mecca's reputation suffers even in comparison to the other largely Hispanic desert communities that seem to serve as Palm Springs barrios. Dead bodies used to be dumped with some frequency in the vineyards fringing the town, earning Mecca a reputation as a place one wouldn't want to visit after dark. It is reputed to have a thriving drug trade, as well, with fields of cannabis sprouting from the salty soil and methamphetamine labs hiding in the desert. "Because it's so isolated," Israel, my tow truck driver told me, "you can't even smell what's cooking there."

Manuela didn't deny the rumors. "We do have that reputation. I think the community knows who they are, and they just keep away from them. And I know that the police know who they are, too, and they're doing their best to eliminate it. Actually, you know, the school is a safe haven. They leave us alone."

Mecca is also ninety minutes from the United States-Mexico border, which the residents see not as a division between two worlds but as an ever-blurring line. The vast majority of Mecca School's students are not U.S. citizens. Most of their relatives are still in Mexico. Every weekend, about one-fourth of the families in town head south of the border. When they come back, they bring a little of their homeland with them, which is why this town is the cultural equivalent of the Azteca restaurant's Mexican-American menu.

"It's like a small part of Mexico, especially if you come in the afternoon," said Manuela. "In Mexico, in the afternoons, you'll see a lot of people sitting on their porches, talking to their neighbors. This is something that you see here. It's a very social little town. And this school is the focal point of Mecca. Any event that we have—the Halloween Carnival, Cinco de Mayo—is here."

I wondered out loud. "Which is bigger here—Cinco de Mayo or the Fourth of July?" In the early days of Mecca, July 4th was an annual happening of significant proportions. There was always an ice cream social and a fireworks display. But that was before the town became a bridge between two nations.

Manuela pondered my question for a few seconds, and then: "I would have to say Cinco de Mayo."

Cinco de Mayo does not, as some believe, commemorate Mexico's Independence Day, which is celebrated on September 16th. No, on the fifth of May Mexicans remember the Battle of Puebla, when outnumbered and outequipped Mexican soldiers defeated the army of Napoleon III. "Nobody thought they would win that battle," said Manuela, "and they did."

She might well have been describing many of her students. As we spoke, many of the children's parents were out planting cantaloupes or tomatoes or chili peppers. They were sitting on the back of tractors, sticking seedlings into holes in the ground, plant by plant by plant. One might say the teachers at Mecca School were doing much the same thing.

"I don't look at is as a battle. It's just something that we have to learn—that every time they fall they must get up. And that's something in our culture already. I don't think they give up. And that's what's unique about our kids. If you ask people at the high school, they love the kids we send them because these kids want to learn. We have a lot of our teachers, about five or six of them, who have gone through the system and gotten an education, and now they're back here teaching in their own community. And that's great to see. I mean, that's one of the greatest gifts. . . ."

It almost looked as though Manuela had the beginnings of a smile on her face. I announced what I was thinking. "You like your job."

And here she unveiled a beautiful grin. "Oh, I love my job." And then she told me a story.

Every battle has its heroes. At Coachella Valley High School, where Manuela sends her graduated students, such a man is Colonel Chauncey Veatch, who served as an officer in the infantry and the medical service corps for twenty-two years before retiring from the army in 1995 and turning to teaching. He teaches social sciences—American and world history, U.S. government, economics, career preparation—in a high school where 99 percent of the students are of Latino descent and most come from migrant families. He also teaches English as a

second language classes in Mecca. Veatch is one of those
teachers who seems to have inherited a God-given talent to ed-
ucate and inspire—America's most important resource, especially in its most marginalized places.

"I want to be a dream maker for my kids," he likes to say. "I
want them to set high goals for themselves—professionally and
personally. I want to do everything I can to help them realize
those dreams." And he adds, "A teacher is ultimately judged by
the achievements of his students."

Twelve of Veatch's students have participated in engineer-
ing and Latin American studies classes at the Naval Postgradu-
ate School. Eight of his students have taken classes in Arabic,
Korean, French and Russian at the Defense Language Institute. Veatch's Cadet Corps marched in the Rose Parade. Half
of his students claim they want to become teachers themselves.

Veatch has been honored as the Bilingual Teacher of the
Year, the Migrant Program Teacher of the Year, the Mexican
American Chamber of Commerce Educator of the Year . . .
and finally, in 2002, the National Teacher of the Year. This
earned him a trip to the White House, where President Bush
presented the coveted crystal apple to him during a Rose Garden ceremony. Veatch was allowed to take two students with
him. One of them, Manuela proudly explained, was a kid
from Mecca, a boy named Ramon Castillejo. He came from a
migrant family and, under Veatch's supervision, joined the
Cadet Corps and became an outstanding student, tutor and
community volunteer. He now attends college at Long Beach
State.

"At the White House ceremony, someone mentioned that
Chauncey was a hero," said Manuela, still smiling. "And he

pointed to his students and said, 'Well, I'd like you to meet *my* heroes.' "

Which is how the young son of migrant workers from Mecca found himself being applauded by the president of the United States.

EPILOGUE

SEQUOIADENDRON GIGANTEUM

It was Friday, September 13th, and for the first time in fifty days, I had nowhere specific to go. Home was on the agenda, but my family wasn't due to return for another couple of days, so it wouldn't yet be home at all. I set a course west, out of the desert and toward the coast, and I found myself meandering, almost as if I was letting Phileas navigate the way.

I seemed to be searching for a closing metaphor, which wasn't likely to emerge from Tinseltown, so I cruised through Greater Los Angeles—Pomona and Pasadena and Burbank and the like—with speedy intent. When the unfamiliar snarl of traffic dwindled to a mere sneer, I exited to refuel. As the numbers clicked higher on the fuel pump, I rummaged through my souvenirs from the road. A set of wildlife postcards drawn by Donna Chase in Siberia. A candlestick holder crafted by Jennifer Zingg in Paris. A cassette of polka music recorded by the Prague Czech Brass Band. A "Cargill AgHorizons" cap from Vienna. A necklace of Krishna *japa* beads. A city flag from Cairo. A POW/MIA sticker from Bagdad. A "Tardy & Absent Slip" from Mecca School. A remnant of a vandalized WELCOME TO CONGO sign. A book of matches from the London Depot, which advertised WARM BEER. LOUSY FOOD. INDOOR POOL.

I had traveled more than ten thousand miles through half of the fifty states, and certainly it had met the challenge as an exotic excursion. I had dined at a Paris café, imbibed at a London pub, achieved enlightenment in Athens, watched the great river flow past Cairo, found King David in Jerusalem and made a pilgrimage to Mecca. I had marveled at what might be called the Seven Wonders of my Small World—the Pillars of Rome, the Castle at Versailles, the Madison Buffalo Jump, Fort Defiance Park, the Cane Ridge Meeting House, the Great Grain Elevator, the Palace of Gold. I had encountered a cast of characters as varied as the landscape—devout ranchers and devoted nudists, farmers and fiddlers, miners and migrants, artists and activists, throwbacks and thoroughbreds, hillbillies, hippies, hermits and Hare Krishnas.

But beyond diversity, I was hoping to locate an overarching theme to my experiences, a chorus amid the cacophony of sampled subcultures. In the unwieldy style of nineteenth-century literature, the final chapter of *Around the World in 80 Days* is titled "In Which it is Shown That Phileas Fogg Gained Nothing by His Tour Around the World, Unless it were Happiness." Not true for me. Pleasure, yes. But I had gained something else. The sum of a nation's parts had given me a sort of holistic understanding of the American whole. Yet as the end approached, I was still trying to discern the lesson learned.

North now, on I-5, and into the San Joaquin Valley. The ride seemed all pavement and dust, and it seemed to match my thoughts, which were flat and hazy. At a point almost in the dead center of California, I came across an exit and options. West would take me to the coast, homeward. I was but a few hours away. But I directed Phileas (or maybe Phileas directed me) eastward, inland, through Visalia and Lemoncove and Three Rivers, and then up, and up, and up.

Eventually, I found myself clinging to the side of a mountain, a long and winding road at ten miles per hour in the southern Sierra Nevada. It was the kind of ascent that allows you to look straight down at several points to see the path you completed fifteen minutes earlier, and the view was almost inconceivably majestic. The mountains surrounding me were granite behemoths draped in lush green forest, except for their peaks, which were bald like massive monks' heads. The only thing between me and a thousand-foot drop was the tall grass fringing the road. The sign said: FROM HERE ON IN, VEHICLES OVER 22 FEET NOT RECOMMENDED. I had about six inches to spare.

I pushed higher still, almost as if I was climbing to the nation's pinnacle in an effort to get a better assessment of things. This was Phileas's finest hour. And then darkness, a tunnel of trees, conifers that seemed huge until I spied the kings of the forest for whom this national park was named.

The giant sequoias, *Sequoiadendron giganteum*, are bright orange and so incongruously immense that they look as if they were transplanted from another planet. Coastal redwoods are generally taller, but not nearly as bulky. Giant sequoias grow upward one to two feet per year until they are between two hundred and three hundred feet high, and then the growth is outward—about half an inch annually. They are like people in that respect.

Phileas pulled to a stop at the trailhead of the Congress Trail, a two-mile path through the Giant Forest. There stands General Sherman, a cinnamon-barked, 2,000-year-old colossus with one massive thick limb protruding out and up at sharp angles as though flexing a muscle. Some trees are taller than its 275 feet. Some are thicker (it is 102 feet around). But none more impressively combines height and girth. Composed of 52,500 cubic feet of wood, General Sherman is simply the world's largest living thing.

Here, ironically, as I concluded my small world tour, was my metaphor.

The supporting buttresses at the base of the largest sequoias look like enormous elephant feet. In fact, watching people stroll along the trail, past the sporadic thick-trunked leviathans of the Giant Forest, is visually akin to watching a beetle skitter beneath a pachyderm. These trees are nature-made superlatives. I could imagine great titans of an ancient age picnicking beneath them, perhaps biting into the World's Largest Kolache. Indeed, everywhere I looked—and every fact I gleaned from the Sequoia National Park guidebooks—reminded me of a snippet of discovery from the past fifty days.

The sequoias are so large that they overwhelm the senses and overshadow the other sentinels of the forest, some of them—like evergreens two hundred feet high and five feet thick—impressive in their own right. My mind's eye recalled quiet Vienna, sleeping in the shadow of South Dakota's largest grain elevator. And the trees seem as though they must have been here forever, but they are likely just the third generation of sequoias in the area. I thought of Carly Danhof-Bellach in

Amsterdam, granddaughter of Dutch immigrants, yet an entrenched American.

There was a time when any sequoia of significance was given a name—Centennial, for instance, or the McKinley Tree. But most remain anonymous, or at least unidentified. Like Xander, Fun and the One-Armed Man, a name is just a disguise for a life form open to interpretation. In 1956, President Eisenhower designated one named tree—the General Grant Tree—as the only *living* national shrine to honor those who have given their lives for the nation. I recalled a tiny dying tree in Bagdad—a local shrine to Dennis Pike, but no less lofty.

Not every sequoia grows large. It depends on the location and the conditions. The right tree in the wrong place grows old but is confined by its surroundings. Sequoias have been known to grow just an inch wide in a century. And, of course, I had seen hamlets whose names signify grandiose aspirations—Calcutta, Moscow, Jerusalem—but you can't carve a kingdom out of a West Virginia hollow or the Maine outback or a curve in a lonely Arkansas highway.

Sequoias grow only on the western slopes of the Sierra Nevada, where the average winter may bring 250 inches of snow. They grow in groves, but most of them appear to stand alone, as if claiming their own isolated space amid the dense forest—much like the remote farm in Siberia, Maine. In fact, the man who is said to have "discovered" the Giant Forest in the 1860s, a fellow named Hale Tharp, once moved into a fallen, hollow sequoia, adding a fireplace and using it as a summer residence. Siberia's Donna Chase would have been right at home, fiddling among the giants.

Falling over is the typical cause of death for sequoias,

largely because their shallow roots are susceptible to erosion and damage—natural or human caused. But there is life from death. The toppling of a damaged tree often opens a hole in the forest canopy, allowing much-needed sunlight into the darkness and giving young sequoias a chance to reach maturity. Which sounds a bit like Cairo, the capital of Little Egypt, whose fall from glory allows it to give life as a cautionary tale.

Among the earliest residents of this hard-to-reach section of the Sierra Nevada were lonely sheepherders, mostly French and Spanish Basques. Because there were no controls over land use, the land was overgrazed and precious mountain watersheds were destroyed. I recalled Rome, where Jesse White, the cattle rancher descended from Basque sheepherders, was claiming a right to self-determination along his river corridor.

Although the wood of a mature giant sequoia was eventually found to be weak and relatively unprofitable, nineteenth-century lumbermen turned the Big Trees, as they were called, into little things—fence posts, railroad ties, cigar boxes. In 1889, The Sanger Lumber Company built a fifty-mile-long flume to transport the timber, which led to the destruction of the largest sequoia grove of all. John Muir soon took up the conservationist cause, efforts that eventually resulted in creation of the national park. Said he, regarding the effort to kill the kings of trees, "As well sell the rain clouds and the snow and the rivers to be cut up and carried away, if that were possible." The Athens Generating Plant, a modern-day Sanger Lumber along the Hudson River, suggests it may be possible, indeed.

Fire is, of course, the natural thinner of any forest—every few years, on average, among the sequoias. The giant trees possess thick, fire-resistant bark, but they are not immune to the flames. As I ambled along the trail, I spotted dozens of charred giants, still standing but blackened, like walking wounded. Some were lost, burned into submission, standing hollow and empty, like the Castle in Kentucky's Versailles. But often a sequoia will cling to life even after fire has gutted it, even after it has been emptied of its vitality. These indefatigable trees amid the California mountains reminded me of Congo, the should-be ghost town in the Appalachian hills. In fact, sequoias even take advantage of fire. They will often wait until a blaze has cleared out the underbrush before dropping their seeds—hundreds of thousands of them—on the newly burned forest floor. Odds are that some of the seeds will take hold—new beginnings amid dire circumstances, a situation that calls to mind the over-the-border influx into Mecca.

I continued along the trail and noticed the air thickening with the smell of smoke. Here, some sequoias were so scorched that they looked like stalks of charcoal. Others appeared to have avoided the fires entirely, but appearances can deceive. While examining a particularly substantial sequoia, I noticed a quiet trail of smoke swirling behind it, some fifteen feet up. Moving closer for a better look, I found myself ankle-deep in ash, gazing up at a tree that was still smoldering, the fire inching its way up, getting narrower and narrower as it peeled off a layer of skin. But the tree was very much alive.

This was my metaphor in full. The big trees and the tiny hamlets tell the same story. Mine had been a journey through stories of survival, of trials by fire, of enduring the elements and sustaining existence, if only barely. The road is life, as Jack Kerouac once avowed, and the road has taught me that it isn't necessarily the accomplishments that inspire, but rather the effort. It is the lesson that small worlds tell large tales—

about saving a town, defending a river, suffering the seasons, maintaining a way of life, embracing a hope, chasing a dream.

There used to be a Mark Twain Tree, a giant sequoia of nearly unmatched proportions. But it was cut down to convince the skeptics. Its twenty-foot-wide cross-section was displayed all over the world for publicity purposes, not unlike Twain himself. Still, the nonbelievers suspected they were being deceived. The "California hoax," they called it. Apparently, something that unique, that unexpectedly grand, was so foreign to their small world of understanding that it couldn't possibly be appreciated secondhand. Their only recourse was to go see the wonders for themselves.

Imagine that.

ACKNOWLEDGMENTS

This is a chronicle covering a broad canvas, but the task was made much easier by the existence of previous in-depth studies into the various subcultures sampled here. In particular, I found a handful of books fascinating and eminently useful. These include *The Riverkeepers* by John Cronin and Robert F. Kennedy, Jr.; *The Persistence of Ethnicity* by Rob Kroes; *Owyhee Graffiti* by Michael F. Hanley IV; *Sequoia and Kings Canyon* by William C. Tweed and Malinee Crapsey; *Let My People Go*, edited by Jan Peterson Roddy and featuring photographs by Preston Ewing, Jr.; Daniel Rothenberg's comprehensive study of migrant laborers, *With These Hands*; Nori J. Muster's chronicle of her Hare Krishna days, *Betrayal of the Spirit*; and *Monkey on a Stick: Murder, Madness and the Hare Krishnas* by John Hubner and Lindsey Gruson.

Of course, the task wouldn't have been possible at all without the welcome and honesty shown by the many people whom I met along the way. Donna Chase, Preston Ewing, Jr. and Lou Ann and Denise Pike were particularly gracious with their time and hospitality. I am grateful, as well, to Joel McElhannon; Pam and Jesse White; Brenda Clements; Joe Danhof and his granddaughter Carly; Scott Borg; Myra Cluts; Mark Nemec; Chad, Greg and Lois in London; Jennifer Zingg; Wes Purcell; Betty Allman; Trish and Lanny Earlywine; Carrie Feder; Owen Lipstein; Peggy, Jimmy and the rest of the bare-bottomed bevy at Juniper Woods; Amy Northrop; Gin Bills; Jack Jones and his sister Maxine; Sherri at the Jerusalem Circle H; Harrol at the Jerusalem post office; Betty and Darrell Reid; Jeannette Walters and her daughter Kathryn; Mabel

Clarkson and her daughter Sharon; the late Johnnie Wood; Manuela Silvestre; Jim Outback; Israel the tow truck driver; the Krishna devotees at New Vrindavan; and the sundry denizens of the London Depot.

Thanks, too, to Robert Preskill, Amanda Ayers, Mitchell Ivers and Hillary Schupf for guiding the book's travels, and to the kind folks at Winnebago Industries, particularly Kelli Harms. The Rialta—my good friend Phileas—was the perfect companion.

Finally, I will never be able to fully express how much I appreciate my sainted wife Amy. She is my partner, my editor, my muse and, after a long journey, a sight for sore eyes.

INDEX